More Build
It BIG

101 Insider Secrets from Top Direct Selling Experts

Direct Selling Women's Alliance

KAPLAN) PUBLISHING

This publication is designed to provide accurate and authoritative information in regard to the subject matter covered. It is sold with the understanding that the publisher is not engaged in rendering legal, accounting, or other professional service. If legal advice or other expert assistance is required, the services of a competent professional person should be sought.

President, Kaplan Publishing: Roy Lipner
Vice President and Publisher: Maureen McMahon
Acquisitions Editor: Michael Cunningham
Director of Production: Daniel Frey
Production Editor: Karen Goodfriend
Cover Design: Gail Chandler
Typesetter: Caitlin Ostrow

The Direct Selling Women's Alliance, mydswa.org and Principle-Centered Coaching, are trademarks of the Direct Selling Women's Alliance. Other product, service, and company names mentioned herein may be the properties of their respective owners.

Published by Kaplan Publishing
a division of Kaplan, Inc.

Printed in the United States of America

06 07 08 09 10 9 8 7 6 5 4 3 2 1

Library of Congress Cataloging-in-Publication Data

More build it big : 101 insider secrets from top direct selling experts / Direct Selling Women's Alliance.
    p.   cm.
    Includes index.
    ISBN-13: 978-1-4195-2003-7
    1. Direct selling. I. Title: One hundred one insider secrets from top direct selling experts. II. Direct Selling Women's Alliance.
    HF5438.25.M84 2006
    658.8'72—dc22
                                 2005024573

■ Acknowledgments

We dedicate this book to the individuals and companies that are the lifeblood of our wonderful direct-selling profession. Your passion to serve others is a source of inspiration to us all!

The dream of catching a butterfly expresses a childlike desire to capture something wondrously elusive—like beauty or love—if only for a moment, and then joyfully watch it fly free. Writing a book that captures the wisdom of 80 individuals is truly as delicate and magical as catching 80 butterflies!

This book wouldn't exist without our remarkable editing team and their butterfly nets. Our heartfelt thanks goes to Susan Raab, our Senior Editor, who gave 100 percent to this project. She held our vision to the highest standards, and her dedication to excellence combined with her newfound love of our profession took this project to new heights. We also appreciate the able touch of Sally Smith, who smoothed our expressions and made them shine.

We sincerely thank Michael Cunningham of Dearborn Trade Publishing, who believes in the industry and in the DSWA. In the spirit of service, he and the rest of the Dearborn team have worked tirelessly to support this project and promote our books around the world.

We send our deepest gratitude to our contributing leaders and experts. They are the shining stars of our profession and work daily to inspire, teach, and support direct sellers around the world. By living and working in the spirit of service and excellence, you are leading by example and holding those in our industry to a higher standard.

There are no words that can express the appreciation we have for the DSWA team. Suzi Mark and Judi Finneran worked quietly and tirelessly behind the scenes to ensure that the outcome is something of which we all can be proud. They exemplify the highest ideals of support and service. Without their willing spirits and unwavering commitment, this book would have never come to be.

We send our love and appreciation to our families, who continue to support us on this journey. Each has played an active part in the growth of the Alliance and in the creation of this book. We thank our parents who have offered heartfelt encouragement and support through the years while modeling how to live a rich and meaningful life. We thank our husbands—Mario, Saffery, and Maui—for always standing by us and for believing in our vision to make a lasting contribution by sharing our gifts. Our amazing children—Isea, Kahea, Kaala, Alex, Paola, and Dane—continue to be the light of our lives. We are proud of who you have become!

Lastly, we give thanks to God for walking with us daily and putting us in a place where we can make a difference. We are blessed every day and know that You have challenged us to not only dream, but to fulfill those dreams. We joyfully release these dear butterflies into Your care.

Blessings and aloha,

Nicki Keohohou
Jane Deuber
Grace Keohohou Lee

■ Contents

■ Preface

What Is Direct Selling?

Today, more than ever before, people are considering the possibility of starting their own businesses. The lure of independence, prestige, freedom from time constraints, and fulfilling work pulls seductively at our heartstrings as an alternative to being unfulfilled and underpaid.

However, the truth is, starting a traditional small business can be backbreaking work, requiring long days that stretch late into the night, never-ending amounts of capital, and strong mental stamina to juggle the many roles and responsibilities of today's entrepreneur. Is this any way to live? We believe there is a better way.

Enter the direct-selling business–small, lean, and incredibly efficient. As a direct-selling professional, you choose from hundreds of fine companies selling every product or service imaginable from women's apparel to state-of-the-art nutritional products. In exchange for a minimal investment (many times less than $100), the company agrees to research, design, test, manufacture, store, ship, and in many cases service their product—all at their expense. You, in turn, agree to become their "marketing department," acting independently to share the products and find new customers, who then become your clients. For every sale you make, you are paid a commission ranging from 20 to 50 percent. As a direct-selling professional you have the opportunity to work part-time or full-time. You can expand your business enterprise by engaging and training other people who like you, love the products, propagate their enthusiasm for the business, and gain new customers. For this you are paid additional bonuses.

It doesn't stop there. Your company has a stake in your prosperity and goes to great lengths to inspire you with incentives ranging from free products to all-expense-paid getaways to exotic destinations. Companies understand their success depends on your success and provide ongoing support in the form of training material and live events designed to inspire you to continually grow and learn. Unlike traditional entrepreneurs who usually fly solo, you are never alone in your direct-selling business. You always have someone to support you along the way. In fact, you'll form lifelong friendships with some of the most incredible people you'll ever meet.

If you are one of the hundreds of thousands of individuals thinking about starting a small business, be sure to look before you leap into the life of a traditional entrepreneur. You might be surprised to learn the trappings of a conventional business limit your freedom instead of enhance it. Why not consider starting a direct-selling business of your own? Perhaps, like thousands of others before you, you'll discover more rewards than you ever thought possible.

■ Introduction

If you own a home-based business, or have thought about starting one—direct selling or otherwise—this book is written for you. Like its predecessor, *Build It Big*, these pages reveal 101 innovative insights on how to succeed in your entrepreneurial endeavor. What makes this book so unique is that it provides the best ideas on a range of topics, shared by the women and men who don't just talk about success—they live it. Although this book was written specifically for the more than 46 million people worldwide who are independent distributors with direct-selling companies, the information applies equally to anyone who owns a small business or is looking to begin one. Through these insights, you can discover an enlightened perspective of every facet of growing your business, from getting started to becoming a leader and coaching your team to greatness.

The idea and design for our first book came not from the boardroom of the DSWA, but from the loyal members of our Leaders Task Force. We posed the question, "If you could design the ideal book on direct-selling success that you would recommend to everyone on your team, what would it look like?" Their answers shaped the vision for a series of books that are easy to read, comprehensive in subject matter, innovative in content, inspirational in nature, and valuable beyond measure. As indicated by the international success of *Build It Big*, we are delighted that the vision has become a reality. Now, in *More Build It Big*, we are proud to have exceeded the quality, innovation, and relevance of the first book.

The direct-selling leaders who contributed to this book were selected not only because they have attained considerable success in direct selling, but also because they have done so with a spirit and sense of integrity that exemplifies the best of our profession. These leaders oversee a collective organization of nearly half a million distributors, with teams ranging in size from 400 to 40,000. They've walked in your shoes, experienced your joys, and triumphed over the same challenges you face every day. These leaders want you to learn from their mistakes and generously offer their tried-and-true secrets to success.

The speakers and experts included here are the most sought-after trainers in our industry. Their energy, enthusiasm, and ability to teach and inspire transcends the words of their most treasured insights on how to grow your direct-selling business while living a more fulfilling life.

In exchange for the time you invest in reading this book, the readers of the first book confirm that you'll gain a new sense of pride—a feeling of excitement to be a part of this great profession. As you follow our contributors' recommendations, you'll find your dreams and deepest desires becoming clear and your determination strengthened. You will very likely adopt a new mindset about your business and how to succeed, as well as incorporate new habits into your daily life that will move you closer to your dreams. Furthermore, you will discover insider secrets that will inspire you to greater confidence in both yourself and your business, making it easier to share what you do with others.

We'll also go on to give you the answers to some of your most pressing challenges including how to: increase sales volume; sponsor more team members; juggle family and business; and create a team culture that inspires others to achieve their heart's desire.

Most importantly, if you truly drink in the wisdom shared in these pages, this book will inspire you into action by offering you practical, proven strategies you can implement in your business right away. We have provided clear, concise action steps at the close of every insight that can be completed within 48 hours. Many of our readers have shared that these action steps are the keys to making the most of the book.

Before you turn the page to begin your journey with *More Build It Big*, know that the resources and support do not stop here. We have designed an entire Web site at http://www.morebuilditbig.com for your learning enjoyment. There you will find handouts, checklists, and supplementary materials that go beyond what we could provide you in each brief insight. We offer these as a show of our commitment to make your experience one that will have a lasting and meaningful impact on your business and your life.

So, let's begin your journey toward becoming more of the person you know you can be. On the other side of these pages is an opportunity to live a more confident, meaningful, and purposeful life!

■ How to Use This Book

How can you make the most of the material presented here? First and foremost, *finish the book*. Don't allow yourself to be among the majority of book buyers who never make it past the first ten pages. You're not like them. You're not a quitter, or you wouldn't be in this profession to begin with. Second, pace yourself. Some of you have such an insatiable thirst for information on how to succeed in direct selling that you will be tempted to blaze through the first six insights, never bothering to stop and write down the action steps you are committed to take. Others will approach this book nonchalantly, allowing it to gather dust on your bedside until you've had a rotten day and come searching for answers. Our challenge to you is to not fall into either of these groups, but to find a comfortable middle ground that keeps you consistently moving through the book, implementing the ideas and bringing forth the results you know you deserve.

There are many ways to use the book to your advantage. You can partner with another direct seller and commit to read one insight per day. Then meet for breakfast or lunch every two weeks to discuss how the actions you are taking are impacting your success. If you are a leader, select a particular insight and use it as the educational focus for your meeting. Ask team members to read it and implement the action steps prior to the meeting and then share their experiences. You can join one of the many *Build It Big* circles, popping up throughout the country. These groups of direct sellers often start in local DSWA chapters, which meet regularly to share and support one another and implement the ideas presented in this book.

Finally, designate one special journal as your *Build It Big Journal*. In it, record the ideas and tips that you want to capture; your commitments and action steps that grow out of each insight; and your thoughts, experiences, and growth. Before you know it, you too will ***Build It Big!***

1 *Direct-Selling Excellence*

*T*hose of us who are in the direct-selling profession feel enormous pride in our ability to positively impact the lives of millions of people around the world. This chapter provides a straightforward, unfiltered look into the direct-selling universe, populated by 50 million people worldwide. The authors who have shared their insights were called upon to express their thoughts and feelings about a profession that they have not only chosen as a career path, but one that they have also grown to love.

If you are not yet part of the direct-selling profession, we encourage you to read this chapter with an open mind and an open heart. What you discover may correct misconceptions that you may have and enable you to take the first steps on an exciting adventure that can change your life.

Those of you who have already taken the leap will find confirmation that your experience is shared by many others. This chapter will confirm your sense that direct selling enables you to live and work according to your own values, arranging your life around that which is near and dear to you. It will reinforce your sense of pride that you have chosen to forge a path that allows you to realize your unique vision and dreams, and, most importantly, the insights will encourage you to continue to strive for and embody excellence in your career choice and in your life.

■ Direct-Selling Excellence

By Kim Leopardo
Modeling the traits of excellence

MODELING FOR INSPIRATION

Although millions of women have found their lives' fulfillment in direct selling, urban legend prevents millions more from discovering the freedom and satisfaction of this wonderful career choice. Whether you're just starting out or already leading thousands, *by adopting and modeling the traits of direct-selling excellence, you can counteract negative perceptions, help others to embrace a career in direct selling, and grow into the best leader you can be.*

EXHIBITING OUR PRIDE

Direct sales is an industry based on helping each other work toward a common goal. When we model the following traits of direct-selling excellence, we are not only helping each other, but we are exhibiting the pride we feel in being a part of this great profession. In the process, we're helping other women to join us on our career path, and thus fulfill their visions and dreams.

Model abundance. If you're a team of one, treat the universe as if it's the first member of your team. Believe and act as if the universe has been wonderful to you, is conspiring to do something great for you today, and will provide even more in the future. As you add team members, trust that they are there to help you, not compete with you. At every opportunity, give credit to the universe and to your team, remembering that you always get back more than you give.

Model excellent leadership. Lead yourself. Become the leader you would follow. Who you are is what you attract. You will soon attract a team that mirrors your attitude.

Model humility. Be grateful to learn anything from anyone. Whether you're new to direct selling or are a seasoned leader, discover new ideas and improve yourself. Embrace change. Tell your team, "What an excellent idea! I've never thought to do it that way." Internalize the knowledge that you can be wrong and never hesitate to admit it.

Model gratitude. If you have a team of one, be appreciative of yourself. Never pass up the opportunity to tell your team members how proud and privileged you are to have them in your life.

Model support for your company. Believe in your company, its products, and its policies, and communicate your faith in them to your team.

Model a positive attitude. Remember that you are responsible for your own success. When you see the glass as half full, so it shall be. When you need guidance, ask for help. When someone looks to you for guidance, give it to her freely and cheerfully.

Model good communication. Direct selling is about building relationships, and relationships are built on communication. Maintain personal contact with your clients, your hosts, and your team through phone calls and notes.

Model selling and recruiting. To talk the talk, you must walk the walk. Treat your business as a business, stay organized, and set and reach your booking, selling, and recruiting goals.

Model healthy boundaries. You aren't a therapist, but you are a great salesperson, team member, and leader. Know when you can help and when you can't, and communicate your boundaries with care and concern.

Actions for Excellence

John Maxwell, author of *There's No Such Thing as Business Ethics*, says, "Though you cannot go back and make a brand new start . . . anyone can start from now and make a brand new end." Start creating your "brand new end" by taking these steps in the next 48 hours:

1. Look back over the past week and think about all of the people who observed your life. What did you model during the week? List the ways in which you are pleased with how you conducted yourself in all the moments of your week. List the traits you modeled for others that weren't ideal.

2. Assess the balance between your life and your work. List where you are investing your time, and if needed, change your priorities to reflect your values and satisfy your heart.

3. Select one trait of excellence that you will model in the coming week. Write down the situations and scenarios where you will have the opportunity to model that trait. Then, make the commitment to take action! ■

■ Define Your Core Beliefs

By Kathleen Heyn
Building others by shoring up their beliefs

BUILDING A SOLID FOUNDATION

Your internalized beliefs about direct selling will make or break your attempts to recruit new team members. If you experience doubt about whether this business is right for you, those misgivings will be communicated to your prospects—even if you never verbalize them.

Your inconsistent or conflicting beliefs may manifest as hesitation, discomfort, or lack of pride, and will lead others to perceive you as untrustworthy in regard to the opportunity associated with your business. ***Examining and strengthening your beliefs in direct selling will have a positive impact on your prospects, which in turn will lead you to recruiting success.*** Your core belief will be a solid foundation that will affect every action you take. Your passion and belief in the business will grow proportionately to the service that you provide to those you encounter in your life. Your business will become your passion and your purpose, and when that happens, everyone wins!

PEELING THE ONION

Your attitudes and beliefs directly affect your actions, which eventually impact your results, and thus, your lifestyle. You are in your current position because—either consciously or subconsciously—you planned to be there.

In truth, beliefs are simply perceptions. When an event occurs (fact) and you attach a feeling to it (emotion), it becomes a perception (how you view the event) and ultimately a belief. Unfortunately, our perceptions are often inaccurate because our emotions color the facts. Enveloping ourselves in false perceptions or inaccurate beliefs can impede our ability to build a successful business.

Recruiting is based upon trust and belief—the belief you have in the product, company, and profession, as well as the belief that others have in you, the sponsor. When these beliefs are formed, the recruiting process can begin. Uncover your core beliefs about the direct-selling profession *before* moving forward with your business and enrolling others into your organization.

The process of discovering your core beliefs depends on your ability to "peel the onion." The outer layers of the onion are the emotions you attach to an event, such as frustration at not meeting your monthly goal or anger at a team member who didn't keep her commitment to book three new presentations. The next layer consists of your perception or interpretation of an event. Perhaps you perceive that your monthly goal is unrealistic or that your team member isn't working very hard. The final layer reveals your core belief: "Women who reach their monthly goal are lucky" or your team member "isn't cut out for direct selling."

When you peel the onion, you discover, layer by layer, your belief in yourself, your belief in the profession, your unmet goals, and the obstacles that prevent you from fulfilling your dreams. Once you uncover and acknowledge your core beliefs, you can pinpoint areas where you can work to increase your belief in yourself, in your products, in your company, and in the profession.

Once you've examined and shored up your core beliefs, you will be able to communicate a consistently positive and trustworthy message to your prospects. Identify the ways in which you can add value and be of service to others as you build your business. Then find strategies to incorporate them into every business opportunity. In doing so, you will no longer perceive the process as one of recruiting people into your business for additional profit; rather, your core belief will manifest as an attitude of helping and serving others. Then, when you do offer your business as the vehicle to help women reach their dreams, it will be a genuine offer of an opportunity for them.

Getting to the Core

Uncovering your core beliefs and challenging them is an evolutionary process that takes time. To get started, take these three steps today and tomorrow:

1. *Make a commitment.* Draw up a written contract with yourself that states your intent to uncover your core beliefs and your commitment to bring energy and honesty to the process.

2. *Find resources.* Make a list of resources—books, CDs, audiotapes—that will help you shore up any wavering beliefs in yourself, your product, your company, or the business.

3. *Find a role model.* Take a mental tour of your upline and make a list of women who exemplify solid core beliefs and an attitude of service to others. ■

■ The Myth about Being in Business for Yourself

By David Bach
Teaching people how to finish rich

CHALLENGING THE MISCONCEPTIONS

Whether you're considering going into business for yourself or you're working to build a team, you understand the allure of making your own schedule, being your own boss, working from home, and having independence. Unfortunately, a fear of the unknown or an unwillingness to take risks often keeps people from acting on their desire to own their own business. Through reading this book or through working with your prospects, you can *dispel the myths of entrepreneurship and, as a result, create an atmosphere for an informed decision-making process about business ownership.*

Let's consider some of the many myths that discourage people from even considering going into business for themselves. Separating the facts from the fictions can totally transform your attitude and make the difference between never getting started and finishing rich.

> *. . . In fact, many businesses today are started with less than $1,000.*

Myth No. 1: You Need a Lot of Money to Start

The reality of most small businesses is starting them takes less money than you think. The average start-up cost of the companies on *Inc.* magazine's 2004 list of America's fastest-growing small businesses was $25,000, and many of them were started with $5,000 or less. In fact, many businesses today are started with less than $1,000.

Myth No. 2: You Need to Have Experience

> **T**he bottom line is this: In most cases, you need no more than one to two hours a day to get a business going on the side . . .

Friends and relatives may warn you that you need to have experience in business in order to be able to start one. Don't let these people steal your dreams. While experience certainly helps, action beats inaction any day of the week. Besides, you don't have to go it alone. These days, it's easy to be in business for yourself but not by yourself. As you'll discover, there are so many resources out there to help you build a home-based business and second stream of income you may wonder why you waited so long to do this.

There are countless companies in the business of helping you get your business off the ground with training and mentoring systems designed to help you succeed. In addition, the government now offers training and there are many volunteer organizations staffed by veteran entrepreneurs whose experience you can tap.

Myth No. 3: You Need a Lot of Time

The naysayers who, I promise you, will come out of the woodwork the minute they find out you are planning to start a business on the side will insist you don't have time to start a business. "You're too busy," they'll argue. You have a job, kids, household chores, whatever. The bottom line is this: In most cases, you need no more than one to two hours a day to get a business going on the side, which is why I say you not only should but can do it without quitting your day job. If you commit two hours a day to a new venture, that's 60 hours a month or roughly 720 hours a year. If you put that kind of effort into starting a business on the side over the next five years, I promise you—you'll succeed. What would you have to give up? Television and maybe a little sleep? Wake up an hour earlier each day and skip the

TV at night and you'll have the time. If you can't commit to an hour or two a day to start a business, you're not ready to do this.

Myth No. 4: Nine Out of Ten New Businesses Fail

The biggest myth about starting your own business is you have a 90 percent chance of failing within one year. This much-heralded statistic doesn't match up with what we see in the real world. According to the Small Business Administration, two-thirds of all new businesses survive at least two years and about half survive four.

Myth No. 5: You Need a Lot of Stuff to Get Started

The idea that you need a business plan and business cards and stationery and a phone line and an office and so on and so forth to start your business is simply not true. The only things you absolutely need to start a business are passion, commitment, desire, and a willingness to take action. I know this from experience. I started and ran Finish Rich, Inc., to the point where it was bringing in $1 million in annual revenue, without having an office, a business plan, business cards, or stationery. What I did have was passion and commitment.

> **T**he only things you absolutely need to start a business are passion, commitment, desire, and a willingness to take action.

Myth No. 6: You Have to Be Passionate about the Particular Business You Choose

I'm a big believer in the idea if you do what you love, the money will follow. But I also recognize this cliché has held many people back from starting their own business. Why? Because they don't know "what they love" or because they believe "what they love" can't make money. If your goal is to earn an extra $500 a month, that in and of itself can be enough of a reason to start your own business! People become successful in business all the time even though they aren't really turned on by the actual product or service they happen to produce or sell. What they're passionate about is being an entrepreneur and being their own boss. If you really want to be your own boss and are dedicated and willing to work hard, then you have what it takes to start your own business.

■ Shoot Out of the Starting Block

By Gayle Driscoll
Bringing smiles of success to direct sellers everywhere

FAST-TRACKING NEWBIES

As a leader, it is essential that you give each new team member the opportunity to start on the fast track to success. ***Create and implement a fast-start system so that every newcomer can show what she's made of.*** At the end of 90 days, you're likely to have a productive team member who is ready to ease off her initial sprint and continue with the endurance of someone who is comfortable moving into leadership. Your system will bring you increased retention, higher sales volume, and a growing and happy team. It will also ensure that you focus your efforts where they have the most leverage: working with strong members.

SPRINTING TO SUCCESS

The first component of your quick-start system is establishing your new team member's level of commitment. A commitment is an agreement or pledge to do something in the future—*no matter what*. This is different from a well-meaning promise or good intention in that a commitment causes you to act, regardless of any circumstance that may get in the way.

Once your new team member's commitment level is established, it's time to sign a partnership agreement. Communicate your willingness to champion her every step of the way, and make sure she understands her commitment to herself.

After the partnership agreement is signed, conduct a thorough training to provide your newest member with the tools she needs to launch her business. Creating rich possibilities for your new teammate will inspire her to go to work. To ensure that she gets off to a quick start, help her develop daily or weekly intentions. By asking her to assign a target completion date to each undertaking, you solidify her commitment and give her a glimpse of the finish line.

Examples of daily undertakings include:

- Order your product and set up your auto ship.

- Study the company's training materials and Web site.

- Create a names list.

- Order three-way calling for your phone.

- Establish your corporate Web site.

- Order your business cards.

- Listen to motivational CDs.

- Read chapters in a book.

Establish a follow-up date or time for your next training or coaching call. If she's completed her undertakings, give her the enthusiastic praise she deserves and encourage her to celebrate her achievements. Follow up with another request that moves her business plan forward. If, on the other hand, she hasn't completed her undertakings, bring her back to her original commitment, goals, and benchmarks—her Why for starting this business.

In addition to helping your new team member meet objectives, the process of following up on her undertakings serves to test her commitment level. This test relates to another aspect of getting a new recruit off to a great start: matching your time to her efforts.

Your new team member must understand that your commitment level is based on her commitment level. She takes a step, you take a step; she takes a step, you take two; she takes one, and you take three. She needs to internalize the importance of massive, consistent, and persistent action. When she follows through, you know you have a winner.

But if she doesn't follow through, you need to react in kind. If she stops moving forward, you stop, too. She must realize that you are working with others who are committed, and that if she remains committed, you will be there for her as well. If she fails to commit, then you need to move on and work with the willing. It's much more enjoyable, rewarding, and fun to work with those who you don't have to drag across the finish line.

You know your new team member will make it around the fast track when

- she has a clear vision of what she intends to accomplish;

- she has created a plan for the attainment of her goal;

- she is motivated by her vision;

- she maintains her enthusiasm, her persistence, and her good attitude; and

- she accomplishes all of her assignments on time and is accountable for her actions.

On Your Mark, Get Set, Lead!

In the next 48 hours, begin to create your own system for fast-tracking your recruits by

- outlining your own vision, goals, and benchmarks;

- developing a template of daily and weekly actions that you can use when working with your new recruits; and

- reevaluating your efforts on behalf of each of your team members to ensure that you are leveraging your energy to reap the most rewards. ■

■ Bring Your Values to Life through Direct Selling

By Joy von Skepsgardh
Living the gift of a value-driven profession

GETTING INTO ALIGNMENT

Whether or not we're aware of it, we each have our own hierarchy of values. When you go about your day without a spring in our step, chances are that you're living life out of alignment with your values. ***When you take the time to identify and prioritize your values, you're better able to commit to living within your own truths.*** In the direct-selling business, you have an opportunity to design a business and a lifestyle that embraces and demonstrates your personal values. When you are living your values, you feel "on purpose" and fulfilled.

So, what are values? They are simply the qualities that you treasure, admire, appreciate, believe in, and cherish. Simply put, a value is what is important to you.

One of my most important values is freedom. By engaging in my referral marketing business, I create my own schedule, which varies daily. I have the option of when I want to work, the freedom to choose my own marketing methodologies, and the flexibility to change and flow with the shifting activities involved in my business. I am free to work from home, on the road, or outside on the patio if I so choose. I can share my products and professional opportunity while I travel, and I can teach others how they can have more freedom in their lives.

IDENTIFYING AND PRIORITIZING YOUR VALUES

There are dozens, if not hundreds, of potential values. They can include beauty, financial freedom, community, spirituality, honesty, service, integrity, commitment, nature, environmental preservation, free time, discipline, romance, family, independence, animals, adventure, cars, artistic expression, fresh ideas, cleanliness, health, laughter, travel, and security. A value can be a personal quality, a person, a place, or a thing.

For example, one woman might value family. With a young son, husband, and mother-in-law under one roof, she is living in alignment with her value because she works from home and is able to be with those she loves while growing her sales volume monthly. She can nurse her child and rock him to sleep in between phone calls. She can simmer a hot soup while catching up on her e-mail. She enjoys the gift of family and work side by side.

Another professional direct seller may value health. To her, exercising daily, having times of silence and stillness, and eating pure foods bring her great pleasure. Because her direct-selling company is involved in health products, she can share this passion with others and be an example of true vitality to her customers. She also associates with like-minded people and finds new clients at health classes, on hikes, and during retreats. She creates a style of doing business healthily, as a natural extension of her values.

A direct-selling professional who values friendship can build an organization of friends. She can do business while sharing personal insights, and offer true customer care because she enjoys her customers, meeting new people, and socializing her way to financial abundance.

It's Your Turn

If you had a treasure chest of your values, what would be inside it? Take the time to list between five and ten of your core values in no particular order. Be honest with yourself; don't compare yourself to anyone else. Deep down, you know what feels important to you.

Next, write each of your values on a 3" × 5" card. Create the hierarchy of your values by rearranging the cards until you are satisfied that your cards are in order of importance for who you are at this time.

Now, ask yourself, "Am I living in integrity with my values?" Remember, direct selling gives you the opportunity to better align your work habits to fit your values. What changes are you willing to make? If your values are in opposition to your lifestyle, you are not being honest with yourself, because your daily choices do come from an internal value set.

Next Steps for Living Your Values

1. Now that you have completed the exercise, identify three things you can do to honor your most important value.

2. Implement one thing into your business within the next 48 hours, and schedule the other two things into your calendar for completion within the next month.

3. Keep your index cards on your desk and commit to "reshuffling" them once a month to discover new priorities that surface. ■

■ Will It Be an Entrance or Exit?

By Doug Firebaugh
Fun, faith-filled, and on fire

OPENINGS EVERYWHERE

Have you ever walked through a door before? We all have, and we do it daily. Doors are an entrance or an exit to where we are going, or coming from. We have doors in our homes, in our cars, and just about everywhere else we go. Doors are a part of our daily life, and our direct-selling business.

You may not realize it, but you have a door you walk through every morning, and everyone on the planet walks through that door. But this door is a door that is a little different than any other door you will face today.

This door is invisible. You may not realize it, but every morning when you wake up, you have two invisible doors facing you, before your feet ever hit the floor. They have been there all your life, and can impact and affect your life beyond anything I could ever write or talk about. These doors are powerful entrances to life and all that goes with it. But these doors are special, as they have writing on them, and in big, bold letters.

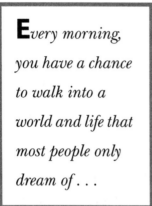

Every morning,
you have a chance
to walk into a
world and life that
most people only
dream of . . .

One door has "Success" written on it, and the other door has "Struggle" written on it. One door leads to a life of success, wealth, and treasure overflow. The other door leads to a life of struggle, worry, and survival. If you walk through the door of Success daily, then you have entered into a life of success. If you walk through the door of Struggle, then you have entered into a life and world of struggle. **Both doors are the entrances to where your life is headed, and what you can expect out of today.**

Most people today walk through the door of Struggle. Why does this happen? It is a learned behavior. We are programmed to think a certain way, view things a certain way, expect things in a certain way, and to take action in a certain way. All of these things were learned from what we heard growing up. Many times, we are taught that the door of Struggle is "just the way it is," and there is no alternative to that door. There *is* an alternative, and it is an entrance that many people have chosen to walk through daily. They have let go of the learned sayings that dominate most people's lives.

What are those sayings? You know, the ones we all grew up hearing:

- "What do you think, money grows on trees?"

- "What do you think I am made of, money?"

- "We cannot afford that."

- "If you don't wish for much, you won't be disappointed."

- "Hold on to what you got. You may not get anymore."

- "Times are tight."

- "Life is tough."

- "We just cannot seem to ever get ahead."

Every morning, you have a chance to walk into a world and life that most people only dream of, if you decide to. It is a world that is soaked with possibilities and hope. This entrance leads to the lifestyle that everyone dreams of, but few ever live. And it can become a part of your life, if you decide to walk through that door. And your life will be changed beyond recognition. Why? *You* will be changed beyond recognition. What lies behind the Success door is a life-changing power, and a life-changing way of thinking. That is why most people in direct selling do not succeed like they could have. They were walking through the wrong door. And whatever door you are walking through in the morning, is where your life and business are headed.

Choosing Your Door

Tomorrow morning, when you wake up, you will be facing two doors. One has Success written on it, and the other has Struggle written on it. Which doorknob is your hand going to be reaching for? Which entrance are you going to be walking through? What is going to be your world tomorrow? Will it be Success? Will it be Struggle? People respond to you in this business from what they perceive. Do they perceive you as headed straight to Success, or straight to Struggle? That all depends on the entrance that you walked through this morning.

Your thoughts are the keys that open either an exit from Success, or the entrance to it. The decision is yours. ■

■ Go the Extra Mile

By Grace Keohohou Lee
Vice President and Cofounder of the DSWA

THE DIFFERENCE BETWEEN GOOD AND GREAT

Today, customers have myriad options to purchase products. Often, the deciding factor in making a purchase is the level of service a customer receives. When the customer is discerning, poor customer service means missed opportunities for sales. As a direct seller, you have the opportunity to provide customers with consistent, individualized attention—something they don't receive when shopping in a store or online. ***By going the extra mile and providing exceptional customer service, you will garner repeat business, referrals for new customers, bookings with new groups of customers, and the satisfaction of knowing you're doing a great job.***

Think of a company—a restaurant, store, or bank—where you enjoy doing business. Why do you like being their customer? Are the employees friendly, courteous, and knowledgeable? Imagine for a moment that you are there right now. How do you feel?

What does good service really mean? It means giving your customer your personal attention, making her feel as though she is your *only* customer, and delivering more than she expects. In short, good customer service means making a friend of your customer and letting her know that you have her best interests at heart. Here are some tips for providing good service:

- Remember her name and use it frequently.

- Remember what she has purchased.

- Learn her likes and dislikes.

- Send her thank-you notes.

- Contact her regularly.

- Put her needs high on your priority list.

- Inform her of specials and sales.

- Be available to meet her needs.

- Follow up when you say you will.

- Remember facts about her family or hobbies.

- Sell her a product that is flattering.

- Be organized and thorough.

- Be a friend.

- Return her phone calls promptly.

- Demonstrate that you want to fulfill her needs.

The difference between good service and excellent service is the amount of initiative you take. As Roger Staubach said, "There are no traffic jams along the extra mile." It is your willingness and ability to provide your customer with something that she appreciates and doesn't expect. Customers love those little extras. Here are some ways to make shopping with you a delightful experience:

- Gift-wrap her order in a pretty bag with shred and a ribbon and deliver it to her office. She will feel like it is her birthday.

- Offer a gift with her purchase of over $50.

- Enclose a motivational quote in a personal note to let her know you are thinking of her.

Today's Steps along the Extra Mile

1. Review the list of extra-mile services, and select three to add to your business practices this month.

2. Consider developing an index card system or a database containing personalized information about each of your customers.

3. Purchase your gift bags, research your motivational quotes, or pull together the premiums you will need to implement your services. ■

Sensational Shows

2

*I*magine, for a moment, that you are among a group of people who are relaxed, enjoying great conversation, ready to have a good time, and gathered to learn about your products and opportunities. With solid preplanning, and a bit of luck, you have a standing-room-only crowd. Occasionally, though, only a few have come to meet you. Regardless of the number of people in the room, one element remains constant—the opportunity to present your product to potential customers is a privilege for which Fortune 500 companies pay thousands, and sometimes millions, of dollars.

To assist you in leveraging this opportunity, the leaders and experts who contributed to this chapter have provided their best advice for scheduling in-home shows, coaching hostesses, and maximizing the sales opportunity. The result is an incredible compilation of practical, proven insights you can implement immediately for greater results.

This chapter is uniquely valuable in that it holds fresh ideas for all distributors, whether in the party plan or network marketing segment of the profession. The industry-wide trend toward group gatherings, during which the focus remains on the product, is not only good for sales, but also provides fertile ground for finding potential team members. So cast off any label you may have taken on and be open to these innovative ways to grow your business. As the saying goes . . . It's like getting paid to party!

■ Fill Your Calendar with Appreciation

By Steve Wiltshire

Warming our industry with an attitude of gratitude

MOVING FROM WARM TO HOT

You've diligently made your calls, booked your parties, and held your presentations. You've reached the end of your warm market, and you're facing the challenge of booking more parties. *To reinvigorate your bookings, create an Appreciation Party–an extraordinary experience for all of your hostesses and friends–as your "thank you" for their support of you and your business.* Not only will you build your reputation for giving great parties, but you'll also attract more bookings.

While your company's standard structured party is based on a formula for success, it isn't intended to be a straightjacket. *You can be creative.* You don't always have to hold parties at the home of your hostess. You don't always have to fill the room with new people. You can have parties at your own home for people who have helped you. Just as people who have purchased from you before are most likely to do so again, hostesses are likely to book with you repeatedly–especially if you show them that you value their friendship and support.

CREATING AN EXTRAORDINARY EXPERIENCE

1. **Schedule two dates** to host an Appreciation Party for your previous hostesses, guests, and friends. Think up a theme for the event that will move, touch, and engage them. Make yours an event they will not want to miss.

2. **Design a flier** that incorporates your theme and promotes the experience rather than the product. For example, you might create a flier for a "Friends' Night Out," and mention that festivities include door prizes, food, and merriment. Enclose your theme flier, company postcard invitation, three on-time drawing tickets, and a splash of confetti in a colored envelope.

3. **Develop your invitation list.** Ask yourself, "If I could host a party, inviting only those who I knew would accept my invitation without hesitation, who would I choose to invite?"

4. **Think about each guest** before calling to invite her. What do you know about her past or current life situation? Use that knowledge to design your phone script, placing all the focus on the guest. Your phone call will be much more fulfilling when you have an immediate connection with your guest.

   Listen closely and be passionate when you share your invitation. Let her hear your excitement at the prospect of seeing her at your "Friends' Night Out Party." Invite her to bring a friend. Remind her that the only thing she has to bring is a smile and her personality!

   If your guest isn't available when you call, come up with a voice message that will entice her to return your call. Try an acknowledgment, a little bit of mystery, and some enthusiasm. Say, for example,

   "Hi, Jill, this is Sally. I've been thinking that I haven't seen you in a while. I'm hosting a 'Taste of Italy Party' for a group of my special friends and I want you to join me. I know life is busy so I'm going to give you three times when you can reach me in the next few days: (*offer three times you'll be at your phone*). I sincerely look forward to a rich conversation with you and enjoying your friendship soon."

5. **Visit those who can't attend.** If an intended guest can't make either of your scheduled dates, you can still express your appreciation by bringing her a card or a gift along with a few samples of your new products. That personal connection authenticates your invitation and gives you the possibility for sales, bookings, and sharing your business opportunity.

6. **Design a WOW party!** Prepare extraordinary activities, and make sure your party theme shines through. Design a demonstration that's participatory, fun, and informative. Lastly, ask yourself, "If I was a guest at a party, what would make that party so exceptional that I'd want to duplicate the experience?"

7. **Put on your party hat** for the big event. Be authentic, connect, and enjoy! Be sure to have your next three available dates in mind, because your calendar is sure to fill.

Today's Three Steps to Thanks

1. Pull out your calendar and set aside two dates for your Appreciation Parties.

2. Think of an exciting, enticing theme that will draw in your guests.

3. Write down a list of former hostesses and others who have shown you support in the past. This will become your invitation list. ■

■ Vitalize Your Connections

By Pat Dempsey
Connecting for a lasting impression

LIFEGIVING LINKS

In all your relationships—from your customers and team members to your upline and company—your interpersonal skills either make or break your success. When you have no connections, you have no business! In fact, your direct-selling career rewards you in unswerving proportion to the meaningful connections you create with others.

Do you make more and better connections every day? Perhaps you believe the skill of vitalizing connections is something that doesn't come naturally to you. Perhaps you haven't taken the time to master it, have let your skill grow rusty, or simply don't slow down enough to do it! And unless you have a heart of gratitude and joy, your ability to vitalize your connections will be limited.

As a direct seller, you must create vital connections every day. Slow down, honor others, and take the time to listen. *Lay the foundation for a deep and meaningful connection by expressing how much you value each person you meet.* Sometimes you can create kinship by expressing your appreciation for someone directly, but more often you can build a powerful bond simply by giving her your full attention and deeply listening to what she has to say.

Each day, ensure your success by creating vital connections that have a positive impact and make a difference in women's lives. Every customer, hostess, fellow consultant, and even your home office staff deserves the very best you have to offer. When you create vital connections, you not only create valuable contacts for your business, you also enrich your life with more friends, more partners, and more meaningful interactions.

BUILDING CONNECTIONS WITH YOURSELF AND OTHERS

Are you ready to create vital connections? Take an inventory of yourself and make sure you're prepared.

Prepare Your Mind

- Are you taking advantage of the many opportunities for ongoing self-improvement and education regarding your business?

- Are you up to date with all the latest product information, specials, and promotions from your company?

- Do you have the confidence that comes from *knowing* that you regularly and successfully work the business yourself?

- Have you prepared and practiced your 30-second commercial, your personal story, and success stories that vitalize your descriptions of benefits and opportunities?

Prepare Your Heart

- Are you well connected with yourself? Do you take the time to care for yourself both spiritually and personally?

- Are you receptive? Do you graciously accept the input and encouragement you need from others? Are you ready to deeply listen to your contacts and identify and validate their true needs?

- Do you have an attitude of gratitude? Are you truly enjoying the journey?

Prepare Your Appearance

- Are you dressed for success? Is your clothing appropriately professional, neat, and clean?

- Are you wearing your smile? Do your eyes tell the world you're happy, confident, and successful?

When you're prepared, you find opportunities for making connections everywhere you go—from your regular routine of running errands, driving your kids, and enjoying social and community get-togethers, to local networking events, team meetings, regionals, and conferences.

Vital Connections Today and Tomorrow

1. Once you've answered the questions and assessed your preparation, identify three ways you can be better prepared to connect: one mental, one emotional, and one physical. Visit http://www.dswa.org for tools that aid your preparation. For example, you can prepare yourself mentally with articles from the Learning Library; emotionally with live teleclasses or archived class recordings; or physically by attending a DSWA Chapter meeting or Success Circle.

2. Develop an affirmation that supports the improvement in your emotional preparation; for example: "I give thanks for

everyone I know and everyone I've yet to meet because they bring joy and happiness into my life."

3. Select a special broach or necklace, and hold it as you repeat your affirmation.

4. Wear the broach or necklace to energize your awareness of every opportunity you have to create a vital connection. ■

■ Catch and Coach Your Busy Hostess

By Debbie Rotkvich
Inspiring hostesses to go for the gold

THE 72-HOUR WINDOW

What's the secret to high sales? Your company's top-ranked saleswoman would probably attribute her success to working closely with her hostesses. Chances are, though, that your best potential hostess is also your busiest hostess, and that her schedule often prevents you from being able to coach her to a high-volume party. *Discovering your hostess's motivation and positioning yourself to receive her guest list within three days of booking gives you the leverage you need to help her follow through with the party.* Your successful coaching efforts will result in higher attendance, greater sales, and a sense of pride and accomplishment for both you and your hostess.

Motivation Breeds Success

The first step in coaching your hostess is to determine her motivation. She may be longing for free products and discounts. Perhaps she's helping the original hostess by scheduling a show of her own, or helping you grow your business. Once you understand what makes her tick, you can provide your hostess with the incentives to maintain her excitement and enthusiasm throughout the planning process.

Get That Guest List

Receiving your hostess's guest list as quickly as possible is key to holding a successful show. Although your extra effort may be required, it's time well spent; your busiest hostesses are often those with the biggest network of friends. One strategy that works is to hinge the original hostess's benefit on the second hostess's cooperation:

> "Carol, can I count on you to get this guest list back to me within the next three working days? I'm asking because, in order for Linda to get credit for your booking, I need to have a copy of your guest list when I close her show. I close every show quickly so the hostess and the guests can receive their products in a timely manner. Can I count on you?"

Some may laugh and others may be hesitant, but by stating your expectation up front you lay the foundation for her to take your show seriously. Follow up by asking her if she would prefer to e-mail you the guest list or mail it in a postage-paid envelope that you provide. Further entice her by saying, "Carol, when I receive your list by the third day, I'll have an extra surprise for you at your show!"

Review the contact information you will need for each guest, and explain the law of averages—that less than one in three invited guests will attend. Together, decide on an attendance goal.

Keep in Touch

Between the booking and the show, use every means of communication—e-mail, voice mail, and personal notes—to remind her of her goal. A week before her event, ask your hostess to call the guests who haven't responded to her invitation. This simple reminder can often make the show a success.

Catching and Coaching Today

1. Write the suggested script on an index card and carry it with you. By glancing at it from time to time, you'll soon have it committed to memory.

2. Consider requiring that each future hostess submit her completed guest list within three days in order for the original hostess to receive credit.

3. Discover the motivation for every hostess currently on your calendar and coach her toward that goal. ■

■ Optimize Your Guest List

By Katherine Sigrist
Sharing her savvy for successful shows

NO GUEST UNBIDDEN

If you successfully book shows, but experience a high number of hostess cancellations or chronic low attendance, you may be overlooking the importance of the guest list. *By setting aside time to coach your hostess into building a great guest list, you'll increase hostess follow through.* By prequalifying the show's guests, you'll increase show attendance, thereby generating more sales, bookings, and recruits.

DEVELOPING THE IDEAL LIST

40-Plus or Bust!

As soon as your hostess has selected her date, schedule a 20- to 30-minute face-to-face meeting with her to develop her guest list. If an in-person meeting isn't possible, hold a phone conference.

Start the coaching process by explaining that 40-plus guests is your goal. Support her in the brainstorming process by suggesting groups of potential guests that she may have forgotten: personal friends, co-workers, neighbors, relatives, church members, organization members, former classmates, friends and relatives from out of town, mothers of her children's classmates, and so on. Take your time with this important step. The resulting piece of paper is your ticket to success!

Handling Resistance

Occasionally, a hostess may resist providing you with the names and contact information of her guests. To overcome her resistance, explain how the guest list can make the difference between a low show and a great show.

If she still resists, respect her privacy and let her get the information out to her network of friends in the manner she chooses. Remind her, though, that studies indicate that the primary reason for cancellations is that the hostess failed to get the invitations out in time. Share that you respect her busy schedule and simply want to make the process as convenient and as easy for her as you can.

Find the Stars

Your next step is to identify future hostesses and potential team members from among the names on the guest list. Have your hostess use a green highlighter to mark the names of her 15 favorite people. As hostess, her job is to call each of these women in the next two days, extend a personal invitation, and get a commitment from each to attend and to bring her favorite person with her. Have your hostess tell each person she calls that when she brings a friend, she will receive a special treat. Encourage your hostess to make a few calls while you're there, so you can coach her on effective invitations and put a few successes under her belt.

Ask her to follow up by mailing an invitation to each person on her list. Give her an additional ten invitations to carry with her. When she sees someone she has left off her list or meets someone new, she can invite her to the show.

Ask her to keep a list of who is coming, including the names of the friends they are bringing. For those unable to attend, there are two options. The hostess can collect an order from them, or you can call them on her behalf. The goal is to collect five or more outside orders before the party even takes place.

Once you have the completed list, ask your hostess to tell you about the people on it:

- Who loves to have home parties?

- Who enjoys entertaining?

- Who is most likely to book a show of their own?

- Who could use a girls' night out?

- Who would benefit the most from receiving free items?

- Who might be looking for a second source of income?

- Who needs a little more excitement in her life?

- Who needs to find fulfillment or create a new dream?

- Who already loves our products?

- Is there something special about anyone else on this list that you think I should know about?

After noting her responses, use a yellow highlighter on the three or four names of guests who would make great hostesses and a pink highlighter for the guests who may be interested in the business opportunity. Offer an incentive to your hostess for securing a booking or setting up an opportunity appointment before her show date.

Eliminate Listlessness Today

1. Get on the phone and book four parties to hold within the next three weeks.

2. Set up a 30-minute coaching appointment with each hostess.

3. Use the color-coding system and questions provided to make the most of each guest list. ■

■ Psych Up for Success

By Jodi Wilson Siegel
Embracing your greatness, sharing your joy

WARMING UP FOR THE BIG EVENT

When you get into a positive mindset for your presentation, you can skyrocket your success. Relive the 30 minutes prior to your last presentation. Did you shove your products into the trunk, label material while putting on your mascara at the stoplight, and arrive at the hostess's or prospect's door thinking about the video you should have returned yesterday?

If this is your pattern, you're not even coming close to fulfilling your potential for sales and sponsoring. Although you might not realize it, you're treating your presentations as an afterthought. You're missing a key element in your performance: *mental preparation.* Can you imagine a gymnast training for years, and then skipping her warm-up routine at the Olympics? Of course not! ***When you go through your warm-up routine to get yourself psyched before your presentation, you will earn a gold medal for sales and recruiting, and you will get in the mindset to reach your full potential.***

GOING FOR THE GOLD

A study of Olympic athletes by Orlick and Partington showed that, "of the three states of readiness assessed (mental, physical, and technical) only mental factors were statistically linked with final Olympic rankings." Your presentation starts well before you arrive at your destination. Take 30 minutes prior to your departure or while you're in the car to psych yourself up for success. Here are a few ideas to help you get your game face on, so you can achieve champion status in your company:

- **Boost your energy during the drive.** Create a CD of your favorite heart-pumping music. Play happy, energetic music that enlivens your mood.

- **Drop the daily hassles of life** and commit the next two to three hours to your hostess or recruit. Leave your other roles behind and become a professional consultant or network marketer. After all, your business can serve as a great temporary escape from life's worries!

- **Focus on your goals.** Place a picture of your current goal in your car. Glance at the picture and imagine how you will feel when you achieve your goal.

- **Think positive thoughts.** Positive emotions can help sustain motivation and enable you to approach each presentation with enthusiasm and energy. If you find yourself dwelling on negative thoughts, put on the mental brakes. You control your thoughts. Turn any negative thought, such as "I don't want people to think I'm pushy," into a positive one, such as, "I can't wait to make a difference in a new friend's life!"

- **Visualize your presentation.** Through your mind's eye, watch yourself acting confident and poised. See your guests or recruits interacting with you and enjoying themselves. Visualize pens out writing big checks and your prospect's enthusiastic response to your company.

- **Review key portions of your presentation.** The more often you say your presentation out loud, the more natural it will sound. While you're alone, use a tone of voice and inflection that is over the top. Feel the emotion!

- **Eliminate "wish" and "hope" from your vocabulary.** Avoid "hoping" it will be a $1,000 party or "wishing" that your prospect will agree to become a part of your team. Wishing won't make it happen. Be prepared to take action to achieve your goals.

■ **List positive personal characteristics.** Our industry celebrates individuality. Rejoice in what makes you special. Focus on your strengths and build up your confidence.

■ **Stay pumped.** Even when you are tired, bored, or discouraged, you can choose to see the positive. Your energy and passion for your company are key ingredients in determining the success of your presentation.

■ **Relive the moment.** Like an Olympic gymnast relives her best performance, take a moment to relive your most successful presentation, when everything came together. Recall the feeling of "being in the zone," the feeling of connection, and the feeling of success. You'll walk into your presentation with the confidence of a gold medalist.

Prepare for Your Next Presentation Today

1. Research music that gets you pumped. Create a special "driving to the presentation" CD. Make sure that it gets your toes tapping and your head moving!

2. Create a list of your attributes. If you have trouble coming up with a list of positive personal characteristics, ask a friend, spouse, colleague, or parent to make a list for you.

3. Ask yourself, "How do I feel and act when I am at my best?" Take some time to think about your best party. Write about what you were thinking, what you were feeling, and how you were acting before, during, and after your best party. Focus your energy on what lights you up—and make *every* party your best party! ■

■ Pitch with Accuracy, Speed, and Power

By Ronna Lichtenberg
Helping women pitch with panache

GETTING IN THE STRIKE ZONE

Your prospect wants to know just three basic pieces of information: the benefit to her if she buys from you; the Post-it® note version of your offering; and why your offering is better than another competing product. *That's it.* In fact, that's all your pitch needs whether you're selling products, raising funds for a charity, or asking your spouse to endorse your plans for the weekend!

Sure, you must be able to provide detailed backup and additional information, if your prospect asks for it. But **keep the message of your pitch simple and clear, centered on what she needs to know to make an informed decision.**

POLISHING YOUR PITCH

At the heart of every pitch are three basic elements: your best understanding of what your prospect needs; the in-a-nutshell version of what you're offering her; and why what you're offering fulfills her need better than her alternatives.

Putting your pitch on paper allows you to physically see what you've got, read it aloud, and hear how it will sound to others. Writing helps you refine your ideas and see where you need more detail or support, a change of tone, or sometimes even an entirely new approach.

Draft your pitch with your best understanding of what your prospect needs and how your offering fulfills that need. Make sure to explain why you think she needs it. Many pitchers mistakenly assume that their prospect will immediately recognize and understand the benefit. But just because you think what you've got to offer is good for your prospect doesn't mean she will automatically see it that way, too.

Next, focus on the content of your offering—the relevant details that your prospect will find most appealing and that best meet her needs.

Finally, make sure you include an explicit discussion of why your offering is better than the alternatives available to your prospect. No pitch exists in a vacuum; whomever you're dealing with always has other options. When you take the time to explore why you're the best one for the task at hand, you demonstrate real caring about the relationship. You've taken the time to think through your prospect's needs and to see the situation from her perspective rather than your own.

Sometimes the reason you're better than the alternatives may be as simple as what you're offering is more convenient. Sometimes people choose their bank because there's a branch with an ATM on their corner or to exercise at a particular gym because it's within a few blocks of their house. Closer, cheaper, more convenient are all common reasons one alternative seems more attractive than another.

Power Up Your Pitch Today

Brainstorming and sorting through ideas helps you identify the most powerful and accurate ones. To find the best elements for your pitch, complete the exercise below.

1. Ask yourself, "What problem will my offering solve?" Write all the answers you can think of.

2. Go back over your answers and circle the three most important ones.

3. Ask yourself, "How will my offering make life easier or otherwise better for my prospect?" Write all the answers you can think of, being as specific as possible.

4. Go back over your answers and circle the three most important ones.

5. Ask yourself, "Why is my solution better than anyone else's?" Write all the reasons that come to your mind.

6. Look over the list and circle the three most compelling advantages.

7. Look back at the three answers you've chosen for each question, and now pick the single most compelling point from each one. You now have your three-point power pitch!

Excerpted from *Pitch Like a Girl: How a Woman Can Be Herself and Still Succeed* by Ronna Lichtenberg © 2004. Permission granted by Rodale Inc. ∎

∎ Pleasure Your Prospects to Win Loyal Customers

By Tami Carbone
Turning shows into memorable experiences

MOVING FROM PRODUCT TO PLEASURE

The best product in the world is simply that: a product. Your enthusiasm and your skill in showing your product are admirable, but product knowledge alone isn't enough to engage your customers and take your business to the next level. ***The key to growing a successful business is to fulfill your customers' basic human needs—including the need for pleasure.*** By creating an experience that meets the emotional needs of your customer, you create pleasure in her life—pleasure she will want to re-create with your products and services again and again. It's a pleasure that she will want to bring into her home and share with her family and friends.

Peak performance expert Tony Robbins identifies six basic human needs:

1. **Comfort and Certainty.** The ability to reduce, eliminate, or avoid stress; or create, increase, and intensify pleasure.

2. **Variety and Uncertainty.** The need for surprises, differences, challenge, and excitement.

3. **Significance.** A sense of being, feeling important, and a sense of purpose.

4. **Connection and Love.** The need to experience bonding, sharing, and feeling part of oneness; being cared for and cared about.

5. **Personal Growth.** To become a better person, improve our life skills, and to excel in life.

6. **Contribution.** The desire to help others, to make our world a better place, and to change someone's life, if even for just a moment.

Looking at each of the six basic needs in the context of your business sets the foundation for connecting with your customers.

EMOTIONAL CONNECTIONS

Provide your customer with relief from her hectic life by fulfilling her need for **Comfort and Certainty.** Work closely with your hostess to create a sales environment that is welcoming and comfortable. Keep the lights dim for your introduction and presentation. Eliminate disruptive sounds. Make sure the room temperature is neither too hot nor too cold. Provide inviting seating that allows everyone to feel connected to the group. Most importantly, display your products so they are appealing to the eye yet not overwhelming to the mind.

The need for **Variety and Uncertainty** keeps us on the edge of our seats and waiting for more. Bring the customers into your presentation. Ask lots of questions. Have customers share their ideas. Invite them to make connections with other customers. Offer a variety of products, so there's something for everyone. Make your presentation fun, exciting, and unpredictable.

Deep down, each of us wants to feel **Significant.** Make each customer feel special. Remember and use her name to give her a feeling of significance. Every person loves to be complimented, especially in front of her peers. Compliment her on her questions or answers, her smile, her eyes, or her kindness. Practice treating everyone you meet to a sincere compliment.

The deepest human desire is one for **Connection and Love.** First impressions are everything, so get your customer at "Hello." We often underestimate the power of a touch, a smile, a kind word, and a listening ear, all of which have the power to turn someone's life around. Face your customer directly and look straight into her eyes. Speak to her with a compassionate tone of voice. Be present in the moment. Each of these simple acts will help you to establish connection.

Give your customers the **Personal Growth** they desire. Make your parties more about teaching and sharing and less about selling. Give your guests techniques that they can use with your products that will bring them pleasure. Give them information they can share with others.

The need to **Contribute** is what fills the heart. A full heart goes a long way. To start your party, ask each customer to share her name and one thing that's special about her hostess. This brings out smiles, tears, and laughter. The hostess feels significant and the guests feel as though they've contributed.

When making your presentation, keep in mind that you have the opportunity to transform the emotions of your customers, which in turn will transform your business.

Today's Actions to Begin Meeting Needs

1. *Practice* being conscious of your environment and the people who surround you. Notice when you feel pleasure and think about which of your needs are being met and how.

2. *Write* one thing you can do during your next presentation to meet each of the six needs of your customer.

3. *Observe* how small acts of kindness are received and how they shift the energy of your presentation.

4. *Celebrate* that you have a business that rewards you for being of service to others. ■

■ Stop Selecting and Start Asking

By Sandra Bergstrom
Bringing fun and beauty into homes across America

LOST FOR WANT OF ASKING

In direct selling, bookings—appointments to show your product to one or more people—are the first step in the all-important cycle of sales and sponsoring. While it may seem overly simplified, *the key to your direct-selling success lies in developing the skill and the courage to ask* **everyone** *you meet.*

When asking for bookings, we naturally tend to target women who are excited about our product. We might overlook the woman sitting quietly in the corner because she didn't buy anything and we anticipate a negative response. This assumption translates into a missed opportunity. Perhaps she's secretly wishing she could earn free products! When you set aside the anticipation of failure, you can seize every opportunity to book a show. Make each and every person feel important by offering her the choice.

Three Steps to Successful Booking

Increase your confidence to ask everyone by following these proven steps: **Attract, Excite,** and **Book.** Just as you would stumble and fall if you tried to leap to the stage without using the steps, you must first attract, then excite, your potential hostess before closing the deal and setting the booking date.

1. **Discover Her Interest.** Active listening is the key to attracting your potential hostess. By asking questions and actively listening to her responses, you will make her feel important, build your relationship with her, and maybe even uncover her motivation for booking a show of her own. Does she want to earn free product? Is she ready for a night out with her

friends? Is she motivated to help the hostess earn a particular gift?

2. **Create Excitement.** Once you understand her motivation for hosting a show, create excitement by sharing how she will benefit from a show of her own. Suggest, for example, that a party would be a great way to make time to get together with her friends. The more you can tap into her excitement by sharing benefits that interest her, the more likely you are to book a show with her.

3. **Get the Date.** After identifying her needs and communicating the benefits of a show, close by asking your potential hostess for a booking. Keeping in mind that a booking is not a booking without a definite date, *be specific*. For example, "When is the best time for you, the beginning or the end of the week?" When she responds, "The beginning of the week," say "I have an opening in two weeks on a Monday. Would that work for you?"

1-2-3 Steps to Success

1. Stop being selective! Make a commitment to ask every person at your next presentation to schedule a show of her own.

2. Practice the art of listening so that you can identify the unique interest or motivation for each guest.

3. Celebrate your efforts rather than your results. Focus on developing the art of asking and the bookings will come. ∎

■ Maximize Your Show Sales with One-on-One Contact

By Barbara Fishpaw
Teaching the art of building a successful business

OVERCOMING THE FEAR

Successful direct sellers understand that the one-on-one time with customers is the most important part of your show. But many demonstrators—especially those who are new—find this one-on-one time the scariest part of the party or presentation. When you're unsure of how to build relationships during a show, you can lose the opportunities for personal contact that you need to make your show a success. *Learn to maximize those opportunities for building relationships and put what you learn into practice.* When you do, you'll have higher sales, new friends, and lifetime customers.

BUILDING RELATIONSHIPS TO BUILD SALES

During a presentation, have you ever asked your guests if they've attended one of your company's parties before? When someone answers affirmatively and you inquire who the demonstrator was, if her response is, "I don't remember," an alarm should ring in your head and red lights should start flashing. You would never want this to happen to you! Instead, you want to create a positive and memorable impression during your presentation—and especially during the order-taking part of your party. Your future success in direct selling lies in your ability to personally connect with these women, who are your customers, your future hostesses, and your future team members. After all, do you want your guest for an evening or for a lifetime?

One-on-One Tips

■ Participate in conversations during shopping time to establish yourself as "one of the gang." Contributing to the fun will make you memorable, and guests will feel more at ease when they approach you to give you their orders.

- Give a sincere compliment to each guest. Don't reserve your gratitude until she places an order.

- Use your guests' names in conversation whenever possible. If you're not good at names, distribute name tags or break the ice with a "name game." For example, say, "Using the first letter of your first name, tell us a word that starts with that letter and describes our hostess."

- Make eye contact when your guests come to you to place their orders.

- Thank your guests for their business with a friendly smile and a helpful attitude.

- Role-play a one-on-one order building conversation with someone on your team who has a high customer purchase average. When you have memorized several conversation starters, your confidence level will increase and you will look forward to working one-on-one with your guests.

Order-Building Tips

- Be prepared. Are you aware of all current company specials? Are your name, phone number, and e-mail legible on the customers' receipts?

- Stay close to the action. Be within ear-shot and sight of your guests so not only can you take orders, but you can also jump in at any time to plant a booking, sales, or sponsoring seed.

- Give each guest a blank piece of paper along with her order blank. Encourage her to write down everything she likes. Say, "If you're like me, you'll see so many items you love, you won't be able to remember them all when it's time to fill out your order blank. Why not list the items on your paper first? Then, we'll decide what you can't live without and I'll help you complete your order ticket." When she shows you her list, you'll get valuable information as to her tastes, and can comfortably lead her to conversations about bookings (if she has more on her scrap paper than she is able to purchase, say, "Why not consider booking a party and getting the rest of the items for free?") and sponsoring (if she has a really long list, it's obvious she loves your product, so you may ask, "Have you ever thought of doing something like this?").

■ While reviewing her selections, try some of these one-on-one order building conversation starters:

— "This is our most popular item and it will go perfectly with ____, which you've already chosen."

— "I understand why you like ____ best. May I show you my favorite item in our line?"

— "You've qualified for our company's monthly special!"

— "Remember, we have several payment options."

— "I personally own and love this item."

— "Do you have any upcoming occasions when you will need a gift? I would be happy to help you with that now, to save you time later."

— "I couldn't help but notice all the items on your paper. Are you thinking about booking a party for (hostess name)?"

■ Never judge a person by her looks and decide for her whether or not she can afford her purchase. Looks can be deceiving.

Don't Delay, Start Today

1. Schedule a role-playing session with someone on your team who has a high customer purchase average so you can practice conversation starters.

2. Add a wish list to the catalogs you'll be using during your parties during the coming week.

3. Play a name game at your next show or purchase self-stick name tags. ■

■ Coddle Your Customers

By Jenny Bywater

Known as "Jenny B" in the party plan industry

THE POWER OF REPEAT BUSINESS

If your continual search for new hostesses leaves you feeling like a hamster running in its wheel, you may need to work smarter, not harder. Large companies know that servicing an existing customer base is more cost-effective than generating new leads. Likewise, *by diligently following up with former customers, you can generate a new revenue stream with relatively little effort,* and extricate yourself from that hamster wheel.

YOUR CUSTOMER CARE PROGRAM

When was the last time you contacted a customer who placed an order at a party? Build residual income by developing your own customer care program. Here's how:

Create a System

Organize a system that allows you to collect and easily access your customer information. Keeping it simple will help ensure that you'll follow through. Develop a computerized database, design a spreadsheet, or even collate a file of index cards. Regardless of the tool you use, develop a system to regularly enter customer information and design a method to sort the records for specific calls and mailings.

Collect Information

Give each of your customers a customer care card that includes a space for her name, phone number, address, e-mail, date of birth, and anniversary. Include a space for her to fill in her "wish list" items, so you'll know the products she'd like but hasn't yet purchased. Also incorporate three checkboxes: one asks for permission to include her in mailings and e-mail notices; one asks if she's interested in getting free products; and one asks if she's interested in earning an extra $100 per week. A checkmark in the first box puts her on your mailing list, while a positive response to the second or third box gives you a reason to call her. Take the cards home and add the information to your customer care system.

Start a Preferred Customer Club

It's easy to encourage repeat business by rewarding your customers. Give each woman a preferred customer card and mark off squares as she makes purchases. When the card is full, she earns an enticing reward.

To generate excitement among new customers and get them to spend a little more money, give them a card and explain that you'll mark one square for every $20 they spend. Then say, "On orders you place tonight, I'll mark off double boxes. This means that, when you spend $40, I will mark off four boxes!" Then, if a customer's order is $34, say, "You are only six dollars away from getting four boxes marked off. Is there something else you were thinking of getting, or do you need any gifts?" With the proper phrasing, you encourage greater sales!

Contact Your Customers

Now that you have the mechanism for great customer care in place, it's time to develop a plan for consistently contacting your customers via phone calls, mail, or e-mail. Use some or all of the following strategies:

- Send a birthday or anniversary discount card that's valid during the month of the event she's commemorating.

- When a party postpones, get on the phone and contact your preferred customers. Offer to mark double boxes on her reward card if she places an order that night. If you leave a message, offer a few specials and double box mark-off if she calls you back by the next day.

■ Prepare mailings to keep in touch. Set a goal to make a specific number of customer calls each week, and mail only to that many customers. As you make your calls, mail to the next section of your customer list. Continue this process until you've made it through your entire list. Then, start over with a new mailing!

■ Use customers' wish lists. If someone's product is on special, drop her a postcard, call her, or both.

■ Save the cost of postage and send e-mails on a regular basis. Keep your notes personal and infrequent enough so that they're not perceived as spam.

Working Smarter, Not Harder, Today

Don't wear yourself out drumming up new business. Take the lead of big companies and build residual income from your existing customer base. If you don't contact them, someone else will! Here's how to get started:

1. Decide on a system that makes it easy to enter and access customer information.

2. Develop ideas for your preferred customer club and design your customer care and club cards.

3. Get started; call five previous customers today! ■

■ Ask for What You Want

By Denise Michaels
Author of Testosterone-Free Marketing

YES, VIRGINIA, YOU CAN ASK!

You've made your prospecting calls and met with a potential team member. You've answered her questions, explained the compensation plan, and developed a friendly relationship with her. What comes next? *Ask her to do business with you!*

Experience has taught me that asking for the sale is something many women dread. After coaching over 1,200 people in marketing, I've discovered why. The real question should be, "Why not?"

Like most women, you were probably raised with the notion that asking for what you want will turn you into a pushy, used-car salesman type—or even worse, a demanding shrew. As women, we were taught to wait and let people come to us. We want to attract or draw people to us. Most of us are uncomfortable asking blatantly for what we want. We get tripped up by waiting for customers to come to us just like we waited for the cute boy in high school history class to call for a date.

The behaviors we learned as "nice girls" no longer serve us as entrepreneurs. The beliefs we grew up with can hold us back in our businesses. *Your business cannot grow beyond the level of your personal growth.* Being an entrepreneur requires different skills from being a wife, a mother, or even an employee. ***You must develop new perceptions, make new choices, and take different actions to be successful.*** Instead of waiting supportively in the background, you must do your job as a leader and *go first*. Politely ask for the business. It's expected!

When you ask for the business, you spend less time building relationships that never progress to doing business together. Your organization grows faster. Your confidence soars. You stop bouncing from one product to another, hoping the next one will magically sell itself. And, you will have mastered the most important skill in the direct-selling business: Selling. It all happens the moment you ask.

REVEALING YOUR POWER TO ASK

Master these three phases of asking so you can build your business big:

1. **Pay attention to buying signals.** If the person you're sitting across from is smiling, nodding her head, and generally in agreement with you, she's probably ready to buy. Trust your intuition about her. If you feel uncomfortable about asking for her business, check whether beliefs you developed as a girl are still affecting you subconsciously as a woman.

2. **Make different conscious choices.** When you're in the direct-selling business, the highest and best use of your time is *selling*. If you avoid asking for the business and instead endlessly discuss products and services or benefits and promotions, you may be making choices based on what feels comfortable. Making a new conscious choice means *breaking through your fear barrier and comfort zone on purpose to improve your results in business*. Choose the beliefs that best support you *now*.

3. **Take action: Ask!** It's easier when you're prepared. If you're unsure of exactly what to say, ask your company or upline support team to suggest ways to ask for an order and to invite a person to join your team. Commit three of these to memory so you'll be able to share them even when you're nervous. Then, after you've satisfactorily answered your prospect's questions and noticed her buying signals, make asking for the business a natural part of your conversation. Smile with good eye contact to show you are confident. Lay the distributor agreement or order form out in plain view, put a pen in front of her, and *ask for her business*. Expect the best! When you ask with assurance and anticipation, your offer is even more attractive.

Creating New Perceptions, Choices, and Actions

In the next 48 hours, take advantage of every opportunity to win your inner game.

1. When you're closing with a prospect, be aware of these two powers working as feelings inside you: *your intuition* about her readiness to buy and *your beliefs* about asking for the business.

2. When your intuition is positive, make a new conscious choice: Step out of your comfort zone and rely on your new, empowering beliefs.

3. Take action and *ask for the business!*

4. No matter how your prospect responds, *celebrate!* Next time will be easier, and the more you do it, the more at ease you will feel. ■

■ Increase Your Show's Success with Outside Orders

By Gloria Brice
Savvy in sales and service

OVERCOMING ATTENDANCE WOES

Show sales are an excellent—and, for some distributors, the primary—source of distribution. Over the course of an afternoon or evening, you meet an average of eight people who have come to learn about your product and to have some fun. Typically, the higher the attendance at a show, the higher the sales and the greater the income it creates for the distributor.

Today, however, many people are so overscheduled that they are challenged to show up for a home demonstration. The resulting low attendance can negatively affect sales and be discouraging to both you and your hostess. ***When you incorporate outside orders—those taken by the hostess before or after her show—as a strategy for a show's success plan, you can turn a marginal show into one that's extremely profitable.*** As a result, you'll have higher sales and a happier hostess.

By encouraging the hostess to increase her sales with outside orders, you also plant the seeds for her to consider your business opportunity. While gathering outside orders, your hostess is actually selling and demonstrating product. As she does so, she becomes more aware of its benefits. She also develops seeds of confidence that will bloom if she becomes a distributor. By asking her friends to help her, she is further positioned for success because she instantly has future hostesses and distributors!

TRANSFORMING MARGINAL INTO PROFITABLE

Once your future hostess has selected a date, work with her to set a show goal. Create an expectation for outside orders by saying, "Sally, outside orders can play an important role in your show's success, especially if we gather them from people you invite but who can't attend. Thinking of all the people you'll see between now and your show, about how many orders would you like to have before the party starts?" Multiply that number by the average order amount and you'll arrive at your goal for outside orders. When you arm your hostess with the necessary tools, such as catalogs, order forms, and a large envelope, you'll have set the stage for sales before the show even begins.

At the show, give your hostess a gift for the amount of outside orders she has already collected. Potential hostesses will understand that obtaining outside orders is expected and rewarded.

Outside orders can also come to the rescue of a show that does not turn out as either you or your hostess had hoped. Let's imagine that you have done your best and followed the recommended steps for coaching your hostess. You arrive at the show enthusiastic and prepared. The hostess has cleaned her house, prepared snacks, and is eager to earn the free products you have talked about. But only two people show up and the sales total doesn't qualify for a show. She is disappointed, you are disappointed (but you do *not* show it), and you feel a bit weary during your hour-long drive home from the show. What can you do to lift her spirits and turn the situation around? Coach her on how to collect outside orders *before* closing her show!

- Encourage her! Explain that some of your most successful shows were only marginal until the hostess began collecting outside orders. Make your hostess aware of the free or discounted product she can receive and help her establish a goal for postshow orders.

- Explain the number of orders and bookings she needs in order to meet those goals.

- Supply her with the tools she needs to collect outside orders. For instance, if your company is offering specials, give her fliers and a list of selling points. If you have a product that can be easily demonstrated, give or loan one to your hostess so she can "show and tell."

- Suggest she ask two or three of her friends to help her gather outside orders.

- Offer a reward for meeting her outside order and booking goals.

Ordering Up Success Today

1. Contact each of your upcoming hostesses. Outline the benefits of preshow outside orders, offer a reward for reaching outside order goals, and supply packets of catalogs and order forms to get them on their way.

2. Contact three past hostesses and tell them you would like for them to try a method that can help increase their show sales and earn even more free product. Then outline the preshow and postshow outside ordering strategy.

3. Share this method with distributors on your team. ■

3

Networking and Prospecting

*T*he top leaders who contributed to this chapter were asked, "How have you been able to build such large organizations?" What do you suppose was their overwhelming response? If you imagine their answers revealed a secret phrase that magically lures unsuspecting prospects into their business opportunity web, you would be wrong. Nor did they share that their success comes from employing the latest Internet recruiting tool or leads from a hot new vendor. While many top leaders are using technology and leads to grow their organizations, nothing seems to surpass the importance of good old-fashioned networking and prospecting. In short, their advice is, "Get out and talk to a lot of people about what you have to offer!" When you do, you will be inspired to solidify your belief in what you offer, network in the spirit of service, and look for a mutually beneficial exchange with others.

If these are the very secrets to success in direct selling, why are so many distributors still wrestling with fears and self-doubt that keep them from opening their mouths and talking to strangers?

To answer this important question, we've assembled top leaders who exhibit impressive levels of achievement in the areas of prospecting and networking. What you may find surprising about these insights is that they express the importance of elevating a simple chance meeting into an opportunity to connect on a more meaningful level.

■ Warm Up to Friendly Conversations

By Ilene Meckley
Top trainer for the direct-selling profession

RESISTING THE URGE TO RUN AND HIDE

If you are like many women, sharing may be more than a bit scary for you. Childhood messages of "Don't talk to strangers" or "Don't speak unless spoken to" are ingrained in your subconscious. Even when talking to people is the single most important thing you can do to build your business, when the opportunity arises, your heart pounds and you have a sudden urge to run and hide. The art of conversation is the key to sharing what you have to offer. Whether you are looking for your next team member or simply want to share your product, *learning to make friendly conversations with perfect strangers is one of the best skills you can develop as a direct-selling professional.* The key to opening up is in seeing the benefit that others gain from what you have to offer. When you share with others in mind, you reap the rewards of greater confidence and a growing, thriving business.

Conversational Openers

The conversational opener and "warm chatter" used to introduce yourself to a prospect forms a critical bridge between greeting a stranger and getting a friend interested in your business. Here are some tips that can help you open new doors by opening conversations.

Find common ground. Establish rapport by finding out what you have in common. Your interaction will turn into a pleasant encounter with two people who have a mutual interest. No matter what the outcome, she'll be glad she met you and the awkwardness will fade into appreciation.

Don't have a hidden agenda. Share what you do naturally through the course of the conversation, rather than waiting until later in the encounter and ending on that note. Ending with your business offer may appear as though that was the sole purpose of your conversation, which may leave the other person feeling undervalued and uncomfortable.

Be sincere and genuine. As the saying goes, there is nothing engaging about perfection. Your success does not depend upon you memorizing a script or delivering a flawless 30-second commercial. If you start feeling nervous or tongue-tied, say, "I'm sorry. I'm getting a little confused with my words here. I'm really new at sharing about my business. Thanks for letting me practice with you."

Make others feel good about themselves. Nothing sounds better to a person than to hear her own name, and nothing feels better than a sincere compliment or talking to someone who is genuinely interested in what you have to say.

Talking Points for Today and Tomorrow

1. At your next opportunity, whether at the grocery store or a networking event, seek out quality conversations with three people with whom you would like to do business.

2. In your interaction with them, do these three things: listen with genuine interest; offer a sincere compliment; and find something you have in common.

3. Be joyful and appreciative that you are in a business that pays you to make new friends. ■

■ Create a Compelling 30-Second Commercial

By Gayle McDonald
Building her organization with lightning speed

"WHAT DO YOU DO?"

Like many direct sellers, you understand that networking is essential to your success. It connects you with future customers, hostesses, and team members. Armed with business cards and brochures, you go hunting, with high hopes of making connections that count.

But brochures and business cards alone cannot secure new contacts. You'll also need an engaging 30-second commercial to respond to the question, "What do you do?" If you don't get the response you want or need for success, perhaps you need work on your 30-second commercial. *A sharp, clear, compelling response to "What do you do?" is your ticket to turning on lots of new friends to your business and product.*

When you think of your 30-second commercial as a warm verbal handshake for making new friends, you'll find yourself looking forward to sharing it with others.

BUILD YOUR COMMERCIAL

What is a good 30-second commercial? A brief and clear presentation of the benefit you offer and an explanation of what makes you unique.

If you think your introduction needs a little polishing, here are a few simple guidelines that will help you respond to the all-important question with confidence and ease:

1. **Get right to the point.** Make the first seconds count by putting benefits up front. Don't make the mistake of taking too long to get to the point.

2. **Tease them—don't bore them.** Don't try to tell the *whole* story in just 30 seconds! Tell your listener just enough so that she is intrigued and wants to know more about what you do.

3. **Share the difference you make.** Paint a picture in her mind of what it would be like to use your services. "Women call me when they want to transform their daily routine into pampering rituals that reduce stress and maintain balance." Or, "Women call me when they want to start a home-based business to earn additional income and eventually leave their 9-to-5 jobs." If she can see herself benefiting, she will want to know more.

4. **Share what problems you have solved.** Facts tell, but stories sell. Bring the benefit you offer to life by sharing a real-life story. "Many of my clients have not only seen a reduction of fine lines, but their skin has a healthy glow that makes them look and feel more beautiful." Or, "I just recently helped a team member execute a plan that allowed her to take her entire family on a two-week vacation, paid for with her business income."

Sharing with Everyone

Once you have crafted your 30-second commercial, practice it whenever you can. Strike up conversations with grocery store cashiers, bank tellers, drugstore employees, sales girls, teachers, and moms at the park, the PTA, and Little League games.

Because you'll meet a variety of people with varying interests, have a few versions of your commercial ready to go. One might focus on the fun of a product demonstration, another might be oriented to product results, and another may present the benefits of the business opportunity. By having several 30-second commercials prepared, you'll be able to share them with ease and confidence.

The Ultimate Prize

While sharing what you have to offer, learning about the other person, and making a personal connection are important goals of your networking efforts, one final element is absolutely key: getting her card or name and number!

Have plenty of business cards with you at all times. As you extend your card, smile and say, "It's been so nice talking with you. If you'd like to give me your name and phone number, I'd love to connect with you in a day or so." Be prepared with a small pad and paper in the event she doesn't have a business card to give you. Smile and say, "Is it best to call during the day or the evening?"

Actions to Take Today and Tomorrow

1. List the three types of commercials you want to create; for example, one for your product, one for your business opportunity, and one for group presentations.

2. Write out each commercial and practice it with friends.

3. Keep fine-tuning and changing each commercial until it feels natural and elicits a reaction that says, "That's interesting, tell me more." ■

■ Create a Buzz through Community Action

By Jackie Baugrud
Joyfully making a difference in other people's lives

READY TO START HUMMING

You took the first step by making a commitment to a direct-selling company with products you like. Now you're ready to turn this into a business, but you don't know how to let people know what you have to offer. Networking is essential to the business of direct selling, but it can be very intimidating for the first-time entrepreneur. ***By becom-***

ing a celebrity in your own backyard and by considering yourself an ambassador of goodwill within your community, you can start creating a buzz about your products. In the process, you'll gain a reputation in your community for being someone who can be counted on and trusted, and you'll become the "go to" person for your product.

POLLINATING PERSON-TO-PERSON

To become the first person on everyone's mind when they have a need for your product or service, you must visit them where they bloom. Here's how:

Get out and meet people. It sounds like a cliché, but your community offers boundless opportunities to network. If you aren't already involved in your child's school, in your church, or in a service group, it's time to get started. Volunteer for committees or projects that stir your passion to serve.

Make a connection. Think back to an event where you met someone memorable. What was it about her that resonated with you? Was it her smile, her attentiveness, her positive attitude, or her interest in what you had to offer? What made her memorable to you will make *you* memorable to others.

When communicating with someone, focus on listening to her. What are her needs? If, while she's talking, you're thinking about how you can sell to her, you're not listening. To establish a memorable connection, be genuine, be interested in what she has to say, and have a warm smile. Show your most positive attitude—others are naturally drawn to happy people.

If you don't know what to say when you meet people, script it! Write it down and practice. Having that script in the front of your mind can help push your fears to the back.

Make your mark. You can make a difference in your networking group in these six ways:

1. **Be generous.** Donate prizes to silent auctions and benefit drawings. If the cost is reasonable, sponsor a team. Offer to do a fundraising campaign using your products and give the group part of your commission.

2. **Do it well.** If you offer to do something, do it well and on time. Give more than you receive and expect nothing in return.

3. **Give it away.** Offer an occasional free seminar to the members of the group. Teach them about the benefits of your products and ways to use them to make their lives easier. If another member of the group offers a compatible product or service, partner up for double the value and double the results.

4. **Fundraise.** Help a special interest or charity raise funds by offering to donate a portion of sales made to members in a designated month.

5. **Communicate.** Send regular correspondence—such as newsletters, new product announcements and special promotions—to members. Use a variety of formats, such as postcards, fliers, and e-mails, and always include your name, e-mail address, and Web site.

6. **Personalize.** Send personalized notes to those people who you meet along the way. Always include your business card and any pertinent information they can use.

Share your enthusiasm. While you are getting your name out there, attend company and team events to learn more about your products and services. This will get your energy and enthusiasm flowing, and you can take that excitement back to the local groups you're serving. Your community will want to hear more about what you find exciting.

Gathering your Nectar Today and Tomorrow

Networking can happen anywhere and everywhere. Be prepared and be ready for it!

1. Buy or make something—a pin, purse, or shirt, for example—that draws people's attention. Wear it as a conversation starter at least three days in the coming week.

2. Make a list of the opportunities to serve in your community, and rank them according to your passion. Commit to calling your top two during the coming week.

3. Have something ready to give someone who asks for more information. Put together an information packet and pledge to carry it with you at all times. ■

■ Let Friendship Lead to Fearless Phoning

Beth Jones-Schall
Sharing the spirit of success

GOOD CALLS FOR GOOD RELATIONSHIPS

Surveys show most direct sellers have a fear of phoning customers and prospects. Our hearts beat faster, our palms sweat, and in an instant our phones turn into 20-pound dumbbells we can't find the strength to lift.

If you are among the many who would rather do anything else but make calls to prospects and customers, then consider this . . . *your key to fearless phoning is to envision a friend at the other end of the line.*

Let's take a look at eight simple steps to build friendships with your customers and end phone fear forever:

1. **Befriend your hostess.** Make it a point to develop a relationship with your hostess and your phone calls will become welcomed communication from one friend to another.

2. **Connect with guests before the party.** Begin to build a relationship with guests even before you meet them by making

"ice-breaker" contact a day or two prior to the party to introduce yourself. Ask each hostess for the names, phone numbers, and e-mail addresses of her guests. Then e-mail or call each one to introduce yourself and let her know you're looking forward to meeting her at the party. Your guests will feel more connected to you and more confident in attending the party when you've taken the first steps to build the relationship.

3. **Ask guests to introduce themselves.** The night of the party, after you have introduced yourself, have each guest also do a quick introduction. Have each one tell how she knows the hostess, share a little about her family, and describe what keeps her day busy. This puts the spotlight on the guests and helps you find something you have in common with each one—a key element to establishing rapport.

> **T**hank-you calls set you apart in this profession as someone who puts a high value on personalized service and relationship building.

4. **Plan for one-on-one consulting time at the party.** One of the most important relationship-building times at a party is just after your presentation while the guests are shopping. Position yourself with an empty chair next to you where guests can sit while you review their order. This will give you a valuable minute or two (at most!) to confirm and compliment her selection and make a personal connection.

5. **Make thank-you calls the day after each party.** Your customers will be pleasantly surprised when you take the time (usually less than a minute per person) to call the day after to say thank you, it was nice meeting them, compliment their selection, and let them know you look forward to keeping in touch with them. *Thank-you calls set you apart in this profession as someone who puts a high value on personalized service and relationship building.* Your customers will so appreciate your

thoughtfulness—even if left on an answering machine. The sound of your voice along with a sincere thank you will go a long way in building a relationship. Plus thank-you calls are *fun* to make because you aren't asking for anything—you're saying thank you! Don't be surprised when your customer asks if she can add something to her order or if she could still book a party. It's a response to your sincere interest in her.

6. **Send monthly communication.** Market research suggests that if you are not in front of your customer once every four weeks, she will forget about you. A brief monthly e-newsletter with tips, ideas, and your available dates is an effective way to be in front of each customer monthly and continue to build a relationship with her.

7. **Make customer-care calls.** You'll enjoy making periodic customer-care calls when you've taken steps 1 through 6 to build a relationship. Your call is a courtesy to your customer to check on her needs and see how you can be of help. Because she knows you by this point, you won't be bothering her, you'll be serving her.

8. **Acknowledge birth dates.** Collect and log the birthdays of your best hostesses and customers so you can send or e-mail each one a card on her special day. Friends always wish friends "Happy Birthday!"

Building Friendships Today and Tomorrow

1. Review the relationship-building steps above and choose two to add to your next show. Integrate them into your show plan.

2. Spend a half-hour today and again tomorrow making thank-you calls that build friendships with your hostesses and customers. ■

■ Discover Where Customers and Clients Lurk

By Peter Mingils
Respected provider of quality leads

OPENING YOUR EYES TO HIDDEN TREASURES

You probably think about it most of the time. Questions of improving your business haunt your waking thoughts as well as your dreams. "How do I sell my next product?" "Who will buy it?" "How do I get my next client or distributor?" "How do I build a bigger team?" There seem to be more questions than answers. Here's a starting point for finding those people who will want to join you as a customer or as a partner.

Begin by thinking about what you *really* want. You will find that what you *really* want is similar to what millions of people in your marketplace *really* want, too . . . and, your products and your opportunity can help those millions get what they want. This generates confidence that *just about anything you do can help increase your business.* The numbers are in your favor!

At the root of obtaining all the things you want is the prospect of building a large customer base and an effective team. There are many ways to overcome this challenge. The important question for you will be **what works best for you and your team.**

GUIDE TO FINDING WHAT WORKS FOR YOU

Building your business requires what is in your head and what is in your purse, and you probably have a lot of experience in using both. Just remember to keep your brain turned on at all times and your hand over your wallet. Basic business sense and common sense go a long way. Here are some of the simple Do's and Don'ts you can work on and have fun with:

Do

- *Contact your faithful supporters.* Who do you know that uses or buys your product already? Some people call this their "warm" market. There are always some people who think you're terrific and would love to help you. You already know who to approach directly and who to approach softly. Ask your groupies to pile on and enjoy the ride, send the others cards. Tell whoever's left that you won't bug them anymore if they go on autoship! You can do just about anything with your wonderful smile and charming personality. Just ask!

- *Advertise and promote.* There are several forms of letting people know you're out there. Some ways cost money, some don't. Try several systems to find what works best for you. Ask people who are already successful at building.

- *Talk to people who are already looking.* You can buy leads and systems that help generate prospects at varying levels of interest. Use what's already working for others.

Don't

- *Don't invent or create something new.* Unless you have experience in a particular area, you will have a learning curve in determining what works that will cost you time, frustration, and money.

- *Don't lead when you should follow.* If something works already, stick with it. Even if it wasn't your idea.

- *Don't follow when you should just say "no."* If you think peer pressure among kids is huge, just wait until your next conference call when upline leaders are promoting the new system or vendor and the order forms are passed around. Too many systems are promoted before they are tested. Or worse yet, some are designed to fail. Not all are like this certainly. Just make sure you resist the temptation to feel disloyal by not following "The System." *Follow proven systems, not the system of the week.*

MEASURE YOUR RESULTS

Work with facts. When investing your resources, which are time, money, and emotional wear and tear, ask yourself these four questions:

1. How much does it cost to get a response?

2. How much does it cost to get a good or worthwhile response?

3. How much does it cost to bring in my next product sale or distributor?

4. How much do I make during the lifetime of that product sale or distributor?

The answers to these questions will help guide you on what's really working or not.

If you focus on how to sell more product and how to develop a bigger team, you'll be focusing on some of the most important things you can control while building your business.

In the Next 48 Hours

1. Find someone who is like you and is already successful.

2. Arrange to meet this person to explore what prospecting methods work for them that may work for you.

3. Identify three methods for finding prospects and outline how you will implement them. ■

■ Become a Talent Scout—Look for Your Next Star

By Karen Phelps
Keeping the fun and profits in your business

CHANGING YOUR FOCUS

Your calendar may be filled with bookings and you may be exceeding your sales goals, but you might not be recruiting team members as quickly as you'd planned. While giving your presentation, *try changing your mental focus from selling to recruiting.* By concentrating on recruiting, you'll build your business by building your organization.

Before your next party or group demonstration, sit down and do some strategizing. So far, your primary goals for your demonstrations have been to share your excitement about your product and generate the sales that result in your commission. You might have thought that finding a recruitment prospect was an added bonus to your sales. What if you changed your thinking, and began to make recruiting your primary goal, with product sales as your added bonus? In other words, why not *become a talent scout and use parties and group demonstrations as forums for finding your next big star?*

The truth is, all that you have to do to generate sales at most parties and group demonstrations is to give a short, enthusiastic presentation. Most companies have products that are easy to demonstrate, and most guests will shop and purchase products whether the consultant is there or not. So why not turn your strategy upside down and use parties and demonstrations as an opportunity to reap long-term benefits through getting more bookings and recruiting prospective team members?

When you're a talent scout, your goals and strategies shift. For each party or product demonstration, have a goal to sponsor someone, get at least two bookings, and have decent sales. By coaching your hostess, you'll meet your sales goal, and by honing your skills in demonstrating the value of your company's hostess program, bookings won't be a problem. That leaves you the opportunity to focus on finding the one person from the group that you're going to sponsor.

With your objective clearly in mind, you can develop the techniques to apply during each and every product demonstration to increase your odds of sponsoring someone.

BECOMING A SPONSORING MAGNET

Use these techniques during your product demonstration to generate enthusiasm among the guests and pave the way to successful recruitment:

- Have a short, focused, well-rehearsed personal story. Make sure you've condensed it to two to three minutes in order to maintain the interest and excitement of your audience.

- At the beginning of your presentation, encourage the guests to watch what you do. You could say, "Some of you may have considered having your own home-based business. Watch what I do tonight. See how easy it is and how much fun I have." As you say this, watch your guests' reactions. Often, you will be able to identify those who have an interest by their heightened interest in your statement.

- Select a guest who you think would make a great consultant with your company. She's the one who is friendly, outgoing, and a lot of fun. Let her know that she would be great in this business and send some information home with her.

- Make your hostess aware of the value of becoming a consultant. Share with her how much money she could have made had she been the consultant at her party. Ask her if she is interested in joining your team.

- As you demonstrate your product, work in examples of the benefits of your home-based direct-selling business. If you're demonstrating a spatula, for instance, mention that you use yours for removing your son's favorite cookies from the cookie sheet. Then add, "One of the things I love about being in this business is that I set my own hours and can pop some cookies into the oven right when my son gets home from school."

- If a guest in attendance is a consultant for another company, congratulate her on her wise decision to become an entrepreneur in direct selling.

Finding Your Star

1. Develop and practice your two- to three-minute personal story. For help, see "Craft Your Recruiting Story" by Maria Dowd in *Build It Big*.

2. Come up with two examples of the benefits you reap from your home-based business that you can work into your presentation.

3. Contact one of your hostesses from the past week and share with her how much she could have made had she been the consultant at her party. Invite her to join your team. ■

■ Transform Fear to Your Advantage

By Debra Shaw

Rattling the cages of the status quo

DANGLING WITH DREAD

When you experience fear, your body actually releases glucose, adrenaline, and other energy-producing chemicals. Your heart rate increases, your breathing becomes shallow, and you become hyperalert. ***You can redirect this energy and use it to face your challenges.*** Fear is an unpleasant sensation, and sometimes we hesitate, waiting for the feeling to subside before we act. But we can't avoid fear. Yes, it's uncomfortable, but it's also a healthy, even necessary, part of living an extraordinary life. The challenge is to act in spite of it. When you summon the courage to travel to the center of your fear, you often find that there's nothing there. But you have to *act* before you can discover that.

When you're hanging from the overhead ladder in a jungle gym, you have to let go of the rung for a moment to move forward. No doubt about it, it's scary. There's an instant when you could fall. But you have to hang with fear to reach the other side. Many of us are just hanging there on the same rung, trying to decide whether we have the nerve to reach for the next one. Some of us simply want to avoid the jungle gym completely and hide in our little caves. But hiding out won't get you anywhere.

If you're not doing things that make you shake in your boots, you're missing some of the fun and even more of the opportunities of living. Grappling with fear yields strength and confidence. Every time you survive a frightening experience, you renounce fear's grip and forgo the impulse to fight. These moments of letting go can yield breakthrough results. Over time, you'll have greater access to the fortitude that permits you to stare fear in the face; no matter how imposing, threatening, or ugly it looks.

BULLETPROOF WAYS TO SURRENDER AND WIN

Harness Your Fear

When we were children, our parents used fear as a tool to keep us from doing something. "You'll break your neck if you climb that tree!" they said. Our challenge as adults is to use fear as the fuel to get things done. Raw, unused fear can eat away at us, causing us countless miseries, even life-threatening illnesses. But when we learn to harness and direct our fear, it provides the power we need to live our dreams.

Focus Outside Yourself

Focusing outside yourself is a great way to stop fighting fear and save your strength. When focused on the benefits of loved ones, many women are masters at halting fear in its tracks. We've experienced moments of heroism when we were able to accomplish something we once thought was impossible.

Build Your Resistance

One particularly effective weapon for neutralizing fear is to desensitize yourself to the situation that triggers the stress. Choose a live situation—something that's really pressing you right now—perhaps pitching the bank for an increased line of credit. Then engage it, first in your head, then through various real-life settings. Begin with the least intimidating and work your way up to the most threatening.

Before you begin, be sure you've done your homework. Nothing defuses fear like knowing your stuff. Learn these four steps:

1. *Find a guinea pig.* Be the first volunteer, deliver the pitch in front of a mirror. Then graduate to your dog, a fellow business owner, your accountant, and so on.

2. *Do a live test run.* Never open up on Broadway. For example, don't give your first pitch to the bank where you really want that line of credit. Instead, practice on a lender you never intend to use. Experience the real-life jitters, ask questions, and get feedback.

3. *Create familiarity to disarm fear and kill surprise.* Visit the locale beforehand. Meet your target—incognito, if necessary. If you can't get to the location beforehand, visit it in your mind. Feel the texture of the fabric on the chairs, smell your target's perfume, taste the coffee being served.

4. *Expect flawless execution.* Feel the fear and the excitement. See yourself, dressed in your best suit—poised, strong, driven—bringing down the house.

   Remember . . . "No guts, no glory!"

Taking the Plunge

1. Find out if your biggest fear is fear itself. As uncomfortable as the experience might be, spend a quiet hour taking an internal inventory of your fears. Are you afraid of monetary

scarcity? Not being loved? Being perceived as incompetent? List three of your fears on a piece of paper.

2. For each fear, write out the worst-case scenario. Use your imagination and really make it bad. Afterwards, using a scale of one to ten, rate the likelihood that that worst-case scenario will happen.

3. Arm yourself with counterarguments, by responding to each of your fears in writing. If your fear is that you won't be loved, your response might be, "I vow that I will always love myself, no matter what." ■

■ Find a Fortune in Referrals

By Leslie Vitzthum
Energizing lives with clarity and passion

WHAT DO YOU DO WITH A DRY WELL?

Here's the challenge: Often distributors think they've run out of people to talk to about their business. After sharing their opportunity with some family, friends, and coworkers, many people hit the wall. They think, "I've already talked to everyone I know!"

Here's an easy-to-learn process that will help you develop ongoing prospects, leading to a continual supply of new customers and distributors! It's the art of consistently asking for (and following up on) referrals.

Asking for referrals is one of the most effective ways to create a never-ending supply of prospects. By incorporating these four, simple referral strategies into your everyday business activities, you and your team will never run out of people to talk to!

PRIMING THE PUMP

Step 1: Learn Your Stories

A fundamental skill mastered by all successful distributors is the ability to share well-packaged stories. Stories must be brief, personal, professional, and passionate. These are the stories you need:

- **Product story**—your product experience and enthusiasm for your product line

- **Business "Why"**—your motivation for building your business and how it affects your life

- **Opportunity**—the uniqueness of your company's opportunity and benefits

Step 2: Work a Never-Ending List

Create a master list of prospects. Include all the people you know personally, the people you do business with, your current customers, and new people you meet.

Systematically approach these people with something new. Ask them for referrals! The secret to finding a fortune in referrals is this: It's not who *you* know, it's who *they* know.

Step 3: Ask for Referrals

When contacting the people on your list, remember that you get what you ask for. Be clear about *who* you're looking for (customer or distributor referrals) and *how* you'd like to receive the referrals. Here are some sample phone scripts you can use.

Customer referrals. During customer follow-up, always focus on your customer's satisfaction first. Once you know she's happy, *always ask for referrals*. You can ask verbally or in follow-up e-mails. I have tagged each part of the script with the *reason* for including that part and bracketed text where you can include your own information.

(Verify that she is satisfied)

"Terry, I'm so happy you love your <products>."

(Validate that many people give you referrals)

"You know I've built my business on referrals." (or, "I plan to build my new business on referrals.")

(Ask for the referral)

"Like most of my clients, I'm sure you have friends who would love <these products> too. Who do you know who would enjoy <your product>? I would really appreciate the referrals."

(Take control of the referral)

"Terry, the best way for me to share the information with your friends is to contact them directly. As you talk to them, please tell them that you'll have your friend <your name> call. Then just send me their name and contact information. I'd really appreciate it."

Distributor referrals. This process is effective because you are not directly trying to recruit her, rather you are asking for her help. If she has a personal interest after you share your story, she will tell you. This example is a phone script.

(Professional opening, getting permission)

"Hello Terry, this is <your name>. I'm calling you for a reason. I have a business idea. Is this a convenient time?" *(Contact agrees)* "Great! I'd like to take just a few minutes to share with you what's happening with my business."

(Share your brief, personal stories from Step 1, and then "pull it away.")

"You may or may not have a personal interest, but I'm hoping you can lead me to someone this would be perfect for. I'm looking for referrals."

(Be clear about who you're looking for. Here are some examples.)

"Terry, I'm looking for . . .

<Entrepreneurs—people who are successful in business and who will recognize this opportunity

People looking to do something part-time that doesn't interfere with what they're already doing.

Women who'd like to work from home and create a business they can work around the needs of their family.>

"With all the exciting things happening with <your company>, I'm looking for people to join me. Again, you may or may not have a personal interest, but I'm hoping you can lead me to someone this would be perfect for. Who do you know? I'm looking for just the right people."

(Take control of the referral.)

"And Terry, the best way for me to share the information is to contact them directly. So, as you talk to people, just tell them that you'll have your friend <your name> call. Then just send me their name and contact information. I'd really appreciate it."

"Take control of the referral" means that *you* have the contact information. So many times people say, "I know just the right person, and I'll give her your information"—but they seldom do. By using the above language, you'll be sure to get the information you need to make the contact.

Step 4: Follow-Up

Once you receive a referral, call and share your brief, enthusiastic stories immediately! Don't delay. Timely response reflects your professionalism, and is critical for a positive outcome. Follow up on all referrals right away! You can use this opening script:

"Hi Pat, this is <your name> from <your company>. I got your name and number from Terry who tells me you may have an interest in learning a little more about our <products or company>. Is this a good time?"

Asking for Referrals Today and Tomorrow

In the next 48 hours, challenge yourself to:

1. Write out your brief stories and memorize them.

2. Practice and get comfortable with the referral language in the scripts above.

3. Create an updated master list of contacts.

4. Call at least five people and ask for referrals.

5. Make a commitment to ask everyone for referrals from now on.

6. Post the following and repeat it to yourself often:

   "I am a master at asking for and receiving referrals!" ■

■ Fall in Love with "Out and About" Prospecting

Ann White
Spirit-driven leader blazing new trails

PROSPECTING—THE LEARNED SKILL

To those of us who faint at sharing our business with our warm market, it is hard to relate to someone who seems able to naturally prospect with ease and confidence. In fact, although I now prospect with ease, I was terrified to do so when I started. What I learned is a new view of prospecting that changed the course of my business and my life. I began to see the wonderful bounty of interesting people who were just unmet friends. Prospecting became a natural flow of daily exchanges, where I invest in others and they invest in me. *I invite you to invest in others and reap the reward of customers and prospects that are waiting for you!*

"OUT AND ABOUT" ATTITUDES AND ACTIONS

Paint a Successful Mental Picture

Before your feet hit the floor, decide to invest in your success today. Review your compelling vision and your daily prospecting goal. Visualize yourself connecting with prospects and reaching your goal.

Wear a Conversation Starter

When you feel good about how you look, your personal impact is elevated. Highlight your look with an eye-catching accessory, such as a pin. It is so much easier to prospect when you feel attractive, so look your best.

Make Prospecting a Lifestyle Not an Event

Lay aside the notion that prospecting happens at special places and times. Allow yourself to see opportunity in your everyday life. Chores and appointments become much more exciting when you realize that you truly can build your business anywhere. During one recent doctor's visit, I sampled and sold to nurses and gained a new business partner!

Living the prospecting lifestyle demands preparation. Keep business cards, a method to collect information, product samples or pamphlets, and the details of your next presentation always at hand. Have a calendar to schedule appointments.

K.I.S.S. (Keep It Short and Sweet)

Your objective is to make a connection and collect follow-up information. The entire one-minute to two-minute prospecting exchange can be summed up in four words—*approach, connect, share,* and *collect.*

1. **Approach.** Determine if the person in front of you is open to your investment. Simply smile and wait. This takes about two seconds. Notice something about the person that you like, such as a scarf, or something that you share, like the weather. Once you receive a return smile, move forward to connect.

2. **Connect.** Establish a further connection. This takes less than 30 seconds. People conduct exchanges with people that they like. Examples of connection starters include an attractive article of clothing, a long bank line, or noncontroversial current event. Use compliments and genuine concern to open her up

to sharing ideas and information with you. In the process, you will want to indicate that you are in a business and that she may want to see what you have to offer.

3. **Share.** Inevitably, your new friend will ask you more about the product or company. Flow into sharing as a natural part of the conversation. Don't overwhelm your prospect with information. Remember, you are in information *gathering* mode. The better job you do of listening, the easier it will be to communicate how your product or opportunity can meet *her* needs. Share what is most important and save the rest for the follow-up appointment.

4. **Collect.** Get key contact information (in 30 seconds or less). Ask for a business card or use preprinted contact cards with space for a name, phone number, e-mail, and address. To request information simply say, "I know you are out and about now. May I have your information so that I can follow up with you later?" while handing your prospect the contact card and a pen. Don't wait for buy-in. Assume that she will give you the information, and she will. Share a little more while she's jotting down her name and numbers. Say, "I look forward to sharing more with you." Don't forget to set a follow-up appointment to occur within 24 hours. Make sure to note a few memorable details about your new friend on her card, and then move on.

Today's Action for "Out and About" Prospecting

1. Paint your successful picture. Make it happen!

2. Wear a conversation starter.

3. Prospect throughout your day.

4. Approach, connect, share, and collect.

5. Relax, and have fun! ∎

■ Tap into the Fountain of Youth

By Grace Keohohou Lee
Vice President and Cofounder of the DSWA

YOUNG MINDS, FRESH IDEAS

Have you been fishing in the fountain of youth lately? The sales force of most direct-selling companies is aging. *The bright future of your business and the direct-selling profession depends largely on the next generation: Generation X.* According to the U.S. Census Bureau, Gen X is comprised of the 47 million Americans born between 1965 and 1975. By learning how they think and what they want, you can engage Gen Xers and recruit them onto your team. In doing so, you'll not only bring youth and energy into your business, but you'll lay the foundation for richly rewarding relationships and a mutually beneficial future.

EMBRACING A NEW GENERATION

Gen Xers Bring Fresh Energy to Your Team

This demographic gained a national identity with the publication of the 1991 book, *Generation X: Tales for an Accelerated Culture*, by Douglas Coupland. Gen X has been relentlessly studied ever since. This generation is characterized by an abundance of energy and time, along with a willingness to commit to projects that serve them financially, emotionally, and socially. They commonly exude a contagious passion and compassion. They hunger for financial freedom, a venue to gain experience, and a flexible schedule that supports their active lifestyle.

The best approach for Gen Xers is to let them know how they can benefit from the business opportunity. They're likely to embrace it and move forward to build thriving businesses. Communication is their strong suit. They've been raised to speak their minds, and their parents have emphasized their ability to achieve their dreams. They can simultaneously share and connect with all walks of life. Just imagine your team infused with high-energy, fun, focused, financially-motivated communicators who are passionate about your products and opportunity.

They'd Rather Be Shopping

The U.S. Department of Labor's 2003 survey showed that Gen Xers reported spending an average of 45 to 50 minutes per day shopping. This group is enticed with high-quality, brand-oriented, image-conscious products.

The direct sales method of distribution is perfect for Gen Xers. They love shopping that is swift, convenient, and fun. Home shows present a venue for them to shop within the convenience of their home, the excitement of freebies or discounted items, and the social interaction they seek out. Shopping online is second nature to them, and they would embrace buying from your Web site with a click of their mouse. Plus, they are accustomed to the two-day to five-day wait for shipping to receive their products, and autoship appeals to them. All three "I would rather be shopping" touch points are offered through this profession, and are effective in their own way.

They Speak Our Language

No slang, catch phrases, or hip clothes are required, just an understanding that image, visibility, quality, and price are key for Gen Xers.

Now more than ever, the direct-selling profession is speaking this generation's language. This is the age of replicating, Web sites, on-line order processing, virtual office and tools, low up-front investment, and no or minimal inventory requirements. Plus, there is a pool of support and resources at their fingertips, as well as a place where they can put their greatest strengths to immediate use. They can use their strong communication skills both in person and virtually to maximize this business on a global scale.

To draw Gen Xers into your business, simply share realistic expectations and work with them to draw an "Accomplishment Map" based on their goals and ambitions. Value their opinions and ideas to show that you care by asking questions and then listening. If you understand personality styles, then you may be familiar with the phrase "Matching and Mirroring." It is an exercise that is commonly used to create rapport with others. As you go, you will grow in understanding and eventually be fluent in what speaks to this generation.

Reaching Out to Rejuvenate

1. Select one idea you want to implement this week to reach the next generation.

2. Write down three things you need to do to act on this idea.

3. Set short-term and long-term goals to connect and welcome people from the next generation as clients and team members. ■

■ Embrace and Enjoy Cultural Differences

By Carmen Saucedo
Latina leader blazing trails around the world

OPENING NEW MARKETS THROUGH SERVICE

Although the Latina community is ripe for direct-selling opportunities, and there has been tremendous direct-selling growth in Latin countries, most Anglo direct sellers are unsuccessful in tapping into the Latina market because they do not understand the culture. *Your Latina customer or prospect views business transactions as extensions of social interactions, so your success lies in understanding that her needs and motivations may significantly differ from those of your Anglo customer.* When you understand the Latina community and tailor your presentations to meet their needs, you obtain better results and open up tremendous opportunities for future success.

> **T**he skin-care class is going to be part party, part family reunion. There is going to be food before, during, and after the party, and sometimes there will even be live music.

Although I am Mexican, when I began in direct sales, I didn't really understand the Latin culture. For example, when I asked an Anglo how she was, she would say, "Fine. How are you?" Yet, when I asked the same question to a Latina in Spanish, she would tell me exactly how she was doing—for at least five minutes! This was puzzling, and it wasn't until I took a college course, entitled "Psychology of the Latin-American Mind," that I discovered that part of my job as a saleswoman was to listen. My client needed to know that I was interested in her illnesses, misfortunes, and events in her life—even though we had just met. I needed to understand my own culture as well as the American culture so that I could perform the service I was set to provide.

Teaching a skin-care class in Spanish means having a celebration. The class is going to be part party, part family reunion. There is going to be food before, during, and after the party, and sometimes there will even be live music. In the American culture, on the other hand, women appreciate you getting to the point, doing what you came to do, showing whatever promotions you have, and getting out of there. Embrace and enjoy the differences between the cultures, and take pride in your sensitivity to the beliefs and traditions of the women with whom you do business.

If you're going to sponsor a Latina, you need to be her friend before you can be her business associate. Over time, you'll grow a long list of friends who will all be clients, and a list of business associates who are friends. In contrast, sponsoring women from the American culture means approaching the relationship as a business opportunity; along the way, a friendship may or may not develop.

To be successful in direct selling in another culture, you have to become one with the culture. Put yourself in the shoes of the person you are trying to connect with and listen to her reasons for wanting to succeed. Never judge her according to her education or the number of tasks already on her plate. When she wants success, she will find the time to do what is necessary to achieve her goals. Just as in the American culture, most Latinas are Supermoms, and it is rewarding to see that they are willing to pursue direct selling and personal development in addition to their other duties.

If you're going to sponsor a Latina, you need to be her friend before you can be her business associate.

Although direct-selling income is often viewed as "extra" in the American culture, in the Latin culture, two incomes are often needed to just barely survive. When a Latina sees the possibility of obtaining the American dream, and wisely communicates and involves her husband and children to make direct selling a family business, achieving her goals and getting the deserved recognition not only improves the family's financial status but also brings them together and makes them proud.

One of the biggest challenges in the Latino culture is communicating the direct-selling vision to the husband, who often believes that you must work hard to earn money, and who doesn't understand that when you love your product and your company, your hard work becomes fun and simple. He finds it incredible that his wife can be so happy, look so good, and come home smiling, saying, "Look, honey, I made one, two, three or more hundred dollars for a few hours of work."

The most important technique to ensuring great sales, sponsoring opportunities, and growing your business in the Latin culture is having sales and bargains for the day, and a special price for everyone. You need to provide gifts for the hostess and think of ways to make her feel special. She is queen for the day, so remind the guests of all she did to put the party together, compliment her on her efforts, and tell her how grateful you are. Then, tell the guests how much they could be earning if this was their party, and that you can help them start their journey to success by joining your team.

> **T**he most important technique to ensuring great sales, sponsoring opportunities, and growing your business in the Latin culture is having sales and bargains for the day, and a special price for everyone.

Working in the Latina market is a pleasure. It's a wonderful feeling to see a woman flower in such amazing ways. Some of the women I've worked with didn't know how to drive a car, much less own one. To see one transform into a successful business woman earning a six-figure income and winning a brand new car, or to go from being very shy to being able to speak before hundreds of people without blinking an eye, makes my job worthwhile. It's incredibly rewarding to witness their families' pride, and watch as they offer the opportunity to others, are esteemed as examples of success in their communities, and serve as mentors to those who follow them.

Building Cultural Bridges

1. Look at the events listing in your local paper for upcoming events in the Latino community. Calendar one or more events, and enjoy learning about and experiencing the culture.

2. Ask your upline to recommend a successful Latina in your organization who can mentor you in reaching out to the Latina community in your area.

3. Locate and begin reading a book on Latino culture. ∎

■ Stand Out with Creative Promotions

Lisa M. Wilber
Making millions while walking her talk

TIE THE KNOT BETWEEN YOUR NAME AND YOUR COMPANY NAME

Earning big money in direct sales depends largely on finding customers and recruits and teaching your team to do the same. Many people in direct sales depend on their family and friends for market share or new team members, but what if you don't have many or have already approached your family and friends and don't want to approach them again? Why not mimic other businesses in promoting your name to your community? ***By tying your name to your company name, whenever someone wants a product from your company, they will come to you first!***

OUTSTANDING STAND-OUT PROMOTION IDEAS

Turn Your Vehicle into a Rolling Advertisement!

You can do this simply with posters in your vehicle windows. There is a kit available to make static cling signs on your inkjet printer for the windows of your car. Magnetic door signs work nicely because they can be installed and removed easily. These can be professionally done or you can buy a kit at the office supply store for you to make them yourself. The most professional and frequently used by big businesses is vinyl signage. With vinyl lettering, the options are unlimited. Complete the look with a vanity plate from your state with the company name on it or a variation of the company name.

Always Wear the Company Name!

Check with your headquarters about having your company's name embroidered on all of the shirts you already own. A professional can scan in your company logo and then charge you a small fee to embroider the logo on the shirts you bring them. Or, you could always wear a name badge or promotional button for your business. Name badges and promotional buttons are often available from your company or at office supply stores.

Be Johnny Appleseed with Your Business Cards!

Set a goal to give out 500 business cards per month, and then do it. Be sure to give each person that you come in contact with three cards: one for her, and two for her friends. When you leave a business card with someone who has given you good service, write on the back, "Your service was excellent! If you are ever looking for a job, please give me a call!" Include a business card with your bills when you pay them—someone opens those envelopes! Always carry a box of push pins in your vehicle and affix six or more business cards to each bulletin board you find. Leave a business card in the pocket of a coat you tried on at the store but didn't buy. Leave cards near ATMs and pay phones. Put business cards in the frame of the mirrors in public bathrooms and changing rooms. Even leave a card under the can of peas at the grocery store! Everywhere you go, leave cards. Just like the seeds that Johnny planted, some of yours will "grow" and produce customers and recruits and others will not. That's why you have to place a minimum of 500 cards each month. Need bigger results? Double or triple your goal.

Join Networking Organizations

Participate in organizations to get your name associated with your company name. Consider your local PTA, Chamber of Commerce, Lions Club, Rotary, Jaycees, ABWA (American Business Women's Association: http://www.abwa.org) and DSWA (Direct Selling Women's Alliance: http://www.dswa.org). When attending meetings, be sure to hand out business cards and participate in any advertising opportunities, such as buying an ad in their newsletter. Also, wear your company name badge when attending meetings. When corresponding with members via mail or e-mail, include your company name every time. The goal is to get everyone to think of you when they see your company's name.

Relentless Self-Promotion!

Find as many ways as possible to get your name and your company name seen over and over again. Send press releases to all the newspapers within 100 miles when you achieve a title promotion, get certified in a training program, or attend your company's convention. Press releases are free, but the newspapers are under no obligation to run your story. So send your releases to *all* the newspapers and sooner or later, some will run it. For even more "traffic," consider joining your state's Adopt-A-Highway program.

What You Can Do Next

1. Select one idea you want to implement this week to creatively market your business.

2. Write down three things you need to do to act on this idea.

3. Set a goal completion date and celebrate having added this creative idea to your marketing plan. ■

4

The Art of Sponsoring

*T*he contributors to this chapter stand strong in the belief that, to succeed in direct selling, you must put people before profits. Sponsoring is an act of service that brings many rewards—from the joy of boosting another's self-esteem to the long-term financial compensation that results from building a large organization. By sponsoring in the spirit of service, you avoid the thwarted dreams and broken promises strewn along the paths of those who are motivated solely from self-interest.

Whether you are new to direct selling or a seasoned professional, you will gain insights into sponsoring, and experience team building through the eyes of those who have sponsored hundreds, or even thousands, of people into their businesses.

It has been said that the greatest gift you can give another is the opportunity to discover their greatness. We believe there is greatness within you, and that these gems of wisdom hold the power to quicken your rise to the top. More importantly, when you apply them to your business and your life, you will experience the life-changing rewards that come from leading others to a transformational opportunity.

■ Shift Your Sponsoring Perspective

By Jane Deuber
President and Cofounder of the DSWA

TRANSFORMING INTERACTIONS FOR RECRUITING SUCCESS

You have a burning desire to grow your business—to walk up on stage and be honored by your company founder. You can practically see the bonus check in your hands, with zeros and commas that bring a smile to your face. But the gap between where you are today and the vision you hold opens wide with team members yet to be recruited. Perhaps you're uncomfortable with sponsoring because you feel you need to be aggressive to succeed. At the other end of the spectrum, perhaps you approach sponsoring with a pushiness that alienates potential team members. *True success in sponsoring comes when you see the process as an opportunity to connect and serve rather than an obligation to share and convince.* When you learn principle-centered sponsoring, any tendency to be overly tentative or intense naturally disappears. By transforming your interaction with your prospect, you improve the likelihood that she will be attracted to the opportunity.

FROM "DOING" AND "SAYING" TO "BEING"

The greatest shift you can make as an up-and-coming leader is to recognize that your role of sponsor is not one of learning the latest closing techniques or polishing your persuasion skills. Rather, sponsoring success lies in standing strong upon the principles that make you an exceptional coach and leader once your prospects are on board. The Direct Selling Women's Alliance advises leaders to apply five proven principles to coach their teams to success. Here, we explore how these principles can strengthen your ability to sponsor. As you read each principle, imagine applying them in your interaction with your potential recruit. What would the process look like? How would you both feel?

Principle #1: Trust

When you apply this principle, your prospect senses that you have her best interests at heart. Your dealings with her will be based on openness and honesty, free from any intention to manipulate, misrepresent, or persuade.

Principle #2: Respect

When you show respect for a prospect, she feels valued and has increased confidence that she has what it takes to succeed in business. Ways of showing respect are to ask for her opinions, honor her beliefs, and see her as a whole and resourceful person who will make a valuable contribution to your team.

Principle #3: Service

Sponsoring in the spirit of service means you have a sincere desire to discover whether your business opportunity meets her current needs. By focusing on how the prospect will benefit, rather than what's in it for you, you demonstrate that you are a caring leader who is committed to making a meaningful difference in the lives of her team members.

Principle #4: Integrity

Integrity is present when your actions are in alignment with your words. Doing what you say you will do—from following up with a phone call to getting her the information you've promised—means you honor your commitments.

Principle #5: Authenticity

To be authentic is to be yourself. Sharing your personal experience from your heart—without ego or exaggeration—inspires confidence and trust.

Imagine yourself taking on these characteristics in your next interaction with a potential team member. You'll create a comfortable environment for your prospect, and give her a glimpse of the experience of working with you in the business. Studies show that, while a love of product and a desire for additional income are among the most commonly quoted reasons for joining a direct-selling company, the desire to work with a particular individual also plays an important role in her decision.

Are you demonstrating the characteristics of someone you would want to work with? If not, make a decision to adopt the characteristics of principle-centered sponsoring and watch the transformation take place. You'll not only experience greater success, but you'll also find the process of making new friends and growing your team more fun and meaningful.

Today's Actions for Principle-Centered Sponsoring

1. While thinking back to your interactions with your last three prospects, take a moment to review each principle and determine which you demonstrated and which were absent.

2. Write down one intention for each of the five insights: one thing you will do during your next opportunity to connect with a potential team member.

3. Notice how you share the business opportunity with others and, when needed, make adjustments to bring you back to the practice of principle-centered sponsoring. ■

■ Manifest the Team You Desire!

By Caterina Rando
Helping you achieve success with ease

RECRUITING FOR THE LONG TERM

In your eagerness to build your business, have you ever recruited a team member who eventually became an emotional burden? ***The time to protect yourself from future burnout is when you're recruiting.*** By becoming clear about the traits you want your team members to embody, and by adopting those traits yourself, you will build a team of partners with whom you can work to achieve your personal and collective goals.

The woman you recruit becomes your business partner and a part of the inner circle of people in your life. This woman will be conversing with you on the phone, e-mailing you often, joining you in your living room for one-on-one sessions or trainings, and coming to your backyard gatherings. You had better be excited about the possibility of having an ongoing long-term relationship with her before inviting her to join your team. Otherwise, it is in your best interest, as well as those you have already recruited, to find someone more suitable.

Finding the more suitable someone involves a two-faceted approach: defining the characteristics that are most important to you in a business partner; and embodying those traits in order to attract the partners you desire.

SEEKING OUT POSITIVE TRAITS

To ensure a flourishing team, now and in the years to come, know the traits that best match yours and become a shining example of them. Here are some traits you may want to look for:

■ **A positive disposition.** No amount of training and practice can turn a natural pessimist into an optimist. Look for recruits who are generally positive and happy, and who are excited about the future and becoming a direct seller.

- **Integrity.** You have to trust the people on your team 100 percent. While trust is built over time, if you have an inkling that a prospect does not operate with total integrity, walk away.

- **Self-motivation.** You can train someone all day Saturday, but come Monday, you cannot make her pick up the phone. She has to do it herself. Look for someone who does what she says she will do and is proactive: someone who calls you back, shows up, and keeps her agreements.

- **Good communication skills.** You don't have to be polished or highly educated to be a successful direct seller. You do have to be able to speak with clarity, certainty, and enthusiasm, as well as look people in the eye and create rapport. Don't confuse language skills with communication skills! Your best recruits are often women who are new to your country and have limited language skills.

- **Professionalism.** Promptness, graciousness, good grooming, good manners, and follow-through are the foundations of professionalism. Someone who has these qualities—even if she has no business experience—is a candidate for your team.

- **A willingness to learn and be coached.** Someone who wants to learn your company's success formula and who is willing to operate within the guidelines your company sets will make a great representative of your organization when she goes out into the community.

- **A willingness to make her business a priority.** You can do this business part-time or full-time, but you cannot do it in your spare time. A woman who is going to be successful makes time for her business.

- **Relevant experience.** You certainly don't have to have any sales or business experience to succeed in direct selling. But the woman who has coordinated the awards program for her daughter's soccer team has organization skills, the woman who greets congregants at her church every week has people skills, and the woman who volunteers once a month at the animal shelter keeps her promises. All of these experiences are relevant to direct selling.

It's Your Turn

You attract who you are. Once you've determined the character traits that you'd like in your business partners—communication skills, professionalism, or a quirky sense of humor—it's time to do a personal inventory and start living what you want to attract. Hold yourself to a higher standard and let the manifestation begin!

Creating Your Team from Within

1. Write down a list of qualities that your ideal business partner would have. Are there qualities other than those listed that are important to you?

2. Prioritize the traits you're looking for in your team members. What's the single most important characteristic? What's the next? And the next?

3. Make a commitment that, every day for the next 30 days, you will review your list of criteria to impress them into your mind. Your subconscious will begin to look for people who match your criteria, and you will begin to attract these people to you. ■

■ Advance Your Recruiting with Appointments

By Jeanette Holtman

Changing lives one appointment at a time

QUICKLY FINDING THE GEM

Are you actively working your business—connecting with new people, enjoying good sales—but can't seem to grow your team? Chances are, you're missing an important step: getting the appointment on your calendar. *Take consistent, gracefully persistent action to make an appointment and advance your relationship with the prospective recruit until she makes a decision.* As a result, you'll more quickly find the prospect that will join your team and she will gain an understanding of your level of professionalism and commitment.

SETTING UP THE MEETING

Industry statistics tell us that one out of ten women who are interested will join our team. But, without an appointment to communicate in person, we end up answering questions sporadically, in multiple phone calls that can cover days, weeks, and even months. Over time, the prospect's interest cools off and we've lost a potentially great team member.

When should I call to set up the appointment?

Call to set up the appointment within 24 hours of meeting your prospect. By setting the expectation that you *will* be calling, you lay the foundation for the next step. You might say something like, "Here is a brochure and DVD with some information that I think you will find interesting. When do you think you will be able to take a look at this information, so I can give you a call?" Set a specific time tomorrow or the soonest possible day to follow up, and then be on your way. Most importantly, honor your word by calling at the agreed-upon time.

What should I say when I call to schedule the appointment?

Don't ask if she looked at the information, because 90 percent of the time, she hasn't looked at it yet, and then the conversation stops. Instead, simply ask for the appointment, which is the goal of the call. Here's a sample script:

> "Hi, this is _____. We met at Linda's yesterday, and I'm calling to see if we can set up a time to meet this week for 30 to 45 minutes over coffee. I'll give you information about our program to take home, and you can ask any questions you may have. What is your schedule like? Would daytime or evening be better for you?"

Be sure to paint the picture of what will happen when you meet— a neutral location, sharing information to take home, and answering questions. Don't start answering questions over the phone. For example, if she asks about the initial investment, respond, "That's a great question! The starter kit is about $200 and you'll have that investment back in a couple of shows. The idea here is to make money, not spend money. We'll talk in more detail when we get together. Do you have your calendar handy?" Don't be elusive, but always go back to the goal of the call: to set the appointment.

I know that I need to schedule an appointment. Why don't I do it?

- *You're not sure what to say in the scheduling call.* Use the script above or write your own simple script. Remember that your goal is to set the appointment, not to sell the opportunity over the phone.

- *You're afraid you might be pressuring someone.* You can't predict "who will" and "who won't." Your job is to offer information to everyone without prejudging, follow up to set an appointment, and then provide information. You allow the other person to be an adult and make her own decision.

■ *You don't know what to do when she says yes to the appointment.* What you lack in skill, you can make up for in numbers. If you hold lots of appointments, you're bound to recruit someone! Over time, you'll refine your skills and your ratio of those who join to number of appointments will improve.

■ *She lives too far away.* If she lives within a couple of hours, ask to meet halfway. If she says No, that is your first clue as to her interest level and initiative. If she's out of state, follow up to schedule a phone appointment. With the written information handy, you can "meet" as if you were sitting together.

Today's Actions for Scheduling Success

1. Make a list of women who have recently expressed interest.

2. Call each of them to set up an appointment for a meeting.

3. Make a commitment that, starting today, you will make the scheduling call within 24 hours of meeting a potential recruit. ■

■ Take the Daily Half-Dozen Steps to Success

By Michael S. Clouse
Empowering the direct-selling entrepreneur

RUNNING THE TREADMILL

Do you ever feel as though you're stuck on the treadmill of day-to-day life, just going through the motions? Your success in direct selling is directly proportional to the degree you're growing and learning, yet you may find yourself so caught up in the mundane tasks of living that you neglect your personal growth and the growth of your business. *By consciously deciding to take small steps toward both personal growth and building your business, you'll make daily progress toward your goals.*

Success and personal fulfillment in direct selling are really just a matter of being disciplined enough to do a little bit on a daily basis. Most of what you need to do falls into two categories: working on yourself and talking to people. Here are the half-dozen small steps you can take every day that will, over time, make a huge difference in your personal life and in the life of your business:

1. Using your personal success planner, spend 15 minutes focusing on your goals. This is your opportunity to review the big picture of why you have a direct-selling business and how you're going to realize your vision.

2. Listen to 30 minutes of an audiotape or CD. Remember to focus on *prospecting*, because you've got to find 'em; *presentation*, because you've got to enroll 'em; and *duplication*, because you've got to turn 'em into leaders who can do the same. Each month, focus on improving one of these three areas of your business.

3. Read ten pages of a good book. Whether you choose to read literature or a self-help book, reading broadens your horizons and gives you food for thought.

4. Expose two new prospects to your business opportunity using a system that anyone can duplicate, such as audiotapes and videotapes, CDs and DVDs, e-mails and Web sites, two-on-ones, or live events.

5. Follow up with your prospects. Get them in and then get them involved. If they see you as a successful business builder—and as a friend—they will stay in the game longer.

6. Follow through with the distributors who you perceive as potential leaders. Meet with them weekly for the first year and invest quality one-on-one time with them as well. Remember, they're not in this business until they're involved.

You don't need to work every day, but on the days you do work, these are the activities that will make you a superstar!

Stepping Up Today

1. Make a commitment to incorporating the daily half-dozen steps to success into each of your workdays.

2. Select a business-related audiotape or CD to listen to over the course of the coming week.

3. Select a book to begin reading that will aid your personal growth. ∎

∎ Engage Prospects with Enchanting Stories

By Mary Nelson
Storyteller extraordinaire

TELL ME A STORY

Whatever your company markets, whatever system your team uses, you must learn to tell *your* story. *Only those who tell great stories achieve great results.* Great stories engage not only the intellect, but also the emotions of the hearer, and emotions verify our decisions.

We grew up hearing stories that motivated, inspired, molded, and enriched us. Our favorite stories changed our beliefs, attitudes, expectations, and our dreams. Stories are made powerful not only by content, but by detail, structure, style, timing, intonation, pace, and passion. Great stories are literally the backbone of life and certainly of our direct-selling industry.

Great speakers can tell a story again and again that always seems fresh and spontaneous. This skill is developed with attention and practice. ***Once you are armed with great stories, your business will boom because you can touch contacts on multiple levels at once, engage them quickly, and help them persuade themselves to join your cause.***

STOCKING YOUR LIBRARY

She who tells the best story wins. You need many stories: about the products, the company, history-to-date, support and training, and the leaders. The more you have, the more easily you can select the right story and style to touch the heart or imagination of each prospect. The best story to open the mind of your bank vice president will be different from one that attracts a stay-at-home mom. Start accumulating your personal stories and getting them ready.

1. Identify the stories you need. List results you need to see, then find stories that fill the need. You need stories to attract new people, to encourage performers, to revitalize flagging team members; stories to highlight product performance, to teach, to harden resolve; stories to drive decisions, and to inspire loyalty.

Identify your values, and find stories that convey them. You must know who you are and why you are in business. Why do you love the product? Why are you passionate about the company? What is the opportunity for success? What training and support exist?

2. Collect the stories. The best stories come from personal experience. Until you have your own, you must draw on stories from your company lore, friends, and family. Over time, your own stories will replace others'.

Record company stories you hear and listen to them over and over. You will tell these until you develop your own. Learn and repeat stories that move you. Know why they touch you, because what touches your feelings will also be important to others.

Develop stories drawn from people who you know—family and friends who use your products and have experienced firsthand benefits.

3. Craft each story. For each story, ask yourself, Why does this appeal to me? How did I feel when I first heard this? What visual picture can I paint? What sound and rhythm can I add? What feelings can I display that make the listener imagine she's experiencing the benefits right now?

Having identified what moves you, begin to identify literary tools that appeal to you. Whether they are idea tools like allegory, personification, comparison, and contrast; structure tools like pace and suspense; or word selection tools like alliteration, rhythm, and cadence, all are useful. Structure your stories to highlight benefits so nobody has to ever wonder what your point was.

4. Learn and practice your stories. Use a recorder and tell those stories over and over until you love the story as you tell it. Stories must be ready at a moment's notice.

When someone's question prompts a story, it should be natural enough that you can pay attention to the hearer and not focus on the story. It must be rehearsed, heartfelt, compelling, and spontaneous all at once. This doesn't happen by luck, but because you have practiced your story many times. It happens because you are constantly working to make it "the perfect story for the person you are speaking to."

5. Ask for feedback. Receive it graciously and use it. Tell your prospects, "I intend to make my business really big so I would love your help. Will you give me some feedback, please?" Ask, "What about what I said interested you?" "What would you like to hear that I failed to tell you?" "What could I do better?"

6. Repeat these steps forever. You always need fresh, relevant stories. If you develop your business by developing the stories that comprise every part of it, you will indeed create a big business.

Actions for Today and Tomorrow

1. List the stories you need for success.

2. Inventory the stories you have and identify which ones you should start looking for.

3. Review two of the stories you use often and brainstorm how to make them more vivid and engaging to your prospect's imagination. ■

■ Build Your Psychological Armor

By Paula Pritchard
Building empires by empowering others

KNOW YOUR NO'S

Rejection is the toughest obstacle we face in direct marketing. It drives away wonderfully talented salespeople each year. How you handle rejection is a critical part of your success. It is something you battle each day to keep in the game.

So you must prepare your defenses against rejection. I call this building your *psychological armor.* I like to envision wearing a suit of armor that protects me from all emotional projectiles—including that most painful two-letter word, *No.*

No is a requirement for success. It is a price we pay. None of us is persuasive enough to get all Yes's, nor are we unconvincing enough to get all No's. ***Make the major psychological shift to understand that you get paid for No's as well as Yes's and embrace them.*** The only difference between those who are successful and those who are not is who tolerated the most rejection and disappointments.

The power over self is the greatest power of all. Once you become self-motivated, purpose driven, and undeterred, you will be unstoppable in whatever you pursue. Success will be yours.

GET A NOSE FOR NO'S

"Success is in the show." It's not how many times people say Yes or No, but how many times you *show* your product or opportunity. Yes's and No's are equal. Let's say you show your product to nine people who say No and a tenth person who says Yes, and you make a $100. Understand that you did not make $100 on the tenth person; you made $10 *every time you made the show.* The No's were just as valuable as the Yes.

Because you get paid for rejection, you must build that psychological armor early in your career while you are still working on your belief level. As your team grows, it is equally important to equip each team member with this same psychological armor. Here's how to build yours:

1. Build strong belief in your company and your product to the point that it becomes a mission. Strong belief in the path you are on and commitment to staying on that path helps make you resilient.

2. Concentrate on keeping a laser focus on your purpose and goals, allowing nothing to deter your progress. Internalized goals are the most powerful.

3. Constantly remind yourself of the most successful people you admire and how strong they have been to push through the same wall of No's as you. Let them inspire and motivate you. Imagine as well how your success will inspire others.

4. When you feel hurt by a rejection, check whether your perceptions are intensifying the experience. Remember there are many reasons someone might say No, and only rarely do these reasons have anything to do with you or your product.

5. Keep yourself motivated by watching, listening, and reading only positive material that keeps you strong. Associate with positive people.

6. Listen to motivational music to keep your emotions positive and on purpose.

7. Imagine yourself wrapped in a suit of armor where you are protected and safe, where no one can hurt you no matter what they say.

8. Know when to take a break and recharge. At the slightest sign of weakness, stop and listen to a tape, a CD, or a mentor until you are back on top of your game.

Strengthen Your Armor Today and Tomorrow

1. Today, take a quiet half hour and capture everything you love and hate about No and rejection. Write it out on paper or speak into a tape recorder. Make sure you feel safe to really let your feelings flow—that you can vent your anger and frustration without disturbing anyone.

2. Tomorrow, take a quiet half-hour to review what you captured. Notice which aspects of rejection are the most painful to you. Promise yourself you will strengthen your armor in those areas.

3. Reread the suggestions in this article. If you don't find any that relate to the specific aspects of rejection you find painful, ask a mentor or your sponsor for help. ■

■ Discover Sponsoring with DISC

By Nicki Keohohou
CEO and Cofounder of the DSWA

ADJUSTING YOUR STYLE

Have you ever met a bright woman who has goals that a direct-selling career could easily fill, but who doesn't understand the value of the opportunity you describe? You're perplexed because you can see a perfect fit, and frustrated because she seems unaffected by your usually contagious enthusiasm. You know that your success in direct selling depends on your ability to grow a team, but sometimes you encounter prospects who just don't seem to get it. Perhaps you haven't mastered the role that personality type plays in sponsoring, and have a tendency to relate to others in your own style, rather than adjusting your style to meet the needs of your prospects. *When you learn to recognize four primary personality styles, you can develop the ability to connect with others so they are open and engaged.* You'll be able to quickly develop rapport—which improves the likelihood of welcoming that person to your team.

CREATING DISC APPEAL

The "D" personality style is dominant, direct, and decisive. She wants a challenge, control, and choices. In your interview with her, weave in phrases such as:

- "You are in charge of your own business."

- "You can determine who you have on your team."

- "There is no stopping you—the sky is the limit!"

The "I" personality style is inspiring and influential. She wants recognition, fun, and approval. With her, you want to share such phrases as:

- "Could you get excited about earning a family vacation?"

- "Wouldn't it be nice to know that you are in a place where you are recognized for your achievements?"

- "Are you ready to have fun while creating the life you've dreamed of?"

The "S" personality style can be described as supportive, steady, and sensitive. She wants to be appreciated and values security. You can make her feel safe and comfortable by using the following phrases:

- "Isn't it great to know that the company has been in business for more than 15 years and that it is very stable?"

- "The company treats their distributors like family. It is a very supportive environment."

- "Can you imagine being in such as positive environment where you can make a difference in people's lives?"

The "*C*" personality style is generally cautious, contemplative, and competent. She wants definitive answers, excellence, and value. Connect with her by using phrases such as:

- "The company has been in business for 15 years. Can you see where that would provide you with the security you need?"

- "The company has a solid infrastructure and has provided the tools we need to build a successful business."

- "What support documentation do you need to assist you in making a decision to be a part of this financially stable company?"

Always build rapport with your prospect prior to your interview. Listen to the speed at which she speaks and match it. Be present with her and in tune with her needs. Be aware of her body language and match yours as closely as possible.

When Sponsoring a D

- Give a short presentation.

- Be an excellent listener.

- Answer her questions.

- Give her the facts.

- Focus on management opportunities, independence, and high income potential.

When Sponsoring an I

- Get to know her first.

- Give a personable interview presentation.

■ Build rapport.

■ Be a good listener (they love to talk!).

■ Have high energy.

When Sponsoring an S

■ Bring her to a meeting as a guest.

■ Build the credibility of the company.

■ Emphasize being part of a family.

■ Let her know she has a support team.

■ Understand that she may have an extended decision-making process.

When Sponsoring a C

■ Share the facts, tools, and processes that are in place.

■ Emphasize professional development.

■ Build the credibility of the company.

■ Expect numerous questions.

■ Be precise about follow-up.

■ Understand that she usually has an extended decision-making process.

Sponsoring with Style Today

1. Identify your own personality style. (See "Discover DISC for New Communication Power," by Dr. Robert A. Rohm, in Chapter 9.)

2. Make a list of potential prospects and try to determine their personality style prior to calling them. Think about

how you will approach them on the phone to set the interview.

3. Set an interview for this week. Use some of the phrases listed here and evaluate your results following the interview. ∎

∎ Offer Added Success to the Successful

By Jacqueline McGrath
Helping others break through their limiting beliefs

INCREASING YOUR CONFIDENCE

Every day, you have the ability to touch the lives of other women and offer them a career where they can achieve their aspirations and reach their dreams. Yet, how many times have you found yourself standing back, letting your chance to impact someone's life pass you by, because she seems too successful to need the business opportunity you have to offer? When you don't offer successful women the chance to join the community of direct sellers, you miss the opportunity to add these potential powerhouses to your team. By learning more about success, you'll come to understand that *accomplished people judge their success by more factors than just their monthly income.* You can feel confident approaching successful women because you know that the opportunity you're offering them can build and expand upon their success.

UNDERSTANDING THE DYNAMICS OF SUCCESS

If you've ever walked into a roomful of guests who are well educated, sharply dressed, and live in an upscale neighborhood, chances are you've assumed that these successful women wouldn't have an interest in a direct-selling career. And, chances are that you've decided not to invite them to join your team. In essence, you've made their decision for them. What you haven't done is recognize the many facets of success.

- **Money isn't everything.** If you were to ask others who are in direct sales why they joined, you'd get many different answers, and only some of them would relate to money. Some women want the fellowship and feeling of community that direct selling brings, others want to raise their families while staying connected to the outside world, and still others embrace the opportunity to challenge themselves. Women who are already successful could get many of their needs—both financial and nonfinancial—met through the business opportunity you offer them.

- **Success breeds success.** Successful people enjoy doing things well, and women who are already successful have proven their motivation and ability to do so. Everyone can do a little better, and sometimes, successful people want to do better than most.

- **Appearances can be deceiving.** Sometimes, the appearance of success can be a façade. We live in a society where many families—even successful families—are living beyond their means. Many people bring home big paychecks, but get little satisfaction or fulfillment from their jobs. Perhaps they'd love to be their own boss and set their own hours.

The bottom line is that *you don't know until you ask!*

When you do ask the successful, reach out with the offer of even greater success—defining "success" in a way that's meaningful to them. Arm yourself with the success stories of the top leaders in your company, but be prepared to share the joys of being able to be home when your kids get home from school. While you don't know for sure what motivates any one person, you can be sure that getting her on your team would contribute to both of your success.

Successfully Asking Today

1. Do some research and collect the success stories of high rollers in your company.

2. Contact your friends at the DSWA to learn success stories of other industry legends.

3. Make a list of all of the nonmonetary rewards you receive from your direct-selling business. ∎

∎ The Four Business-Building Conversations

By John Milton Fogg
Author of The Greatest Networker in the World

DRAWING THEM DEEPER

Has your eagerness to engage ever alienated a prospect? If so, use The Four Conversations to develop relationships naturally:

1. Conversation for Relationship

2. Conversation for Friendship

3. Conversation for Partnership

4. Conversation for Leadership

Each Conversation provides the Foundation for the next. Friendship cannot exist without first establishing Relationship. And if you've ever been in Partnership you know how important (as in mandatory) it is to have your Partner be your Friend.

Each Conversation must be "Complete," before you can move to the next. A Conversation is Complete (not finished or done; there's always the possibility of More and Better) when you say so—when there is nothing missing. It's Complete when You are able to say (as in Declare): "I'm in Relationship with Ralph. Karen is my Friend . . . , Partner . . . ," etcetera.

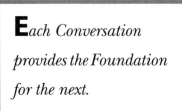

Each Conversation *provides the Foundation for the next.*

There *is* a "number's game" dimension to all of this. The more Relationships you get into, the more Friendships are possible—yes? The more Friends you have the more candidates there are for Partnership. (In Network Marketing, you have Customer-Partners, Team-Partners, and so on.) The more Partners you have, the more and better opportunity for Leaders to emerge.

1. The Conversation for Relationship

Here's where it all begins. Just say "Hi" and you're in Relationship. And is there more? Yes, there is. The more solid you build the Relationship, the better opportunity to move into Friendship—yes? And, that's your Choice—always. You get into Relationship with as many people as possible. You choose to move to Friendship or not, based on your experience of the person.

2. The Conversation for Friendship

What holds most all people together is "Shared Activity." The reason Shared Activity is such great glue for people is the Shared Values involved in Shared Activity. Shared Values are the basis of Friendship.

The Conversation for Friendship is a Value-Based and Value-Led Conversation. You Listen for the other person's Values—those they have you share with them, those you have they like, those they have you want. . . .When enough of those Values are out on the table—from both sides—the building blocks of Friendship are there. Your Friendship becomes "official" when you say, "My Friend Marty."

A Few Realities about Friends. One of the most useful things (in terms of building your business) about someone being your Friend, is the Trust and Regard you have for each other, which allows you to have a Conversation about almost anything—including your product or opportunity—easily, naturally, without fear of rejection.

The recommendation of a Friend is the single, most powerful Marketing "force" in the world. Even if your Friend isn't interested in what you're up to, they know someone who may be and will be happy to refer you and yours.

That's why Friendship is the most powerful Foundation on which to build Your Network Marketing business.

3. The Conversation for Partnership

In Network Marketing (and I say you can say "all of Life" as well) there is No Success except through Partnership. You are either in Partnership with Your Customers, Upline, Team, the Company . . . , or Not. That's it. That's all.

> **T**he reason Shared Activity is such great glue for people is the Shared Values involved in Shared Activity.

Partnership only comes into existence around a "Project." Whether it's the Partnership of Marriage, being a Member of a Team, Buying and Selling anything or a formal Business Partnership, the Partners join to Accomplish something together. Partners *need* each other.

As I've written in one of my e-mail signatures: "The days of 'do it yourself' are *over* . . . The future belongs to those men and women who actively embrace *Partnership*. And a growing group of Partners—working, learning sharing, *Being* together creates *Community*."

The Conversation for Partnership is an Offer you make to the other person—a Proposal. Take this popular example: "Will you marry me . . . ?" We even call it "a proposal."

There are three possible responses to a Proposal of Partnership: Yes. No. Or a "counter offer."

Conversations for Partnership in Network Marketing can occur when You Decide that Your Friend would make a great Business Partner. When you've decided this person has the Values and Vision you want in a Partner, you can make Your Offer, which is to "Take a Look" at the Possibility. That's the Conversation for Partnership.

> **T**here is no success except through partnership.

Remember there are three possible responses and since, in e-commerce terms, the "most desired response" is a "Yes," it makes sense for You to "Make an offer they can't refuse." The most consistently successful way I've seen to do this is to tell Your Friend Why you want him or her for a Partner, and do it with Enthusiasm. Like this:

"Mable, success in my business comes from getting into Partnership with bright, creative, and ambitious people who are looking for the best way to make a huge difference in hundreds of people's lives. That's You Mable! You'd be incredible at this and I *Really* want you for a Partner! Will you give me 20 minutes to show you what I'm up to and see if you'd be as good at this as I am . . . ?"

Remember, this Conversation for Partnership is based on Your Friendship with Mable. She'll answer one of three ways: Yes. No. Or, make you a counter offer. No matter which, Your Friendship is still there. And, because of Your Friendship, the chances of Mable giving you those 20 minutes are very, very good.

4. The Conversation for Leadership

Would you agree that there are no Leaders without Followers . . . ? And if this is so, what is it a leader has that people follow . . . ?

In one word: Vision.

Look at the Great Leaders of History: Gandhi, Churchill, Martin Luther King. Each put forth a compelling Vision of the Future the people followed, willingly, excitedly, by the millions! The Conversation for Leadership is a Conversation of Vision.

And here are two "secrets" I have discovered about Leaders: Their attention is *not* on themselves. Their Visions are about Serving other people. And, once you have had enough successful Conversations for Relationship, Friendship, and Partnership, the Conversation for Leadership comes naturally, automatically, effortlessly because You Are already *Being* a Leader.

Conversations in Action Today and Tomorrow

1. Hold one Conversation for Relationship.

2. Hold one Conversation for Friendship.

3. Hold one Conversation for Partnership. ∎

∎ Exhibit Your Professionalism for Trade Show Success

By Robert and Suzanne McGee
Finding stars through trade shows

MAKING THE MOST OF FACE TIME

Your direct-selling success depends on sales and recruits, and trade shows present a stellar opportunity for exposure to a large group of people to whom you can introduce your company and products. Although your trade show booth helps you meet people outside of your normal circle of influence, unless you have a strategy, maximize your visibility, and follow up with leads, your success is not guaranteed. *By implementing the professional approach that we've found to be effective, you'll make the most of the face-to-face time you have with each person who enters your booth, and will more effectively leverage your trade show investment.*

SETTING UP FOR SUCCESS

Before the Show

There are a wide variety of trade shows from which to choose, so be discriminating in your selection. Consider the demographics of the attendees, the location of the show, and your total costs. You also must factor into the equation the fact that you might not sell anything or sponsor anyone from the show. You must decide whether, under these circumstances, you are willing to make this promotional investment in your business. Start with smaller, local trade shows and work your way up.

At the Show

1. Begin by setting up your booth so that it is inviting to enter and so that your product is easy to see. Most booths are 10' × 10' and a U-shape configuration allows traffic to flow easily while visitors are viewing your product.

2. While setting up your booth, introduce yourself to other vendors. They usually have a wealth of information about which trade shows are best.

3. Have two people working in your booth so that two tasks can be completed at the same time, such as answering questions about the product, tallying purchases, and introducing your business opportunity. The flow of trade show traffic comes in waves, so it's not unusual for your booth to go from empty to very full in a short period of time.

4. Stand at the exterior rim of your booth, so you can easily invite people to come take a look. You *must* be excited and sincerely interested in introducing them to both your product and your opportunity.

5. Be prepared with an enthusiastic and concise story line. You might say, "Have you ever heard of _____? It's a great product that's fun, trendy, and reasonably priced. Please feel free to try it, and if you have any questions, I'll be happy to assist you."

Then, wait just a few minutes and follow up with the second part of your story. "Oh, by the way, in case you know of someone who loves jewelry and would like to have more fun or more money in their life, this is an awesome business. When you are done shopping, I'd be happy to give you some business information."

6. Have packets of information ready for those who want it immediately. For those who don't want to carry it with them throughout the show, be sure to get their contact information, including their e-mail address. Either e-mail or mail the information to them as soon as you return home.

7. Have a clipboard with attached forms that contain spaces for a prospect's contact information. Brightly colored paper and a Sharpie® marker work best. To ensure accuracy, write the contact information yourself while the prospect dictates it.

After the Show

1. As soon as you arrive home, file the leads according to "hot" and "warm."

2. Commit to making follow-up calls within 36 hours. Trade show leads get cold quickly, so use fast and friendly follow-through for maximum results.

3. Record each prospect, including contact phone number, on a master document, slip it into a page protector sheet, and carry it with you wherever you go.

4. Use the extra minutes you have while waiting for an appointment, for a meeting to begin, or for a flight to arrive to make follow-up calls.

Showing Your Stuff

1. Look in your local paper or on its Web site for upcoming events. Find a show where the attendance demographic

matches your customer demographic, take the plunge, and sign up!

2. Even if you can't buy space at a trade show within the next 48 hours, you can spend an hour envisioning what you would do to make your booth appealing, who you would bring to help, and what supplies you'd need to take along.

3. Every trade show visitor loves a giveaway. Do some research on ordering personalized promotional items; give one to each booth visitor who leaves his or her contact information. ∎

∎ Standardize Your Opportunity Meetings

By Kosta K. Gharagozloo
Inspiring financial independence on a global scale

REPLICATING A TURNKEY SUCCESS

Have you ever attended a direct-selling business presentation, and then went back the following week only to find the two presentations had little in common? Have you ever walked away from the second presentation more confused than from the first one?

When sharing your business opportunity with distributors and prospects, ***keep your message clear and consistent.*** The content and setup of your business meetings should be the same regardless of where the presentations take place or who is presenting the information. This is part of what I call the "Franchise Model" approach to direct-selling business meetings.

Let's take a quick look at one of the most effective and successful franchise models around—McDonald's. Have you ever wondered how a chain of hamburger shops run by teenagers can be so successful? The answer is simply because the menus and floor layout are *standardized.*

Before walking into a franchise, the customer knows the basic menu selections and the advertised specials. If not, the customer knows where to look to check for specials and the price board, knows where to go to order, knows where to pick up straws and extra mustard, and knows where to sit and eat. Customers place their orders, pick up their food and condiments, sit down, eat, drop off their trays, and leave. The entire process generally only takes about 20 minutes.

Imagine what would happen to throughput if the franchises in any one city all had different menu selections from each other. What if a franchise in St. John, New Brunswick, had a totally different menu selection from one in Nanaimo, British Columbia, while the franchises in Phoenix and San Francisco offered something altogether different? The customer would be even more confused if franchises located the menu selection and price board in different places. Where would you look? How would you feel?

My idea for holding business meetings is very similar to the Franchise Model: standardization. Identify a business-meeting format, identify the presentation topics, identify a room layout, and stick to it regardless of who is doing the presentation or where it occurs.

When I started my team in 2002, we had nothing but a dream. At our first meeting, there was me, my wife, and one other presenter. At our second meeting, we had me, my wife, my other presenter, and one guest. Today, we average roughly 70 to 110 people at each of our established weekly business meetings in Canada, and more at some of our international ones. Thanks to our standards, the distributor has the confidence to send her prospects to our business meetings in any area and knows the prospect will always get the same high-quality presentation. The distributor can walk her prospect through what to expect without ever having to see a meeting outside her own local area.

ESSENTIAL ELEMENTS EVERY GUEST CAN EXPECT

No matter the city or the presenter's individual style, the meeting format is consistent day to day, week to week, hotel to hotel, city to city, country to country:

- A registration table just outside the meeting room
- A product display table at the front of the room

- Presentation slides that are consistent from meeting to meeting and city to city

- Presenters who share the same high-quality, standardized information

- A compelling product overview

- A few product testimonials selected in advance and guided by the presenters

- A business opportunity overview

- A well-run minimeeting immediately after the main business meeting to explain the compensation package more fully to those who are interested

- A top leader available to meet one-on-one to enroll a prospect

BEYOND QUALITY CONTENT

We've also established standards in other areas. For example, greeters with a professional appearance courteously welcome our guests. Distributors and leaders at the registration desk and doing the presentations wear business attire—no leisure outfits or tee shirts and jeans. First appearances are important and lasting, so these first people a guest meets always act appropriately as "business ambassadors" and are invariably courteous and professional. In fact, we encourage all our distributors to wear business dress and attend the meetings regardless of whether they have guests attending. Weekly attendance at business meetings helps keep distributors in the know about special events such as upcoming meetings with corporate representatives, business-building incentives, or the launch of new product.

Our standards also cover the setup of the meeting room. Because distributors and guests walk in through doors at the back of the room, the main activities of the presentations always take place at the front. Late arrivals can walk in with minimal disruption to the meeting.

To create that all-important enthusiastic atmosphere that gets people into a receptive, positive mindset, uplifting, energetic music plays from the time the doors open to the time the actual business presentation begins.

When people begin to dehydrate, their ability to concentrate diminishes, so the room always includes a water station that is replenished about halfway through the meeting. Just like the water cooler at the office, the water station is a place for distributors and their guests to socialize. We simply ask the socialization be kept to before and after the business meeting, not during it.

Our professionalism extends to our host hotels. We make sure the bills are paid on time, and that our leaders and distributors treat the hotel staff in a respectful and courteous manner. Without the hotel facilities and their support staff, we'd be constantly looking for a place to hold our formal business meetings and those all-important after-the-meeting meetings when the distributor and prospect can really talk at a personal level.

Start Setting Standards Today

As you can see, many things affect your success when standardizing meetings on a local, national, and global scale. Some are simply more obvious than others. Now it's your turn to build your distributors' confidence and unify your team by standardizing your own business meetings. Take time today to schedule a meeting with your team to explore how standardizing business meetings could replicate your recruiting success. ■

■ Build Your Recruiting Pipeline

By Ruth and Dennis Williams
Partnering up to bring people to our profession

CREATING MAXIMUM EXPOSURE FOR SUCCESSFUL RECRUITING

Have you started to recruit a team and discovered that engaging great people is more difficult than you anticipated? Sponsoring is the key to business growth and financial independence in direct selling. Create a recruiting pipeline by harnessing the tried-and-true theory that the average consumer needs approximately six points of exposure before they make the buying decision. *By offering a variety of ways for your prospect to have contact with your business opportunity, you have a better chance to connect with your prospect in a way she prefers and to which she responds.* By growing an organization of business builders, you harness the power of duplication and are able to create long-term residual income from the production volume of those you lead and serve.

FINDING THE RHYTHM

There is a rhythm to building a business. Some people build a little faster, others a little slower; some play with great enthusiasm, while others play very quietly. In our 13 years of building a business, we've learned that prospects need to learn about the business opportunity in the manner that is most comfortable for them. To succeed, your recruits must have a strong conviction that your business opportunity is right for them. Your job is to help them build their conviction.

When recruiting, some distributors lead with the business opportunity and others lead with product sales. We have found that leading with the business opportunity creates a very effective flow of new team members. By continually directing the flow of new business through a system of one-on-one meetings, conference calls, group meetings and events, more recruits stay in the business and succeed.

The following system is an effective way to create a pipeline, in which your prospect increases her commitment to you with every contact and interaction:

1. Begin with a one-on-one presentation over the phone or in person, the purpose of which is to get the prospect to an "in home" presentation or group meeting.

2. Invite your prospect to listen in on a live conference call presentation or to a prerecorded presentation that you or your company may offer through a conference line service. You may choose to three-way the prospect into the conference line to expedite the process.

3. Encourage your prospect to participate in an ABC call or face-to-face meeting. *A* is the leader, *B* is you, the distributor, and *C* is the prospect. It is a good idea to leverage the credibility of *A* when you, as *B,* do not have the experience to close *C.*

4. Invite a small group to your place for an "in home" presentation. This is a very friendly and casual event. Hopefully, the prospect will feel a sense of family with the team members and other guests.

5. Next, invite your recruit to a regional event in a hotel. These events are often hosted by several leaders in the area. The leaders can be from all different organizations. These larger meetings give a professional image of the company and are particularly effective with corporate professionals.

6. Corporate-sponsored events always add more credibility to the program. Corporate regional events, as well as national conventions, are the next stage in motivating distributors.

7. To keep your distributors moving forward, always invite them to educational events, product information calls, training calls, and whatever other tools the company makes available to you.

Remember to raise the stakes each step of the way. For example, do a minipresentation on the phone, but don't discuss pricing or give away materials unless she comes to an in-person presentation.

Likewise, hold a monthly training meeting where you discuss how your company's compensation plan works or how to fill out order forms, but don't train prospects on how to present until they agree to become members of your team.

When you feed prospects into the pipeline of calls, meetings, and events, you are leveraging your time and creating the opportunity to touch more people with less effort. The prospects stay in the system until they either decide to join the company, become a customer, or decline the business opportunity.

Creating Your Pipeline

1. Regardless of your stage of business development, think of your recruiting process as a pipeline.

2. Identify the resources you offer to someone evaluating your business opportunity, and categorize them according to the increasing level of commitment on both sides.

3. Present your resources to your recruits in a manner that matches their level of interest and commitment then raise the stakes as they move through the pipeline. ■

5

Principle-Centered Coaching

Of all the chapters in *Build It Big*, this chapter's counterpart—"Coaching Your Team"—drew the most reader response. It lifted the veil and gave direct-selling leaders a new way to relate to and guide their teams to success. We at the DWSA felt enormous satisfaction at achieving one of our goals: to introduce direct sellers to a coaching model that brings them more success and satisfaction in guiding their teams.

This chapter builds upon the foundation laid in the first book by delving even deeper into the five principles and five skills of Principle-Centered Coaching. You'll discover that this unique approach is a simple model based on the spirit of service. You can easily implement this coaching system and transform your relationship with your team members.

> The coaching skills have revolutionized my thinking, changed the way I work with people for the better, and allowed me to work my business with joy and ease! I deal with situations with calmness, and I find that I don't take things as personally as I did before. Best of all, my consultants and directors feel heard and understood. I am *living* my mission statement to empower women!
>
> **—Linda Wiseman Jones**

The contributors to this chapter have offered you their wisdom in the hope that you will be inspired to adopt the methods of Principle-Centered Coaching to lead your team to success. Just as a well-tossed pebble creates innumerable perfect rings in a pond, so the rewards of coaching in the spirit of service will grow far beyond what you can imagine.

Coach in the Spirit of Service

By Jennie England, PCC, CPCC
Co-creator of the DSWA's Principle-Centered Coaching program

SHIFTING THE FOCUS

As I coach direct-selling leaders in the different aspects of their businesses, I often hear feelings of frustration being expressed in comments like, "My team members say they want to succeed, but I don't see them taking action!" or "My team seems so dependent on me. Why can't they be more self-motivated?" Their statements alone reveal the nature of the problem. *When we focus on what our team isn't doing, we're coaching from a self-centered perspective–an approach that almost always generates feelings of disappointment and disempowerment.* There's a much more fun and fulfilling way to conduct your business. Using the skills of Principle-Centered Coaching, you can coach from a spirit of service, **shift the focus away from what you want to receive, and instead, focus on what your team member wants and needs.** When you do, you will find more joy in your work, more rewarding relationships with your team members, and a better ability to support your team in achieving members' goals.

LEADING WITH YOUR HEART

Do you like to be pushed, prodded, and made to feel that, no matter what you do, it's not enough? Probably not, and neither do your team members. Would you prefer being heard, understood, acknowledged, and supported to reach your goals? Of course you would.

Service is the spirit with which you can inspire, guide, and empower your team. By focusing on giving rather than receiving, you will naturally succeed. As Zig Ziglar said, "You can have anything in the world you want if you just help enough people get what they want." Whether you are the upline or a team leader, using these Principle-Centered Coaching skills is an expression of service that promotes growth and success:

- **Heart-Centered Listening** creates trust, respect, and safety in relationships. It allows you to listen, understand, and guide in a way that serves. The speaker feels heard and empowered, which leads to greater openness, learning, and productivity.

- **"I See You" Acknowledgment** encourages you to look for the best in each team member and validate her qualities and strengths. The receiver feels "seen" and empowered to express her best—and thus moves forward to reach her potential.

- **"You're the Expert" Questions** come from an understanding that your team member knows what is best for her and has answers and wisdom within. These questions and their answers create more clarity, insights, possibilities, and commitment.

- **Agreed Action and Accountability** results from using the previously mentioned skills in a planning session. Your team member, with your support, creates her plan. Because it is hers, she makes a commitment to it, takes ownership, and is responsible for her own success.

- **Compassionate Feedback** supports learning and growth in your team members. It is free of blame and judgment and can expand and enhance the learning for all!

When you use these skills, you honor and respect your team member each step of the way, so that her dignity and self-esteem remain intact. Thus, she is empowered to take action and move forward with new enthusiasm, awareness, and commitment to her own success!

Stepping into the Spirit of Service Today

1. Create your intention to lead in the spirit of service, write it down, read it frequently, and live it!

2. Sign up for the DSWA's Principle-Centered Coaching Skills five-week telecourse.

3. Purchase the DSWA's Principle-Centered Coaching CD and e-book.

4. Hire a coach from the DSWA Coach Referral Network. ▪

■ Let Them Know How Much You Care

By Diane Thompson

Leading the way to a more meaningful life

SETTING YOUR PRIORITIES

Undoubtedly, you care about your team members. The question is, do they know it? Perhaps you don't express your concern and appreciation out of a fear of appearing vulnerable. Maybe you make other aspects of your business a higher priority. It could be that you see your team members as self-sufficient and as able to take care of themselves and their teams. Or, perhaps you simply view your team as a means to an end. Whatever the reason, when you do not show that you care about your team, consultants flounder and leave. *As a leader, you must do your best to show that you genuinely care about your team members as individuals.* When you do, your consultants will feel more connected to the team and will be more likely to stay the course during tough times. They will also be inspired to implement your leadership skills with their own teams.

CARING COMMUNICATION STRATEGIES

You may have heard the phrase, "People don't care how much you know until they know how much you care." I learned this early in my career and it holds true today. That's why I've developed a number of ways to reach out to my organization, which is 12,000 distributors strong. Even with an organization this size, I have found ways to appreciate and show that I care so that even someone I have not met will know they matter to me.

Show Genuine Interest

Listening is a leader's responsibility. Make eye contact and refrain from interrupting her while she is speaking. Use reflective listening techniques. When she's finished, say, "Let me repeat what I heard you say . . ." Repeat what you heard and ask her if that is correct. In this way, you'll tap into her real issues, frustrations, and concerns.

Remember Special Details

For your immediate team:

- Send birthday cards for your immediate leaders and their top leaders.

- Send special notes or a meaningful gift when someone has a hardship.

- Drop a note to the child of an up-and-coming leader, congratulating him or her for being a part of Mom's success team.

For your whole team, reach deep within your organization with e-mails and cards, so that your presence is felt:

- Send e-mails to individuals for accomplishment (I send out hundreds each week).

- Mail personalized cards for a special occasion, such as a high sales achievement or a challenge met.

- Send a congratulatory letter to distributors who have advanced to a higher level of leadership.

- At the very least, send a card when someone calls with a heart-felt story.

Make Note of Her "Why"

For your immediate team:

- Find out her Why during the recruiting process or as soon as possible after she joins your team.

- Keep a record of her Why, perhaps on a profile card or in your coaching materials.

- Memorize her Why. Always be ready to use it in either congratulations on her achievement or turning her around from discouragement to motivation.

Model this approach for your whole team, and train them how to take note of the "Whys" of their team members.

Touch Base Regularly

For your immediate team:

- Start with a face-to-face conversation or a phone conference to help establish your concern and care for her, personally.

- Follow her goals to see how she is doing.

- Enter into a coaching relationship with her.

For your whole team:

- Keep team members in the loop. It's important for them to remember you as someone who genuinely cares and is willing to reach out and sincerely help.

- Send one-to-many communications, such as e-mails and newsletters.

Show You Care Today

1. Review other articles in this book that offer insights on coaching, supporting long-distance teams, developing newsletters and handouts, and holding interactive meetings.

2. Outline a strategy for communicating to your team members that you care.

3. Send out a one-to-many communication and let your team members know that you are available for them. ∎

∎ Help a Team Member Get Unstuck

By Carly Anderson, MCC
Member of the DSWA Coach Referral Network

REDISCOVERING HER GREATNESS

When coaching a team member who feels discouraged, you might feel pretty uncomfortable yourself. Of course everyone eventually hits a plateau in her business. Plateaus are natural, as are hills to climb and peaks to reach for.

To prepare for the plateaus, remember *it is not your responsibility to move your team member forward*. It is your responsibility **to offer her a process that will help her get "unstuck" so she can move forward herself.**

The key to success is to find out what moves *her* from resignation to inspiration. To be in a place of resignation is to have given up because it seems hopeless to keep going. At the other end of the spectrum is inspiration, which taps into a natural, sustainable energy source that makes going forward a joy.

As you lead yourself and others, it's your job not only to stay in touch with what inspires you, but also to keep your team members in touch with what inspires *them*. When someone calls feeling discouraged, here's how to help her renew her movement toward her goals.

FROM RESIGNATION TO INSPIRATION

By listening carefully, asking the right questions, and using the right language, you can move someone from feeling stuck to feeling back in the flow in just three steps.

Step One: Bring Awareness to Being Stuck

Listen for the language of resignation, such as "I can't do this," "This is too hard," "I don't know what to do," or even "I don't have the time to do that." You might even feel the fear in her words.

If you hear this language or sense an underlying fear, ask for permission to coach: "May I make an observation?" or "May I ask you some questions?" If she says Yes, then go ahead. If she seems reluctant to hear you, then honor that and graciously let her know that if she changes her mind, you're available.

If she said Yes, then make your observations in a nonjudgmental tone: "When I hear you say ____, it sounds as if you have _____ and I imagine it feels as if _____. I also hear (name the emotion). Is there an element of truth in that?" For example:

> When I hear you say you don't know what to do, it sounds as if you've given up, and I imagine it feels as if there's nothing you can do to change the situation. I also hear the fear in your voice that this might not change. Is there any element of truth in that?

As you listen to her response, don't take her difficulties personally. Remember that it's not about you—it's about her. Your job is to be present to what's going on for her, and bring awareness in a respectful and supportive manner.

Step Two: Reconnect Her to Inspiration

Now you can take her to her bigger picture so she can reconnect to her reason for being in business: her Why.

Again, ask permission: "May I ask you a question?" Then ask, "What do you *love* about this business?" "What's the *best* thing that's happened to you since you've been in this business?" or "What's most important to you?"

What you're looking for is a question that gets her thinking about what puts a smile on her face. It may be sharing her passion for the product, her personal success story, providing for her family, or making a difference.

Ask open-ended questions and make observations in a way that gives her a choice rather than having it sound as if you have the right answer. If she feels like she has no choice, she might close down and stay stuck.

Step Three: Find an Inspired Action

She might need some back and forth between steps one and two before she is ready for step three. Remember, when we connect to *our own* reasons why we love something, then new possibilities open up. Tap into your *own* inspiration for wanting to help her, and be patient while she discovers her answers in her own time.

Inspired Actions for Today and Tomorrow

1. Become aware of the language of resignation. When we deny what we're feeling, we have no chance of moving to inspired actions.

2. Find out what inspires you—what brings a smile to your face about your business.

3. Notice if you take it personally when a member of your team is not performing as you expect. Instead, find out what inspires you and reconnect with that.

4. Coach *yourself* to take the three steps from resignation to inspiration for the next 48 hours. Your experience will make you eager to share the process with your team. ■

■ Empower Your Team with Forward-Focused Questions

By Robin Blanc-Mascari
Passionately leading others to prosperity

CARING, SHARING, AND MOVING AHEAD

A leader's role in direct selling is to coach—not manage. The difference being that you manage things or events to suit *you*, but you *coach people to help them become what they want.* Our tendency is to direct team members to where *we* think they should be or where *we* want them to be, when the real need is to get them where *they* want to be. Our true role as a leader is to coach our team members in achieving their dreams and goals, not ours. You can best bring this about through forward-focused questions.

How we show we care is directly related to

1. the quality of questions we ask our team, and

2. our *heart-centered listening* to their responses.

We improve the quality of our team's empowerment, our business growth, relationships, and the rest of our lives directly **by improving the quality of questions we ask,** thereby determining the quality of answers we live with.

THE POWER OF FORWARD-FOCUSED QUESTIONS

As described in Principle-Centered Coaching, "You're the Expert" (YTE) questions are open-ended. Different than a closed-ended question that your team member can answer with a simple Yes, No, or other specific response, an open-ended question reveals infinite possibilities in her potential to respond. The beauty of coaching her with these questions is that by tapping into her creativity, her wisdom, and her experience, she experiences true empowerment. Remember that the most empowering solutions are always found inside ourselves, so your job as a coach is to ask YTE questions that bring forth the wisdom existing within each person.

Open-ended questions typically begin with *what* and *how*. The distinction of open-ended questions with a forward focus is that the movement from the question takes us toward where we want to go. For example, compare these two questions:

1. "What were the challenges in your most recent event?"

2. "What did you learn from the challenges at your recent event that will move you toward your desired result?"

The first question has a backward focus, and identifies a challenge from the past, while the second question challenges your team member to discover things in her past to help in her future.

Many confuse *positive* focus with *forward* focus. For example:

■ A positive question: "What was the best part of your meeting?"

■ A forward-focused question: "What part of your meeting was most effective in recruiting new associates?"

The subtle difference is that the first question causes her to analyze her meeting while the second question causes her to analyze her meeting with a focus of finding tools to improve future meetings.

We use questions every day with and without realizing the focus. We can ask, "Did you reach your goal last month?" (closed-ended, backward focus, demanding) or "What results were you most proud of last month that support your short-term goals?" (open-ended, forward-focused, encouraging). Notice how it feels to be asked each of these questions. If our true desire is empowerment and developing interdependent, successful teammates, this very simple difference can have exponentially positive results. No matter whether you're new in the business or a seasoned professional, you can empower your team immediately using these questions.

A WORD OF CAUTION

Having asked a question, the true key to success is Heart-Centered Listening. It's no wonder that we were given two ears and one mouth. Just asking is not enough. Taking the time to have your team member feel listened to and cared about opens up infinite possibilities. Sometimes, you'll need to ask questions that aren't forward focused, so that you can share a moment like taking a rest on a mountain trail to enjoy a stream or a view rather than just charging up the mountain to get to the top. By taking time to truly listen, you show that you value her and celebrate her growth.

For Today and Tomorrow, Awareness Is the Key

1. For the next 48 hours, pay more conscious attention to the questions you are asking and the ones you hear others ask. The first step is awareness—are these questions open-ended, closed-ended, forward, or backward focused? What are the results produced from these different kinds of questions?

2. Now choose to develop a list of questions that best supports your team, ask them, listen to the responses, and notice the results. ∎

■ Reveal Her Re-engaged Vision

By Rysia Crockett
Leading with dignity and class

REDIRECT THE DISCONNECT

You're vigilant in coaching your team, but despite your best efforts, you see a team member begin to disconnect. ***Prevent her from slipping away by guiding her to take a fresh look at her goals, and then recommit to your efforts to coach her to success.*** As a result, you'll form a new partnership with your team member that will bring her back into the fold and support her in growing her business.

A major component of successful coaching is guiding your team member through a process of self-discovery. After the two of you recommit to your partnership, you can use tools to uncover her life priorities, positive attributes, and areas that need improvement. Then together you can map the journey to her desired goal.

COACHING FOR SELF-DISCOVERY

Translate your desire to re-engage your team member into a heartfelt conversation with her. The purpose of your discussion is to encourage her to redefine her vision and to express your commitment to help her achieve her goals. After scheduling a specific time to call your team member, use the following approach:

1. Acknowledge that a problem exists and express your desire to get back on track.

2. Restate the original intent of your partnership and her original dream.

3. Ask for her thoughts.

4. Ask her to restate her dream or vision of success.

5. Suggest that the two of you re-establish your partnership and request her agreement.

6. Present a coaching plan with agreed-upon appointments and time lines.

After initial pleasantries, your part of the dialogue with your teammate might go something like this:

Coach: I've missed working with you. Yesterday, I thought about progress we'd made before you got sick and we got off track. I reflected on your dream to pay cash for your kids' college tuition. I'd like to get back on the path to making your dream come true. What are your thoughts?

Coach: I'm ready to partner with you to make it happen. Share your vision so that I can hear it in your words. What does it look like to walk into the registrar's office and write a check for Tommy's tuition? What's the look on Tommy's face? What are you feeling?

Coach: I'm excited and ready to get started. I have a plan that will allow you to realize your dream, and I'm committed to the process. Are you ready to begin again, together?

Coach: *(Set an appointment to meet.)*

Coach: Thanks so much for agreeing to our new partnership. I'll send you an e-mail with some thought-provoking questions that will be a part of our new beginning.

Follow up with an e-mail and include the following assessment, which will help you and your team member focus on areas for development. Ask that she submit her responses a day or two prior to your meeting.

Questionnaire

Please answer these questions from your heart. Together, we'll use your responses to design a map to reach your goals.

1. What is your victory vision?

2. What's getting in the way of your dream?

3. Do you really believe that you can achieve your vision?

4. What are you willing to give up to make your dream a reality?

5. What are you willing to overcome to achieve your vision?

6. Describe the ways in which you are coachable.

7. Describe your willingness to work hard.

8. In what ways are you willing to step outside of your comfort zone to learn new skills and apply them?

9. Are you a leader? How do you know?

10. What are you afraid of?

Life Priorities

During your meeting, ask your team member to list the things that are most important to her.

Work with her to place her priorities in order of importance. Then, assign hours to each priority based on the 168 hours we have available to us each week. (Don't forget to include sleep.) Once you've determined the number of hours that can be devoted to business, you can use your team member's assessment responses to structure those hours and map out a plan to realize her vision.

Getting Back on Track

Take these three steps in the next 48 hours to prevent a team member from slipping away:

1. Define your strengths as a coach and list three reasons why coaching is fulfilling to you.

2. Identify when and how your team member began to disconnect.

3. Contact her and schedule a phone appointment with her. ∎

∎ Craft Coaching Calls That Inspire Action

By Leigh Kirk
Helping others discover solutions that lead to success

INDIVIDUALIZING TOOLS FOR TEAM MEMBERS

Your direct-selling success depends heavily on how well you communicate with your team. Sustained growth of your business, team retention, and profitability for your team members requires regular coaching calls. ***To successfully coach a large number of team members, you must implement a process to plan and structure calls—a process that tracks who you spoke to and what topics you covered.*** As a result, your team members receive the individualized tools they need to move forward, and you have measurable objectives by which to evaluate their progress.

Having grown an organization of more than 4,800 people spanning all 50 states, I'd like to offer some insights on how to use coaching calls to accelerate your rise to the top.

LAYING THE FOUNDATION, BUILDING THE STRUCTURE

Successful coaching calls that net positive results take effective planning and follow-through. Throughout the process, keep in mind that your goal is to inspire action with measurable results.

Rules for the Relationship

1. Before the first call, set an expectation that you will match your time with her effort.

2. Know your team member's goals and communicate how the coaching call will support those goals. When you know her goals and have them written down in front of you, it will be easy to keep her focused on the action she needs to take.

3. Ask her permission to hold her accountable to her goals. Simply ask, "_____, if I see or hear you doing something that is standing in the way of you reaching your goals, do I have your permission to tell you about it, even if it might be uncomfortable for you to hear?" This sets up open and honest communication, and allows you to be her coach as well as her cheerleader.

4. Your job on the call is to ask questions, listen, and respond. These calls are designed to provide accountability for her goals, and to help her become solutions-conscious, not problem-oriented. Your job is not to try to fix her problems by offering your advice; rather, it is to help her come up with her own solutions and a plan of action.

5. Checking on her progress toward her goal helps you to hold her accountable to making it a reality—which you have already asked for permission to do. If you have set specific goals that are measurable, the questions to ask will be simple. For example:

6. "One of your goals from our call last week was to contact 20 people to schedule presentations. What were your results? Who did you contact? What was the response? How did you handle it? How do you feel about your success last week? What will you do differently this week? What goals will you set this week to help you achieve your goal of _____?"

Elements of a Successful Coaching Call

1. Schedule a consistent day and time for your weekly call—a time dedicated to her business and free from any outside distractions or interruptions.

2. Use a tracking sheet for your calls. Have a place to write down notes about your conversation and a place to log specifics, such as number of: contacts and calls made the week prior; presen-

tations made; people met at those presentations; presentations scheduled for the current week; and total presentations on her calendar. You need to have specific numbers to be able to measure progress.

3. Log her prospective consultants by name. Referring to her list of contacts by name is a meaningful personal touch and effectively communicates that you are interested in her.

4. At the end of each call, have her set specific goals for the following week and a plan of action to achieve those goals. Be sure to write down these goals and action steps so you can hold her accountable on your next call.

5. Always end each call with a measurable action attached to a deadline. Say, for example, "Call ten people today and let me know your results by 10:00 AM tomorrow."

Paying It Forward

1. Identify three of your top performers—those who are consistently working their businesses, creating results, and have goals to advance to higher levels of leadership.

2. Extend an invitation to coach each woman, sharing the value they'll receive and your expectations in return for your investment of time.

3. Set up a tracking system, get permission from each of them to hold them accountable, and solidify their commitment to meet at the agreed-upon times. ∎

■ Prepare for a Great Coaching Call

By Jane Deuber
President and Cofounder of the DSWA

STARTING ON THE SAME PAGE

Although you want to give a team member the best support you can by speaking to her regularly, you may find that your coaching calls ramble on too long and don't pinpoint solutions or identify action steps. You may spend more time "telling and teaching" than "asking and listening." This leaves the team member feeling disempowered and unsure of the direction she should be taking to accomplish her goals. *When you ask your team member to complete and fax a Coaching Call Preparation Form to you before your meeting, you receive essential information to use as a springboard for providing her with focus and direction to determine her next steps.* With a clear process for your coaching call, your team member will feel empowered and supported, and you will leverage your time to benefit both of you.

GETTING IN GOOD FORM

When you use the DSWA's Coaching Call Preparation Form, your team member reaps the maximum benefits from your 30-minute coaching call. It offers seven prompts and spaces for your team member to record her answers:

1. My greatest accomplishments since our last call:

2. What I am most grateful for or proud of this past week:

3. What I wanted to get done but didn't:

4. The challenges or problems I am facing now:

5. The opportunities available to me this week:

6. What I would like to discuss during my coaching call:

7. What I am committed to doing by our next call:

Ask your team member to complete this form and either fax or e-mail it to you prior to your coaching call. To complete the form, she must review and reflect upon her previous week and clarify her goals for her coaching session with you. Plus, it gives you in advance the information you need to outline your coaching strategy.

With the Coaching Call Preparation Form, you and your team member can accomplish these objectives:

1. **Have a more meaningful experience.** With the information-gathering process out of the way, you and your team member can focus on what she needs in order to take the next step.

2. **Hit the ground running.** With her recent wins listed clearly at the top of the form, you can get right to the heart of celebrating her success. This helps minimize chitchat and sets the tone for a great call.

3. **Quickly identify challenges**. A team member who waits until the coaching call to search for and identify challenges tends to stay focused on problems. When she reflects on areas of concern in advance, she becomes more open to finding solutions and has more time to receive guidance and feedback.

4. **Address a specific request.** When a coaching call lacks focus, specific requests can get lost in the shuffle of information gathering and small talk. By stating her intention on her Coaching Call Preparation Form, your team member can draw your attention to details that need to be addressed.

5. **Agree to actions and accountability.** Having her identify and commit to the steps she will take in the coming week ensures that your team member will work on *her* goals, rather than on your goals for her.

Conditions for an Ideal Coaching Call

To ensure a successful call, put the following elements in place:

■ An agreed-upon time and length of call

■ Clarity about the phone number where you can be reached

■ A quiet setting with no background noise

■ No interruptions during the call

■ A complete focus on the call, with no multitasking

■ The team member has completed the Coaching Call Preparation Form and faxed or e-mailed it to you prior to the call

Your Preparation

1. Read the Coaching Call Preparation Form prior to the call and be ready to address specific needs and challenges.

2. Keep the Coaching Call Preparation Forms in a binder, divided into sections by team member, so you can quickly refer back to previous calls to identify trends and developments.

Actions for Effective Calls

1. Commit to elevate your coaching calls by implementing the Coaching Call Preparation Form. Download it from http://www.morebuilditbig.com/gifts.asp.

2. E-mail a copy of your preparation form to each of the team members who you coach, and explain the process and benefits of using the form for your next call.

3. Prepare a binder to store your preparation forms; allocate one section to each of the team members who you coach. ■

■ Keep Your Finger on the Pulse

By Debb Klingel
Building coherent teams for satisfaction and success

THE HEART RATE OF GROWTH

When your team is growing quickly, you might feel blessed that your dream is at last coming true. You might also feel caught in chaos, out of control, and cut off from what you care about most. In the process, you might lose touch with the very people you depend on for your continued success. ***Whether your group is 5 or 5,000, the solution lies in identifying and personally coaching your top performers.*** When you do, your team feels valued and you reap the rewards of your deepening relationship. In addition, your team will remain loyal to you and the company, and be more vested in supporting your success with their effort.

GETTING WITH THE BEAT

Identifying Key Team Members

Choosing the ones to work with may seem daunting. While many on your team profess a desire to grow their business, their desire does not always translate into action or results. Your first task is to decide on the criteria for your coaching investment. Which leaders and rising stars in your organization will make the best use of your personal time and attention?

Current team members. The most efficient way to get a snapshot of your team is to use your monthly production statement. A typical report provides vital statistics, such as the sales volume and sponsoring activity of individuals on your team. Hidden in these numbers are the clues that can help you identify key team members. Think of it as your report card, where you can see areas of success and places in need of your attention.

Using your most recent production report, ask the following questions to spot trends and identify the top 20 percent of your performers—as well as any shining stars:

- Who is producing consistent results?

- Which new team members have gotten off to a quick start?

- Whose sales volume has fallen off and why?

- Who is responding to the monthly corporate and team challenges?

- Who is showing promise that I want to work with more closely?

New team members. Send each new recruit a welcome packet and give her a call. A few questions about why she started and how she would like to see her new venture evolve can uncover potential superstars. When you discover one, set up a call each week to help her grow and reach her goals.

All team members. Watch for the natural leaders at your meetings, and take note of those who consistently volunteer and participate. These observations can help you spot diamonds in the rough and choose the ones who can make the most of your personal attention.

Staying Connected

One way to stay connected with a top performer is to invite her to join the top performers group that you work with personally.

Make it special. Give this group a name, such as Stellar Performers, Rising Stars, or Millionaires in Motion. Share that the purpose of the group is to focus on the areas they need to develop in their businesses. Adopt a monthly or quarterly theme, such as "No Excuses—Just Results!"

Establish entrance requirements. Explain that in exchange for your personalized support, you ask them to commit to certain objectives, such as staying in a problem-solving mode or growing their business. Outline additional, simple requirements, such as

- a desire to work toward a dream,

- a willingness to talk once a week for approximately ten minutes,

- a willingness to design and implement a plan of action, and

- a willingness to undergo a performance evaluation after a determined length of time.

Schedule touch points. Once you have decided together on a goal and established the steps she needs to take, arrange for weekly teleconferences or monthly one-on-one coaching calls to review her progress toward her destination.

Taking the Pulse Today and Tomorrow

1. If you have fewer than five people on your team, write out the criteria you will use to identify your top performers as your team grows.

2. If you already have more than five, choose one new way to identify top performers and implement it within the next 48 hours. ■

■ Motivate Your Team with Recognition

By Chris Harney
Succeeding with an attitude of gratitude

THE SECRET SOURCE OF INSPIRATION

If you're a new leader, you know you must motivate your team, but you might not know how. *By learning that the accomplishment of a goal is the primary motivator for people in direct selling, you're ready*

to put a program in place that honors accomplishments large and small. With your program, you can create an environment of mutual respect that encourages your team members to reach their goals and reap the rewards of success.

While you are a direct-selling leader, one thing will always remain true—*you are in the business of recognition.* In fact, research shows the primary need of all human beings is to feel appreciated. This is why so many people are drawn to the fun, rewards, and excitement this profession has to offer.

One truth about the direct-selling profession that greatly impacts the role of a leader is that this is a "want to" business, not a "have to" business. This means that we, as leaders, need to learn the art of motivating and inspiring a "volunteer army" toward the achievement of their dreams. In fact, learning to inspire your team to perform beyond even their own expectations is one of the most important leadership skills you can develop.

Once you understand what truly motivates your team, you can then create the environment in which success is nurtured and rewarded.

SYSTEMS TO STIR UP SUCCESS

Following these five important guidelines, you can quickly plan effective incentives and recognition:

1. *Understand that what gets recognized, gets repeated.* Choose to recognize positive behaviors in your team members, so you will get more of the same.

2. *Establish clear rules for recognition.* Announce goals and the way you will recognize those who reach them. Then, make sure you follow through. Keep your categories and requirements for monthly or annual recognitions consistent. Remember, your team members can't hit a moving target!

3. *Watch your budget.* Establish incentives that are in line with the income you will earn when team members reach their goals. Offer awards that cost no more than 10 percent of the commission or override that will result. Another good rule of thumb is, don't do

it for 10 people if you won't be able to do it for 100. Some inexpensive ideas are a small gift, business supplies, free product, a breakfast or a lunch with you, an invitation to a pizza night with other top performers, a personal growth book, a shadow day with you, a certificate of honor, or a manicure or pedicure.

4. *Consistently promote your incentives.* Announce all incentive challenges with the same fanfare your company would use to launch their trip incentives. Then keep the excitement going with a theme that is reflected in team communications and at each team event. Keep your incentives, contests, and challenges in the forefront of your team members' minds by frequently mentioning them in calls, newsletters, and meetings.

5. *Recognition is best done with an audience.* A note in the mail is great to develop your relationship with your team member, but public acknowledgment builds your team member's reputation with others. Use broadcast e-mails, newsletters, conference calls, meetings, and trainings to recognize the successes of team members.

Celebration goes hand in hand with recognition. Celebrating accomplishments makes your team members feel special and important. At your next meeting or event:

- Ask everyone who turned in a $1,000 show last week to please stand—then applaud their success.

- Recognize each person who introduced a new recruit to the direct-selling opportunity since you last met. Ask them, as well as the new recruits, to please stand. Then applaud them.

- Create a special seating area for new recruits and their sponsors or play special music when they are introduced. If you want more recruits, find creative ways to recognize both the sponsor and the new person.

- If you want to increase group activity, recognize those individuals with top sales for the month. The top seller should always have special, individual recognition, but remember to celebrate all successes.

- Assign someone to take pictures of those receiving recognition. Put the photos on your team Web site, in your team photo album, or on poster board and bring them with you to team events during the month.

Planning Your Incentives Today

1. Design a recognition program for your team. Decide which accomplishments you will recognize and how you'll recognize them.

2. Send an e-mail to your team members announcing the recognition program. Communicate the ways in which they can earn recognition, what the recognition will consist of, and how it will be delivered.

3. Decide how you will turn public recognitions into celebrations, whether through special music, decorations, or some other means. ■

■ Transform Your Words, Transform Your Life

By Nicki Keohohou
CEO and Cofounder of the DSWA

SHAPING OUR THOUGHTS AND ACTIONS

Some of us have a positive internal voice that encourages us—especially when we are accomplishing great things. We can be our own best cheerleader. We might use positive affirmations, such as "I can do this," "I made this happen," or "I had a fabulous show tonight." Other people ask themselves disempowering questions, such as "Why am I so dumb?" "Why can't I do this?" or "Why can't I make money?" *The quality of your self-talk creates the quality of your life.* If you ask yourself positive questions you get better answers. When you understand that your words shape the way you think, the actions you take, and the way you see yourself and the world, you can choose words that empower you. When you do, your confidence increases, your moods lighten, and you see possibilities where none previously existed.

Direct selling is a relationship business and how you communicate with yourself and others makes a massive difference in the results you receive in business and in life. Many of us use disempowering words and phrases because we were raised around them, we are living or working with people who use them, or we have just formed the habit along the road of life. Using such words and phrases stifles your motivation and negatively impacts those around you. For example, a disempowering phrase, such as "I can't sell," detracts from your success because it erodes your positive mental attitude and chips away at your belief in yourself. It can also discourage your teammates and family, who want to believe in your ability to succeed.

Not long ago, the Carnegie Institute analyzed the records of 10,000 successful people and concluded that 15 percent of success is due to technical training. The other 85 percent of success is due to personality, and the primary personality trait identified by the research is attitude. Your attitude is both defined by and reflected in the words that you use.

CONTROLLING OUR COMMUNICATION

When you incorporate transformational vocabulary into your thoughts and into your communication with others, you are taking control of your thoughts and supporting others to higher success. Become aware of how you communicate with yourself, your team, your family, and everyone you meet. These examples show how you can turn self-defeating phrases into self-affirming phrases:

- "I can't sell" *becomes* "I can share with others and enjoy the process."

- "This is a problem" *becomes* "This is a challenge."

- "I don't deserve that" *becomes* "I deserve success in my life."

- "I'm not smart enough" *becomes* "I have all the knowledge I need to do this."

- "I just don't have time" *becomes* "How can I make the time?"

- "I'm overwhelmed" *becomes* "I have unlimited opportunities and choose to prioritize."

- "I can't afford that" *becomes* "I'm going to create a plan to acquire that."

Your transformational vocabulary can and should extend to those with whom you communicate. For example, let's imagine that you mailed information on your business opportunity to a prospect and want to follow up. In the past, your follow-up may have sounded something like this:

- "I know how busy you are and I hate to bother you, but . . ." or

- "You may not have had a chance to review the information I sent you, but . . ."

When you're committed to using empowering phrases, you might say:

- "I'm calling, as promised, to hear what you felt after reviewing the information." or

- "I am looking forward to hearing what you are most excited about regarding the information I sent last week." or

- "I can't wait to hear how you see this business fitting into your life after reviewing the information."

Take Action toward Positive Transformation

1. Place a wide rubber band around your wrist and wear it 24/7. Every time you catch yourself using a disempowering word or phrase, snap your wrist.

2. Become aware of the words you are using with yourself. On a daily basis, practice saying ten empowering phrases to yourself.

3. At your next team meeting, share examples of transformational vocabulary and ask your associates to make a list of disempowering words and phrases that they use, and have them think of replacements for an empowering approach. ■

6

Managing Your Money

*T*he contributors to this chapter had one thing in mind when crafting their insights: to empower you with the information you need to pocket more of what you earn. From maximizing the tax benefits of a home-based business to helping you adopt a more informed and prosperous view of money, the sound strategies offered here will assist you in optimizing your business and personal finances. We are delighted that the information is presented in simple, easy-to-understand terms that even a novice can grasp.

This chapter contains more than tax-saving strategies and lessons in abundance. These insights also give you a tool for demonstrating the validity of your direct-selling business to key people. Whether you want to gain more support from a spouse, educate your tax preparer, or enlighten your prospect, this chapter provides an informed third-party perspective on the money-saving vehicle that is your business.

But, knowledge without action does not get the job done! Decide now, before moving on to the first insight, to take advantage of the financial incentives your business offers.

The information in this chapter is not legal, financial, or tax advice and is not guaranteed to be correct, complete, or up-to-date. If you need legal, financial, or tax advice, or planning for your specific business and situation, you should consult a licensed professional.

You use this chapter and the information therein at your own risk. The DSWA is not liable for any damages allegedly sustained arising out of use of this information, including any consequential, special, or simi-

lar damages. Use of this information shall not be considered a defense to avoid penalty for any taxing authority actions.

■ Use Strategy to Speed Success

By Cori Rose Dyer
Strategizing her way to the top

FINISHING THE PUZZLE

Meeting the financial goal that inspired you to become a direct seller can be elusive. Like a jigsaw puzzle, every piece must be in its proper place to create the financial picture you desire. Puzzle pieces include great products, solid training, and terrific sales skills. But some direct sellers never locate the final piece of the puzzle that is key to realizing monetary rewards: ***creating and executing a sound business strategy.*** Once that piece is in place, you can move toward your goal with confidence, knowing that your business strategy will exponentially increase the speed with which you can achieve your financial objectives.

KEEPING YOUR EYE ON THE PRIZE

A summation of Webster's definition of **strategy:** The science and art of *using all resources* to execute *approved plans* with the intent to accomplish a *specific goal.*

Establishing Your Goal

The centerpiece of your sound business strategy is a specific financial goal. I got involved in direct sales because I wanted to earn enough money to make my mortgage payment. Perhaps your goal is to have some extra spending money or to bail yourself out of debt. Maybe you want to replace your current salary in order to quit your unsatisfying job, or you could aim high and want to be so rich that you never have to look at price tags.

Attach a financial goal to your motivation; make a firm decision about how much money you need to generate each month to meet your objective. To experience immediate success, you may want to start with a smaller goal and incrementally increase your monthly target. Continually increasing your monthly goal motivates you to find ways to grow your business.

Following Your Plan

The next step of your business strategy is to design and execute a plan to reach your financial goal. Elements of your plan might include

- determining how many sales or new team members you need;

- drawing a chart of your future sales team and, as your team grows, filling in the blanks with names;

- outlining a 30-day schedule of days and hours you are going to work; or

- scheduling your time so that you spend 90 percent of each workday on presenting your products and your business, which includes following up with prior contacts and booking new presentations.

Leveraging Your Resources

The next element of your business strategy is to use all of your available resources—people, time, capital, brainpower, and energy. For example, you should

- understand and fully utilize your company's payment structure;

- spend 10 percent of your workday in meditation, to reflect, think, and tap into your creativity; and

■ tap the resources of your upline and your team, but know that *you* are the only resource you can count on.

The most crucial aspect of your business strategy is your commitment to putting your plan into action. If you have a lofty financial goal, you may need to learn to step outside of your comfort zone. The more often you do those things you perceive as difficult, the easier it will become to fearlessly expand your strategy and create wealth.

Now that you have the final piece to the puzzle, nothing will stop you from reaching, or even exceeding, your financial goal. My initial monthly target of meeting my mortgage payment gave way to earning a six-figure income after my first year in business. Like me, you may be surprised at how the picture changes once you have your goals, plan, and resources in place. Keep in mind that, as with anything worth doing in life, strategy and hard work are critical in achieving your direct-selling success.

Today's Steps for Speeding Your Success

To begin to bring your vision of wealth to fruition, create the building blocks of your business strategy:

1. *Set a long-term financial goal for your business.* This could be funding your family vacation, paying college tuition for your child, or creating an annual six-figure income.

2. *Set an income target for each month of the coming year.* Be realistic, but add incremental increases to motivate you to expand your business.

3. *Schedule three blocks of time* within the next 30 days to design your business plan, list your available resources, and begin to put your plan into action. ■

■ Swim in the Wealth You Keep

By Kathy Robbins
Inspiring you to take care of your money

FILLING THE POOL

If you want to fill a swimming pool and take a dip, you must not only add water, you must plug the drain. Similarly, if you want to accumulate wealth, you not only have to earn money (add water) but you must also control spending (plug the drain).

During my years of direct selling, I have seen countless leaders work hard to earn good money and find themselves no better off financially than were early on in their careers. Whether squandered, wasted, lost, or mismanaged, making a lot of money but keeping very little is too common a reality. The solution to this problem is to ***monitor and control costs as well as earnings.*** The true benefit of controlling spending is the peace that comes from financial freedom.

PLUGGING THE DRAIN

Smart money management stems from these two fundamental truths:

1. It's not what you make, it's what you keep that counts.

2. It's what you do with what you keep that determines financial success.

While there are many actions you can take to control spending, four simple (yet not always easy) things you can do will increase the money you keep and help you make the most of it. The four smart money habits are:

1. Pay attention to expenses.

2. Live on 70 percent of your earnings.

3. Keep good records.

4. Get good financial advice.

Pay Attention to Expenses

It's easy to get caught up in the excitement of your business and not pay attention to expenses. If you have to spend $500 to make $500, you have earned nothing. Be smart with your expenses. Shop for good rates on long distance, cell phone, travel, and any other services or products you use. Ask others in your business what services and products they use.

Live On 70 Percent of Your Earnings

A good book to read on this concept is *The Richest Man in Babylon* by George Clason. Here's how to get started.:

- **Budget your earnings.** Determine in advance where your money will go and make it a non-negotiable monthly success habit. One percentage formula that often shows up is: 10 percent to savings or investments, 10 percent to charity, 10 percent invested back into your business, and the balance is what you live on day-to-day.

- **Pay yourself first.** Make a commitment that you will immediately put at least 10 percent of your commissions into a savings or investment account. This is a principle that all successful money managers follow.

- **Give 10 percent to charity** to fulfill the Law of Reciprocity. This law says what we give away comes back to us tenfold. This habit will pay off in ways you cannot imagine.

- **Invest 10 percent in your business.** While it takes money to make money, luckily, in direct sales it doesn't take large amounts of money. Again, be smart about your expenses.

Keep Good Records

When you keep good records, you can evaluate your expenses and more easily prepare your taxes. With good records you can take all the deductions available to you so you can keep more of your earnings.

Set up a separate checking account for your business, even if your business is just in your personal name. Go to your bank, open a second checking account in your name, and subtitle it "Special Account." Use this account to deposit all commissions and retail earnings and to pay all business expenses.

Also, designate one credit card as your business card. Only business purchases should be put on this card. Pay for this card from your Special Account.

Get Good Financial Advice

Find a good accountant. Ask other people in your direct-selling business who they recommend. You want someone who understands the direct-selling industry and the tax benefits of running a home-based business. You'll find many of them at http://www.dswa.org/accountant_profile.asp, where you can review the list of direct-selling specialists in the DSWA's Financial Services Network.

Find a good investment adviser. Again the best way to do this is to ask for referrals. Take the time to interview the individuals. Tell them what your goals are and ask them how they can help you achieve them. Listen to what they say and listen to how you feel when they say it. If you are uncomfortable, don't use them.

In the Next 48 Hours

1. Review the checklist above and identify the items you want to implement.

2. Number them in order of importance and the order you will complete them.

3. Write one task on your daily To Do list that you can finish in 48 hours that will help you complete the first one you want to implement. ■

■ Claim Your Deductions

By Joseph H. Craft, CPA
Taking the stress and worry out of tax time

PAYING ONLY WHAT YOU OWE

What your accountant doesn't know about your home-based business may be costing you thousands of dollars each year. Recent estimates show that *the self-employed have overpaid their taxes by $160 billion.* ***By learning to identify statements that reveal an accountant is not an expert at home business, you can protect yourself by changing accountants.*** Then you can take full advantage of the tax laws that benefit your business.

RECOGNIZING COSTLY ADVICE

When you can recognize these seven most expensive areas of tax-related misinformation, you'll have the knowledge to judge the expertise of your tax preparer in the arena of home-based businesses:

1. **"Claiming a home office is a red flag."** Although true many years ago, changes in the law have since prevented the IRS from treating all home business operators as suspicious. Today, home office deductions are no more a trigger for an audit than a gift to the Salvation Army. Legitimate deductions include depreciation on equipment and furniture converted to business use, the cost of new equipment, and your housing expenses.

2. **"You can't deduct expenses if you don't make money."** The government wants you to make money and has created tax incentives (deductions) in order to encourage you to invest your time and money in a new business. Why? Home businesses turn into big business and create thousands of jobs. The IRS does not require you to make a profit in order to claim your business expenses. All that is required is the intent to make a profit. Everything you spend in the course of doing business is tax deductible.

3. **"Mileage expenses are not deductible in every business."** If you drive in conjunction with operating your home business, regardless of the type of business, you can claim either the mileage method or the actual cost method of operating your vehicle for business.

4. **"Cell phones are a personal expense, not business."** This may be true, but if you are operating any type of business and you are using your cell phone, it is at least partially deductible. Direct sellers usually deduct the portion of their cell line that is used for business purposes. However, if you are engaged in any business where your cell phone is your business phone, then it is 100 percent deductible.

5. **"Your Internet connection is not deductible."** The same rule applies here as to cell phones: to the extent that you use the Internet for business, it is deductible. This means that if 50 percent of the time you are online you are doing business, you write off 50 percent.

6. **"Your business really isn't a business because you worked less than four hours per day."** The tax code does not require a specific level of effort in order to claim tax deductions. Most people who start a home business do so on the side, working nights and weekends after they get home from their regular job. This means that almost all of the millions of home businesses in this country constitute part-time work. The real rule is that if you are working in your business with the intent to make a profit, take the tax deductions. If your business is a means to subsidize a hobby through tax deductions, then don't take the deductions.

7. **"You can't pay your minor children to work in your home-based business."** As long as they have real duties related to the business and are paid an arm's-length wage, you can pay your child 7 years or older out of your business account and claim it as a tax deduction, which means you have effectively moved income from your higher tax bracket to their lower bracket. If your child is under 18, then you pay no FICA, no Medicare, no workers' compensation, or unemployment insurance. The expense must be an ordinary and necessary expense of operating your business.

Today's Actions for Your Financial Well-Being

1. Review each of the points above and place a check mark next to any statement you have heard from your tax accountant.

2. Think back to your last meeting with your accountant and ask yourself whether she took the time to educate you on how to maximize your home business deductions.

3. If you are not completely satisfied that your accountant is skilled in the area of home business taxation and is willing to educate you regarding your rights, consider seeking a new tax professional immediately. No matter where in the United States that you live, the DSWA's Accountant Referral Network (http://www.dswa.org/accountant_profile.asp) is comprised of qualified professionals who are equipped to work with you. ■

■ Build It Big with Tax Incentives

By Bruce Gardner
Guiding entrepreneurs to hidden financial resources

THE TAXMAN COMETH

Most people dread April 15, and perceive taxes as an evil adjunct to doing business. That's no surprise, given that the average direct seller loses $5,000 each year to Uncle Sam by not properly documenting and deducting business-related expenses. The reality is that taxes can help you build your business. *Once you understand why the government provides incentives to small businesses and learn how to document the myriad of tax deductions available to you, you'll see that tax savings put money back in your pocketbook.*

UNCLE SAM *DOES* WANT YOU

When it comes to taxes, the government is willing to trade some tax revenue today for the hope of greater tax revenue down the road. That's why Congress provides tax incentives to big and small businesses alike. Today, a small business may be a mere blip on the government's radar, but who knows when it's going to turn into a Google, a Microsoft, or an Apple—all home business alumni. Direct selling has made more millionaires than manufacturing, finance, or even the lottery, so the government is willing to roll the dice and give you tax incentives so you can afford to chase your dreams of financial freedom.

Home business operators can realize two different types of tax deductions: direct expenses associated with your business, and indirect expenses assignable to your business. Here are some of the direct expenses that people commonly miss:

- ■ **Web sites.** Whether you build it yourself, hire someone to do it, or pay for a replicated site through a direct-selling company, your business Web site is completely tax deductible.

■ **Internet access.** The portion of Internet access you use for your home business is deductible. If you have broadband and use it half the time for business, this can mean an annual deduction of $300 or more!

■ **Cell phones.** Even if you use your cell phone for personal and business calls, the time that you use it for business is deductible.

■ **Home phone expenses.** If you have a second phone line for your business, it's completely deductible, as are advanced calling features, such as three-way calling and call waiting. Most people remember that long distance calls made for business are deductible, but many forget that flat-rate plans—about $35 per month—can also be deducted. If 60 percent of your long distance calls are business related, that's $21 per month in additional tax deductions.

■ **Laptops and projectors.** If you do sales presentations or opportunity meetings for a direct-selling company, you can buy your own equipment and deduct the cost on your taxes.

■ **Meals and entertainment.** While you can deduct half the cost of most business meals, there are two exceptions that many people overlook. Banquet meals are 100 percent deductible, as are meals served in your own home.

The direct expenses on this list total annual deductions of about $1,500. Depending on your tax bracket, they provide you with $300 to $500 in additional capital. Now, let's look at indirect expenses. You were spending money on these items anyway, so these deductions will, in effect, put additional money in your pocketbook.

■ **Mileage.** Experienced entrepreneurs know that buying or marketing trips that are combined with personal shopping, business banking, and post office trips add to deductible miles while reducing personal mileage. At 40.5 cents per mile (in 2005), home business owners can cut hundreds of dollars off their tax bill.

- **Home-office deductions.** Mortgage interest, rent, insurance, property taxes, home repair, utilities, and other housing expenses can be partially deducted. The percentage of your home that is used for business is taken against these expenses. This class of deduction can be used only against your business net income, or carried forward.

- **Health insurance.** If you pay for health insurance out of your own pocket, or with after-tax dollars at work, you can deduct your out-of-pocket medical insurance premiums. If you are married, you can create a Medical Reimbursement Plan that allows you to deduct copayments, deductibles, prescriptions, over the counter drugs, and in some cases, dietary supplements.

Bottom line? Tax incentives are available to help you pay for the cost of starting and operating a home business. This fact can help when a prospective team member says, "I can't afford to start my own business." You simply respond, "You can't afford not to."

Organize Your Deductions Today and Tomorrow

1. Make a list of your tax-deductible direct and indirect expenses.

2. Set up a spreadsheet or manual system for logging expenses each month.

3. Calendar the day each month when you will log expenses.

4. Visit the Prosperity Center on http://mydswa.org for more tax savings tips. ■

■ Say Just Enough about Compensation

By Jane Deuber
President and Cofounder of the DSWA

THE DELICATE QUESTION OF MONEY

As you prepare for your one-on-one presentation to a prospective recruit, you're committed to providing her with all the information she needs about your products, your company, and your plan, so that she can make an informed decision to join your team. In your enthusiasm to share your business opportunity, you might not take the time to discover whether her primary motivation for starting her own business is money. When you share too much information about your company's compensation plan, you run the risk of talking her into—and out of—the business in a single interview. To avert this risk, *discover the role that the "money factor" will play in her decision to join your company and then tailor your presentation accordingly.* By knowing how to explain your company's compensation plan simply and giving her only the information she needs, you will gain the confidence of your prospect, keep her engaged, and increase the likelihood that she will be inspired to become part of your team.

CUSTOMIZING FOR HER COMFORT

Early in the interview with your prospect, ask questions to discover how much she wants to know about the financial side of the business. Different personality styles require different levels of information. Assuming that you have a working knowledge of your company's plan, you can always safely ask, "What would you like to know about the compensation plan?" Some people want detailed information about how much money they can make before enrolling, while others simply don't care.

In my experience, women are most interested in the benefits of the product and how sharing it and building a business can meet their desire to make a difference in others' lives. On the other hand, many men are very interested in the compensation plan and have a variety of questions about both the short-term and long-term opportunity for creating residual income. Again, find out what your prospect wants to know rather than communicating what you *think* they want to know.

Let's Talk Money

For someone who does want detailed information about the compensation plan, test the waters first. If your compensation plan is complicated, find a way to simplify the message. Give an overview of the plan instead of reading the details to her. If she feels it's too complicated to explain to others, she may run.

For example, you might say, "There are three ways to make money with this compensation plan. You earn a retail profit of 25 percent, up to 10 percent on your group volume, and as much as 5 percent on the sales of those you train and coach."

You will likely encounter a question for which you don't have the answer. If so, don't try to wing it! Let her know that you will get with your sponsor and have an answer later that day or the following day. This sends the message that you are truthful, have support from your upline, and take her question seriously. If your upline is available to answer the question immediately, don't hesitate to call her in right then. Make the most of this opportunity to get the answer you need and have your upline meet your prospect.

How Much Can I Make?

When presenting your income opportunity, you must steer clear of making any kinds of income claims or promises. Not only are income claims unethical and misleading, they can also lead you and your company to court. Showing commission checks, a practice that was used many years ago, has become passé because they are easily misinterpreted.

The best rule of thumb when it comes to offering examples of potential income is to take your lead from your company. Most companies have their legal team carefully provide you with guidelines that present the opportunity in an ethical and accurate way.

Keep your conversation about earning focused on your prospect by asking her how much she would like to earn and then showing her how to do that in the short term as well as the long term. Your role as her sponsor is to help her develop a realistic road map for achieving the income she desires.

Today's Preparation for the Money Question

1. Review your compensation plan so that you're well acquainted with how it works.

2. Ask a friend or relative to play the role of your prospect and practice presenting the compensation basics.

3. Commit to total truth and honesty. It's the only way to go! ∎

∎ Unlock Your Medical Insurance Options

By Vicky Collins, CPA
Member of the DSWA Prosperity Panel

IMPRISONED BY COSTS?

Doctor's visits, insurance premiums, co-pays, prescriptions, dentists, eyeglasses, braces, long-term care insurance premiums—the expenses seem endless. Medical costs may be keeping you, members of your team, and even potential recruits at jobs they hate because you or they are uninformed about options regarding health benefits. Are you trapped by the misconception that there are no tax benefits related to health care costs, that you need to incorporate in order to obtain medical benefits and tax deductions, or that medical insurance premiums are too expensive outside of a large group plan? These false beliefs are costing you thousands of dollars. ***Learn about the options available to you and take action. You'll not only save money, you'll also gain a new sense of freedom*** in knowing you're no longer tied to your job for insurance benefits.

OPENING OPTIONS FOR HEALTH AND PROSPERITY

As a direct seller, you can take advantage of a number of tax-planning opportunities for reducing medical expenses. The following overview includes the types of plans that are available, but you should always discuss plans you are considering with a trusted CPA who is well-versed in home business taxation. The tax laws change rapidly and you must take care when implementing these strategies.

Some of the following plans, as noted, work only when you pay a spouse to work in your business. This means you must maintain a bona fide employee relationship between your business and your spouse. Document the hours and type of work done, and file payroll tax returns, W-2s, and other employer forms. Even though these plans involve more paperwork, the tax benefits are significant, so don't overlook them just because the tasks appear daunting. Most CPAs educated in payroll and home business taxation can provide these services for you.

The tax benefits shown below are based upon the finances of the following sample family:

Married with 2 children	
Tax bracket:	25%
Annual medical insurance premiums:	$6,000
Long-term care insurance premiums paid:	$980
Out-of Pocket medical expenses	$3,000
Self-employment income	$60,000

Health insurance deducted as an adjustment to income. Medical and long-term care insurance premiums paid by a self-employed person are deductible from adjusted gross income to the extent of self-employment income, so long as that person is not eligible for insurance through another plan (including a spouse's plan). This deduction reduces federal and state income tax, but not self-employment tax. *Estimated tax benefit: $1,500 plus $150 for long-term care insurance premium benefit. Note: The IRS adjusts allowable long-term care premiums based on age. Review IRS tables for your allowable deduction.*

Health insurance deducted under a spousal plan on Schedule C. The deduction can be moved to Schedule C when a spouse is employed. The law allows a self-employed person to provide medical insurance for her employees and their families. In this case, the employee is the spouse and the spouse is insuring his family. The value of the deduction increases when it gets moved to Schedule C because self-employment taxes are reduced, in addition to federal and state income taxes. *Estimated tax benefit: $2,300 plus $385 for long-term care insurance premium.*

Medical Reimbursement Plan. This plan can only be implemented when employing a spouse. The plan allows an employee to set aside a certain amount of pay during each pay period. These amounts are then reimbursed as medical expenses when the employee requests reimbursement. The amounts set aside are considered a business deduction on Schedule C, but are also a nontaxable fringe benefit to the employee. The plan must be a written plan and must comply with other Internal Revenue Code requirements. *Estimated tax benefit: $3,500 plus $385 for long-term care insurance premium.*

Self-insured Medical Reimbursement Plan. This is similar to the Medical Reimbursement Plan (so the spouse must be an employee), except that this plan allows the business owner to deduct 100 percent of plan benefits from operating revenues of the company, without using a third-party insurer. *Estimated tax benefit: Varies by year with expenses.*

Health reimbursement arrangements. One of the best plans available, this lets you set aside unused amounts and carry them forward to following years. (This differs from the plans listed above, which all have a "use it or lose it" requirement. The spouse must be employed to use this plan.) Many business owners like these plans be-

cause estimating medical expenses that will be incurred in a given year can be difficult. *Estimated tax benefit: Varies by year with expenses.*

Health savings accounts (HSA). This is a tax-exempt trust that is created for the sole purpose of paying qualified medical expenses of the account beneficiary who, for the months for which contributions are made to an HSA, is covered under a high-deductible health plan. HSAs may be established by the business owner or spouse employee. This can be a very good way to save money on insurance premiums and medical expenses. *Estimated tax benefit: Varies by year.*

Finding Liberation Today

1. Analyze your current medical expenses. Include premiums, out-of-pocket expenses, and deductibles. Calculate the potential tax benefit if you could take these expenses on your Schedule C.

2. Take time to investigate medical insurance options. Several associations offer medical insurance benefits to the self-employed, including the DSWA (http://www.dswa.org/benefits_profile.asp). The expense may not be cost-prohibitive and the benefits may be better than you expect.

3. Make the commitment to set up one of the many benefit programs discussed in this chapter.

4. Seek the advice of a CPA who understands home business taxation. Visit the DSWA's Accountant Referral Network at http://www.dswa.org/accountant_profile.asp. ▪

■ Legitimize Your Business in the Eyes of the IRS

By Vicky Collins, CPA
Member of the DSWA Prosperity Panel

RECLAIMING TAX DOLLARS

A concern of many direct sellers is that the IRS might classify their home-based business as a hobby and disallow deductions against income. Because the IRS tends to look carefully at home-based businesses, you might choose to omit legitimate deductions from your tax returns and needlessly overpay your taxes. *When you understand the criteria that the IRS uses to determine whether an enterprise is a business or a hobby, you can document your business activities and benefit from the allowable deductions to the fullest extent of the law.*

FOR FUN OR PROFIT?

The IRS asks a series of questions when determining whether an activity is a business or a hobby. "Yes" answers indicate a profit motive and take you another step closer to being considered a legitimate business.

1. **Is the business carried on in a businesslike manner?** First, have a genuine intent to make a profit with your home-based business. One indicator of legitimate business is a written plan that outlines your business goals and offers an action plan that will help you attain them. Document the steps you take to grow your business, such as sales calls, product presentations, and communication with clients.

2. **Do you maintain accurate books and records for the business?** Evidence of accurate recordkeeping includes:

— **Separate business checking and credit card accounts.** Avoid commingling your personal finances with your business finances. Maintaining separate records also simplifies tax preparation.

— **General ledger or bookkeeping system.** Record all your business transactions. When you buy something that is personal in nature, do not record it as a business expense. If you buy something for personal use, but wind up selling it, then (and only then) note it in your business books.

— **Records maintained for an appropriate period of time.** If you are audited, your business books and records must be available for inspection by the IRS. This includes financial records and tax returns.

— **Documentation and other support for tax return items.** You must keep your cancelled checks, bills, receipts, and other evidence of income and deductions that are reported on your tax returns.

3. **Is enough time and effort being spent on the business to make profit possible?** A monthly trade show is not enough time. Daily or weekly activity is better proof that you are spending the time you need to operate profitably.

4. **Do you depend on the income for your livelihood?** If the business is your only source of income, it is likely to be considered a business. If you are working to replace income from your job, include this as a written goal in your business plan.

5. **Are losses due to circumstances beyond your control?** Many legitimate businesses incur reasonable losses during the start-up phase. Losses can also be incurred due to circumstances beyond your control, such as a significant downturn in the economy, a product liability issue, or an issue with the company you represent.

6. **Do you change your methods of operation in an attempt to improve profitability?** Regularly review your methods of operation, and document steps you plan to take to correct challenges that keep you from achieving profitability.

7. **Do you or your advisors have the knowledge needed to carry on a successful business?** Having run a successful business in the past indicates you have the knowledge necessary. If you don't currently have the knowledge you need, access your up-line. Document your conversations with them and the steps they recommend to become profitable. Other advisors could include a CPA, lawyer, banker, insurance agent, and other financial professionals.

8. **When you sell, do you sell at a profit?** You should sell your products at the retail price recommended by your company. You can run sales and specials, but do not sell items at or below your cost.

9. **Is your business profitable in some years?** Continual losses are an indication that a taxpayer may be using business deductions to shelter W-2 income or subsidize a hobby.

Where Do You Stand Today?

1. Answer the nine questions the IRS evaluates to determine your intent.

2. If you can answer "Yes" to most of these questions, you can probably relax and stop worrying whether your business will be considered a hobby.

3. If you answered "No" to any of these questions, take steps now to make the adjustments you need to get to "Yes." ■

■ Teach Your Kids the Value of Money

By Dr. Maryann Rosenthal and Dr. Denis Waitley

Instilling sound financial principles in our children

INSTRUCTIONS FOR INDEPENDENCE

Parents today are overwhelmed trying to balance their work and family lives. Feeling guilty about not spending quality time with their children, many parents offer money as a substitute. This practice, combined with a general reluctance to talk about money management issues, is resulting in a generation of financially irresponsible and self-indulged adults. *It's time to put away the wallet and teach your kids about money. There's no better venue for doing so than a direct-selling business.* As a direct-selling parent, you can give them roots and wings, rather than loot and things. Then you can watch your money-savvy children become successful, self-sufficient adults of whom you can be proud!

LESSONS IN MONEY MANAGEMENT

Autonomy and Responsibility

Introduce your children to money as soon as they can count. **Starting in preschool, give them an allowance.** My experience has shown that until a child reaches adolescence—when financial needs become greater—a good rule of thumb is to give your kids $1 per week for every year of age. This means $7 each week for a seven-year-old and $10 each week for a ten-year-old. Keep allowances consistent and the same for sons and daughters. Too often daughters are conditioned to feel that money is given to them, while sons view money as being earned. **Allowances should not be linked to chores or grades.** Extra money for extra jobs, though, is fine.

Goals and Accounts

Teach your kids about financial goals and accounts. With young children, divide allowances into four categories. Give them four labeled canisters or jars in which to deposit their allowances:

- **Spend.** 30 percent of their allowance to spend when and how they desire

- **Save.** 50 percent of their allowance to save up for a special item or outing

- **Share.** 10 percent of their allowance to buy gifts for others or for charities

- **Future.** 10 percent of their allowance for long-range goals

With older children, open bank accounts for depositing their allowance categories. Help your kids set goals for saving. They might want special investment accounts for a particular goal, such as for college or for a car. By the time your children reach adolescence, they should have savings accounts and long-term investment accounts, to which they make regular deposits and from which they do not make withdrawals.

Earning

Get your children earning at an early age. With your direct-selling business, consider creating a family legacy and involve your children in your business as early as possible. Research has proven that children who work and earn while attending high school and college do as well academically as those whose parents provide for all their financial needs.

Healthy Beliefs

Talk to your kids about the value of money. Show your kids some of the family bills so that intangibles become real. They learn that electricity and water take part of the family money. Uncle Sam gets some for police and fire protection and to fix the roads. Some money goes to savings for school tuition and Christmas presents. Then show them what is left and they can get a grasp of what is affordable. By doing this, you're teaching them about budgeting.

With teenagers, talk about what goes into buying and maintaining a car, paying for college, and living on their own. Again, you're showing them something practical about money management, but on a deeper level, you're teaching them how life works: There is no free lunch, and every action or inaction has its consequences.

When you shop, have your younger kids hand the cashier the money so they can grasp the concept of receiving goods for cash. Children learn by observation and repetition.

Healthy Decisions

Show your children how to make choices about money by involving them in a few of the family money decisions. For example, hold a family discussion and ask, "With the money we have for vacation, where should we go?" or "Should we buy an expensive SUV or a less expensive van? The van gets better mileage and with the extra money we could go on a trip."

Investigate ads on TV, radio, and in print. Ask your kids questions: "Will that product make you more popular?" "Will it really do what it says?" "Is that the best price?" "What else could you get for that price?"

Credit

At some point, your teen is going to want to borrow money. Make it a business transaction by explaining how credit works and how much debt is acceptable. Talk about the consequences of too much debt and late payments. Discuss where your teen will get the money to repay the loan. Your teen must pay the loan back in agreed increments within a certain amount of time.

If your teens complain that they don't have credit cards like their friends do, first explain the importance of adult money management and how you want to help them achieve that skill. Then give them some added chores, with the money going into a checking account accessible by a debit card. That way, they can't spend more than they have in the account, and they're responsible for replenishing it. Tell them that, if they handle a debit card well for a year or so, you might consider getting them a credit card, especially if they are planning for college.

Money Smarts for Your Kids Today

1. On a piece of paper, create a circle that represents a money management pie. Cut your pie into six sections, and label each section with one of the topics discussed.

2. Within each section, draw a dot corresponding to how well you've taught your kids that skill. If you've taught them well, make the dot on the outer edge of the slice; if they need additional lessons, make the dot toward the center of the pie.

3. Connect the dots to see what areas need improvement. Set goals for each of the next four weeks to further implement these money management strategies with your kids. ■

■ Hire Your Kids with Uncle Sam's Money

By Rhonda K. Johnson
Making sense of the money side of your business

TURNING FRUSTRATION INTO PURCHASING POWER

Your feelings of resentment and frustration at having to write a check payable to the IRS for your business taxes could be matched by your feelings of guilt and frustration over your inability to keep up with the incessant demands of your children for the endless acquisition of more "stuff." Both Uncle Sam and your children absorb your time and money. To a large extent, you can solve both sources of frustration by *learning how to make Uncle Sam pay you for hiring your kids to work in your business.* Not only will you increase your family's purchasing power, but your children will gain independence and learn business values in the process.

PLAYING TO WIN

After one of my recent speaking engagements, a Los Angeles firefighter approached me with this question: "Are you telling me that, if my son pays my grandson $5,000 per year, there are no taxes due on the money, that we get to keep all of the $5,000, that we can spend it anyway we choose, and then at the end of the year the government will send us an additional $1,800?" The answer to all of those questions is a resounding YES. After a few seconds of silence, he said, "That makes no sense at all." The truth is, little of our tax code makes sense. Think of it as a game. Follow the rules, and play to win.

To qualify for home-based business tax deductions and employ your children, you need to meet a few criteria: You must

- operate a legitimate business;

- demonstrate intent to produce a profit;

- show consistent work activity;

- document business income, expenses, and activities involved;

- hire one or more of your children who are between 7 and 18 years of age (or up to age 23 if they are in college and are dependents);

- pay wages that approximate what you would pay an outside contractor to perform the same duties;

- pay wages to the child using an actual business check; and

- deposit the check into a separate interest-bearing custodial account. (Because your child is a minor, as the parent you have signing privileges on the account.)

These deposited wages do not have to remain in the account. The money may be paid back into the business in part or in its entirety. The money can be used for the CDs and electronics that your kids think they must buy to prevent their world from collapsing. It can also be allowed to accumulate and then used to purchase a big-ticket item, such as a car for your child, or for your child's future college expenses.

Your family employee can perform any of the tasks your business needs in order to function, such as:

- Janitorial services

- Day care

- Answering phones

- Data entry

- Distributing fliers

- Stuffing envelopes

- Washing cars

- Stocking merchandise

- Packing and shipping

Several specific documents are helpful in documenting a legitimate business, and there are resources that provide monthly services and government filings for a nominal fee. It's always a good idea to consult with an enrolled agent or other tax expert to ensure you comply with current regulations.

To properly document the existence of family employees, you must have

- a formal employment agreement for family members;

- a work log of hours and activities for each family employee;

- a separate bank account for each employee;

- a formal payroll system with quarterly and annual reports, including W-2s;

- a state employment number (some states have a minimal fee for a business license and a minimal tax when quarterly taxes are filed);

- documentation demonstrating consistent business operation; and

- evidence of paychecks issued at least once a month.

Full Employment

Employing your children can teach them valuable life lessons, get them to willingly help you with the family business, free up time for you to pursue that business, and help the whole family have more purchasing power. What are you waiting for?

1. Make the decision to maximize the tax benefits your business affords you by committing to take the steps necessary to hire your kids.

2. Make a list of age-appropriate tasks your children can perform within your business and then hold a family meeting and explain that they are now "officially" a part of your business.

3. Set aside one hour today or tomorrow to begin to collect the necessary documentation and continue to invest an hour a few times a week until all elements are in place. ■

■ Fund Your Child's Education with Passive Income

By Sandi Walpert
Offering savvy solutions for your savings goals

STRESS-FREE FINANCING

The cost of a college education is so astronomical that many parents are finding themselves without the resources to finance their child's education. The result? The parents go into debt, the child goes into debt, or the child doesn't pursue a higher education. *Direct Selling—with the right company, the right product, and the right compensation plan—can provide a passive income to build the nest egg necessary for college tuition, and then residual income to provide living expenses while your child attends school.* Not only will your child benefit from the lessons learned by working for your business, but you will have a stress-free mechanism for funding his or her education.

Nine years ago, I knew there had to be a way to provide a better income for my family and a better future for my children. Although I'd had some success with direct-selling companies, I was tired of guessing what was best. It was time to sit down and analyze the situation. I researched many companies, looking at compensation plans, management, product research, demographic trends, company debt, and the uniqueness of the product or service being offered. I looked at my research not as a way to find a job, but to find a foundation for building an empire.

When I joined my company, my sons were ages 4, 6, and 9. My oldest recently turned 18, and, because I positioned him in my company near the top of my team, he has $70,000, earned passively, waiting to pay for his university education. It gets even better. He also has a residual income of $2,500 per month to help pay his living expenses.

BUILDING YOUR EMPIRE

It's possible for you to fund your child's education through direct selling. The key is to start early, choose a company that supports your goals, and hire your children near the top. Here's how:

Decide what you want from your business. Make a list of what you are looking for in an income opportunity, in terms of commission and override structure.

Do your research. Take it slowly, and don't rush your decision. Talk to people in direct selling, gather information from company Web sites, and request marketing materials from various companies. Then, consider the following questions:

- How long has the company been in business? Does it belong to the Better Business Bureau, The Direct Selling Women's Alliance, the Direct Selling Association, or other trade or professional associations?

- Who are the owners and what is their vision for the company?

- Analyze the structure of the compensation plan. Is it competitive with companies that sell similar products? Is there a considerable reward for team building? Is the plan stable, or does the company often change it? If you are unable to work, will your income stop?

- Does the company pay their distributors on time and according to their compensation plan?

- Does the company have a unique product or stand-alone service? Do they follow a trend—such as the Baby Boomers starting to turn 60 in 2006—or a fad?

- What is their track record regarding shipping? A company that has a poor track record in fulfillment can sabotage your business.

Narrow your choices. When you've found two or three companies that have the structure and income opportunity potential to fund your child's education, write their names at the top of a piece of paper. Under each, list the pros and cons. This process helps clarify which company is right for you.

Start building. Once you've signed on with your company, structure your business so that you bring your children in at the top, so they can eventually receive the passive income they need for their educations. Then roll up your sleeves and get to work—building your empire is up to you.

Committing to Action

1. Analyze your current educational funding plan, and how much money you currently have saved.

2. Calculate the approximate cost of sending your child to college, deduct the amount you have, and then divide by the number of years before your son or daughter starts his or her freshman year. This will give you an idea of how much money you have to set aside each year to fund their education.

3. If you decide to fund your child's education through passive income from your business, start planning today. Work the numbers through your current company's compensation plan, and decide whether or not it will support your financial goals. ∎

7

Home Business Excellence

Working from home is the dream of millions of women who, each morning, hurriedly wiggle into their pantyhose, dump cereal into bowls, and dash out the door in time to drop the kids off at school and get to the office before nine. Those of us who have taken the plunge and now work from home often wonder how we were able to run the rat race for such a long time. For those who still hold the vision of leaving their traditional J-O-B behind, we applaud you for keeping the dream alive and cheer you on to success.

Whether you're building your home-based direct-selling business part-time or full-time, the dream can sometimes be a challenge. Visions of building an empire in your bunny slippers quickly fade as you find yourself locked in the bathroom for some "mommy time"— just so you can call your customers and check in with your team members.

The truth of the matter is that working from home requires the skills of the sharpest CEO. Only, instead of shepherding well-groomed, suit-clad protégé, our brood consists of customers we serve, team members we want to support, and bright-eyed, jelly-stained faces that need our love and attention. To help smooth your way, we've gathered top leaders who successfully juggle the roles of mom and entrepreneur. Heed their wisdom, for they are the super-women of our profession, sharing their tips and strategies in hopes you, too, can find equilibrium amidst the inevitable chaos.

■ Structure Your Life for Productivity

By Joyce Feraco
Mastering the art of being an entrepreneurial mom

CULTIVATING SUCCESSFUL DAYS

Often, the biggest downfall of the entrepreneurial mom is confusing activity with productivity. We find ourselves running from morning till night without a moment to spare. But, in order to move from activity to productivity, we must ask ourselves, What results are our actions creating? Does the time we spend with our children create the connection we crave? Does the time we spend building our business create the financial and personal rewards we desire? For most of us, the answer lies between a resounding *Yes* and a guilt-ridden *No*. So, how can we move from a hectic, unstructured, and less-than-productive day toward a more centered, calm, and productive day? The solution to the challenge lies in ***ordering and structuring our time so that we can wake up one morning and realize that we are living our dream.***

PREPARATION, MOTIVATION, AND CELEBRATION

Preparation. The key to making the most of your time is staying one step ahead by anticipating what's needed for the next hour, day, and week.

1. Work from a To Do list generated the day before. List your top ten tasks, making certain that each will contribute to your business.

2. Weed out as you go, and get rid of activities, projects, commitments, and offers that you really don't want or need.

3. Plan a week's worth of menus, and have all of the ingredients on hand. Several Web sites offer recipes for quick and easy meals in 30 minutes or less, and you can always pull out the Crock-Pot™!

4. Play "beat the timer." Many tasks can be completed in 15 minutes or less, so use the timer to hold concise phone calls, straighten files, or organize projects.

5. Realize that children are part of your life, 24 hours a day, 7 days a week. You're a mom! Remember that most of the calls you make are to other women, many of whom also have children. To be able to run a business and be a mother is a great testimony to your abilities—and a great recruiting tool, as well. If you are doing it, she can too!

6. The difference between good and great is working even when you don't feel like it. When it's quitting time, set the timer for 30 minutes and keep working. You'll be one step ahead for tomorrow.

7. At day's end, straighten up your desk, set the timer for 15 minutes, and race to prepare your work for the next day. You'll rid yourself of the confusion of walking into your office and not knowing where to start; instead, you'll simply tackle your To Do list!

Motivation. When you feel as though nothing is going according to plan, it's hard to keep your nose to the proverbial grindstone. Part of structuring your life for productivity is making sure you have a system in place to maintain your drive.

1. Invest in yourself. Attend all company-sponsored events, seek out motivational seminars that interest you, and attend local trainings. There's always something to learn!

2. Combine a family getaway with your business trip. Tack on a few days after your training ends to enjoy well-deserved time with your family. It's never a bad thing when mommy's business and Mickey Mouse go hand in hand.

3. Seek out people who have desires similar to yours, people who inspire you, and people who encourage you to be your best. They'll give you the motivation to continue on your path.

4. Surround yourself with affirmations. A well-placed sticky note can have a huge impact. Put one that says, "GOAL begins with

GO!" on your clock. Attach one to your desk in front of your phone that says, "Reach for the moon; even if you miss, you'll land among the stars." Tack one on your computer monitor that reads, "Struggle and strife come before success, even in the dictionary."

Celebration. Your productive life will bring you many rewards. Acknowledging your successes—both small and large—is just as important as planning your To Do list.

1. Celebrate as you reflect on your home-based business and all of the good it has brought your family.

2. Celebrate simple things in your business, such as the new hostesses, the new customers, or the end of a successful promotion.

3. Celebrate the extra-long nap the little one took, and the help of a three-year-old.

Your To Do List for the Next 48 Hours

1. Get a fresh start and clean off your desk.

2. Register for a motivational seminar, or go online and order an inspirational book.

3. Place affirmations in strategic places around your work area, in your car, and on your calendar. ■

■ The Art of Balance for the Entrepreneurial Parent

By Karen Olson

Juggling family and business with ease

ARE YOUR ROLES AT ODDS?

When you start your home-based business, you might find that your new role as an entrepreneur conflicts with your family's expectations of your old role as a mom. ***When you learn to set boundaries and establish strategies that help you manage both roles, you begin living the life you dreamed of:*** earning additional income while keeping family a top priority and being there for your children.

STAYING IN BALANCE

You are one of the growing legion of "mompreneurs," mothers who choose to combine the rewards of business ownership with the joys of being at home and available to your family. When you set good boundaries and achieve good balance between work and family, you can excel in both business and parenting. To find your equilibrium:

1. Use the door to your office. A door gives you permission to not work when you are on the outside, and a responsibility to work when you are in your office.

2. Invest in your family by having a phone line dedicated to business. Your family shouldn't have to snap to attention when the phone rings. Give yourself permission to let your business phone ring when you're in the middle of story time.

3. Teach your children how to answer the phone. If you aren't able to have a separate business line, make sure they answer with, "Hello, this is the Olson residence." Let your customer's first impression of how you run your business be a positive

one. Your outgoing voice mail message should reflect your professionalism: "Hi, this is the Olson residence and the office of Karen Olson, your HomeMaker's representative."

4. Use your voice mail in the service of your family. It's no longer a family meal when you interrupt it to answer the phone. Instead of making a mad dash to check your messages as soon as you walk in the door, get the groceries put away and the kids settled. Check your messages only when you have the time to respond to them.

5. Choose your role. Try not to multitask business and home at the same time. It's easy to neglect your business by attending to family matters and vice versa. Know in your mind and by your actions whether you are working or parenting.

6. Give your children 30 minutes of your undivided attention when they arrive home from school. Find out about their day and discuss their homework and other after-school activities. During this window of time, you're communicating that your children are your priority, and that they are why you chose to be an entrepreneurial parent. After 30 minutes, your kids will be engaged in a different activity and you can get back to work.

7. Ask family members to help with household responsibilities. Being home all day doesn't mean you have time to complete all household responsibilities on your own. Delegate work that can be done by others so that you have more time for your business.

8. Turn meal preparation time into family time by involving your children in setting the table, cutting up vegetables, and pouring the drinks. When you are home for the evening, make the most of opportunities for family connection.

9. Let your kids know that you have a home-based business so you can be there for them when they need you, and so you can have the flexibility to be involved with their school and sports activities. Also explain that these privileges come with important responsibilities, such as letting you work during business time and being respectful when you are on the phone. Boundaries are great for kids, and you can practice them using your business.

10. Acknowledge and accept change. When you feel out of balance, check whether the needs of your family are changing. Your schedule and priorities will change about every six months, as your children grow. Care needs, homework time, sports, and social activities all have an impact on your schedule. Acknowledge these changes and adjust the way you work your business.

Today's Actions for Increasing Balance

1. Identify two tips from the list above that you want to incorporate this week.

2. Identify two tips that you want to incorporate in the next 30 days.

3. Enjoy your family, your business, and the positive feelings that result from attaining balance in your life. ■

■ Carve Out a Power Hour to Grow Your Business

By Belinda Ellsworth
Building your confidence as a leader

LEVERAGING YOUR TIME

Time: It's the most sought-after commodity in today's world. As I travel around North America speaking and training direct sellers on how to master the disciplines of booking, selling, and recruiting, women regularly ask for my advice on how to find the time to grow their business. In truth, it's not an issue of the amount of time you spend—you can build a large, productive business by working just 15 hours a week. The secret is to *spend the time you have in the most pro-*

ductive way possible. Spend one "Power Hour" each day (five days a week) on your personal business, and then one or two power hours building your team. When you actually make an appointment with yourself to spend four 15-minute intervals, undisturbed, working on predetermined tasks, it's amazing how much you can get done!

Why is the Power Hour concept so effective?

1. *It helps you form good habits.* Schedule your power hour into your calendar as you would a doctor or dentist appointment. In the beginning, you may have to force yourself to sit down, but it will get easier as you build momentum with the system. Those who use the Power Hour system get much more done and are much less overwhelmed.

2. *The secret to success with this system is* focus. During each 15-minute segment, focus only on the topic at hand. If the category is booking calls, spend that 15-minute time frame making only booking calls. Then go on to the next topic and spend 15 focused minutes on that.

3. *This system encourages daily action.* It transcends goal setting and list making, and helps eliminate procrastination. One hour a day, 15 minutes at a time. Too often, we set ourselves up for failure by setting unrealistic goals or making unhealthy lists, so the Power Hour system provides a practical vehicle to help move your business forward.

WORKING SMARTER, NOT HARDER

Here's how it works: Five days a week, spend one power hour on your business. Divide the hour into four 15-minute increments. During the first 15 minutes, make hostess-related calls: hostess coaching and setting up shows. The second 15 minutes, spend time following up on recruit leads: those who have expressed interest or someone you met at a show who would be great doing what you do. Spend the next 15 minutes on customer care calls. Not only will you get additional orders, but you will also collect many new booking and recruiting leads. The final 15 minutes is for personal development and growth: reading a positive book, listening to a CD, or perusing Web sites related to your industry.

If management is your goal, simply double your efforts by investing two power hours: one in your personal business and the other in your group business. Fifteen-minute intervals for team-building could be devoted to following up on group recruit leads, answering questions, or training new team members, and placing business-building calls to members of your team.

The Power Hour system is quick and easy to implement. Simply take four folders and label them with the four topics you consistently work on, such as bookings leads, recruiting leads, customer service or follow-up, team-building calls, and meeting ideas.

Next, get organized. Start by sorting through the stacks of things to do on your desk and placing them in the appropriate folders. Prioritize things in their order of importance. On the left-hand side of the folder, affix a piece of paper that stays there, with all the information you need (names, addresses, phone numbers, and so on). Then, on the right-hand side of the folder, affix a piece of paper that lists things to do. This list will change because, as you accomplish the tasks listed, you will add a new sheet of paper with new tasks and challenges.

Take action! Direct your attention to each folder for 15 minutes. If you don't have a full hour at each sitting, start with just one 15-minute segment, then build on that. Once you establish your files, set your schedule, and execute the Power Hour system, you will feel more in control of your time.

1-2-3 Steps to Productivity

1. Label four folders according to the four areas that consistently need your attention. Attach a sheet of contact information on the left side of the folder and a sheet for To Do items on the right.

2. Clear the clutter off your workspace and file your To Do items in the appropriate folders.

3. Calendar one hour each weekday and designate it as your Power Hour. ■

■ Color Your Hours for Balance and Success

By Christy King
Creatively keeping us all together

HONORING YOUR PRIORITIES

If you find yourself alternating between booking any date your hostess wants out of sheer desperation and being so busy that you find yourself praying for a cancellation, you probably don't have a good grasp of your commitments. If that's the case, your business—and your life—may feel overwhelming and out of control. ***Regain your equilibrium by developing a single-calendar system with color coding,*** which will help you identify, at a glance, what you have planned for the day, week, and month. When you see all of your commitments in one place, you can confidently grow your business and keep all parts of your life in harmony.

A color-coding system in your calendar accomplishes a number of things: it gives you an overview of the many hats you'll be wearing; inspires you to keep your word by honoring the time you have blocked out for your top priorities; and empowers you to quickly assess when you can commit to adding more business, family obligations, or outside activities.

CREATING A COLORFUL PALETTE OF BALANCE

Whether you've come from the corporate world of time clocks and deadlines, or have had your schedule dictated by when the kids need to be fed and when to mop the floors, setting up a system to organize your time is crucial. Start by buying one monthly calendar that appeals to you, along with a set of colorful highlighters, and by scheduling a regular time to plan your monthly activities. Then, using the following guidelines, mark out blocks of time with their corresponding colors.

- **Blue is for peace.** Your spirituality is your lifeline; you cannot possibly give to others if you first have not been filled. Taking the time to read, reflect, and connect with your higher power helps center you for the coming day. Whatever your daily spiritual ritual, partake of it during a time block highlighted in blue.

- **Yellow is for family fun.** Take your monthly calendar and write down all of your family obligations, kids' activities, holidays, and vacations, highlighting them in yellow. If your kids have a busy sports schedule, try to be available for their games, but don't feel guilty if you can't attend everything. Getting young children to understand that Mom has to work may be difficult, but it can be done. Start a "Fun Jar," and put in a dollar every time you work at night. Then use the "Fun Jar" money to do special things as a family.

- **Pink is for loved ones.** It's vital that you schedule time for the relationships that feed your soul. Playtime with girlfriends, visiting a dear relative, or a date night with your spouse recharges your battery and keeps loved ones a priority in your life. Highlight personal connections in pink.

- **Green is for money.** Planning office hours, a day for errands and appointments, and certain evenings to work your parties will help you keep consistent hours for consistent pay. If you keep your schedule uniform each week, you'll find that your household runs more smoothly. Once you've determined which evenings of the week you'll hold parties, highlight them in green. By color-coding these evenings, you can quickly glance at your calendar and see the empty spaces that need to be filled. If you don't have a party scheduled on a work night, get on the phone and schedule parties for those future green spaces.

- **White is for life management.** Leave time for all the things you do daily that aren't necessarily scheduled—cleaning, laundry, shopping, cooking, and meals. This gives you flexibility to roll with the inevitable punches. Learn how much white space you need for balance and honor it.

More Color-Coding Tips

Using a spiral-bound notebook, date the top of each page and write down what needs to be accomplished. Use your highlighters to color code each task as it is completed. Working from a daily To Do list will help you focus and serves as a reference tool if you need to recall when, for example, a call was made or a package was mailed.

Keep a second color-coded calendar of pink and yellow activities on your refrigerator so the family knows where everyone is or needs to be. You can assign an older child to keep the family calendar updated.

Color Yourself Happy Today

1. Have a meeting with your family to review everyone's upcoming commitments and write everything down on your calendar.

2. Determine which days and evenings you are going to work your business.

3. Color code your calendar and make it your goal to *always* have something scheduled in your green spaces. ■

■ Partner Up for a More Prosperous Future

By Barb and Clem Birch
Partnering to make a difference in others' lives

ENGAGE YOUR SPOUSE; ENRICH YOUR MARRIAGE

The benefits of successfully engaging your spouse in your business can be wonderful and exciting. However, doing so can also be potentially damaging to both your personal relationship and your business if not done carefully. ***You are more likely to engage him in your vision if you think carefully and act slowly.***

Partnering with your spouse can give you both more opportunities to grow a larger life together and come to understand what true relationship synergy means.

PLANNING TO PARTNER FOR LONG-TERM SUCCESS

As you walk the fine line between being a partner and maintaining control of your business as CEO, think of it as walking a tightrope in a high-wire act. Prepare yourself. Take a deep breath. Be patient. Don't take a step until you are prepared.

1. *Set your eye on your goal.* Evaluate the activities required by your business. This list may include prospecting, new customer contact, sales and marketing, administration (including accounting, recordkeeping, ordering and inventory control, and so on), tax information gathering and preparation, new associate training and support, ongoing contact with existing customers and associates, goal setting, and managing your vision. Some activities can be delegated, some can be shared, and others are inherently yours. Evaluate activity requirements against your own personal skill set and identify where you need help.

2. *Pick up your balance pole.* This is your business plan, or the description of how you want to run your business. It includes not only the list of activities identified in step 1 but also your "Why." Include how you started your new business to fill *family* needs—additional money, improving self esteem, back-up income, and other issues important to you both. It should also show a division of responsibilities. You and your planned business partner will both need clarity about your respective activities and the role your business will play in your life. Be prepared to clearly discuss why you started your business, along with costs, activities, and prospects for success.

3. *Gently take the first step.* Now make your sales pitch to your intended business partner. Show him that you have a business viewpoint, not an emotional one. Be businesslike and in command, but not cold and bossy. Remember this is a business proposal to your *friend*. Carefully select the location and timing of your presentation. Wait until your spouse is positive about your business. Getting him involved at the wrong time can be devastating. Above all, don't just dump on him what you don't want to do. Your partner could easily misunderstand and feel that you're "using" him to do "your dirty work."

4. *Use balance and judgment.* Finally, ask for his help with those activities that you either feel underqualified to perform or believe will actually get in the way of your progress if you are left to do them alone. If you have adequately prepared and presented your ideas, you should find yourself with a new business partner.

5. *Be persistent. Take each step as soon as you can.* Transitioning from running the whole show alone to having a partner is not a simple or instantaneous event. It is a process that takes patience, vision, and love. It also takes constant, persistent, gentle pressure to become the team you envisioned in step 2.

6. *Be patient. If the rope starts to sway, use your pole for balance.* Remember the pole? This is your business plan—your map for getting to your desired business configuration. If you lose momentum, refer back to this document and recapture your vision. Keep your eye on your goal and just keep moving toward it until you get there!

Actions for Today to Start Engagement

1. Realize that *you* are the owner and Chief Executive Officer (CEO) of your business and the *person in charge*. Go ahead right now and write your name down with the title "CEO" right behind it. Let yourself "feel" what this means.

2. Make a list of the general activities that came along with your business.

3. Identify activities on the list that

   — you don't want to do, or are not the best use of your time;
   — you don't feel qualified to do; and
   — detract from your ability to focus on business activities you are good at and that enhance your business.

4. Match up the *skills* and *interests* of your partner with activities on your list, and star those items you think he would enjoy the most.

You now are creating more of the vision needed for your business plan! ◼

◼ Maintain Your Balance with Family Meetings

By Sue Burdick
Juggling family and entrepreneurship with flair

CREATING A BUSINESS–FAMILY MERGER

Until you can properly balance the daily chaos of family life with the freedom and flexibility of direct selling, your effectiveness in business is compromised. ***You can attain that balance by holding regular family meetings, where good communication and planning will help family members define their roles in the household and in your business.*** When your spouse and children understand the rewards of helping you to achieve that harmony, they will be motivated to do what they can to make your business a success.

Starting a home-based business challenges the family because it disrupts the status quo. Initially, family members may be upset that you can no longer act as a short-order cook at breakfast or as an on-call chauffeur after school. In response, you may try to both fulfill your traditional role and juggle your business responsibilities, or you may feel guilty about your work taking time away from your family. Either approach works about as well as trying to hold a dozen ping-pong balls underwater: regardless of your efforts, some of them will eventually pop to the surface. I've found a third path that works for my husband, our five boys, and me: creating a business–family merger that encourages everyone to play a role in the success of my direct-selling business.

The key to a successful merger is the family meeting. During the meeting, you'll clearly communicate your schedule and manage your family's expectations of your availability. You'll also listen to their needs and devise solutions to conflicts or problems that arise. In the process, you'll enlist their help in maintaining the household and in supporting your business.

READY, SET, MEET!

Call your hubby and the kids together! Here's the agenda for your first family meeting:

1. *Explain your home-based business.* Demonstrate the product, explain the tasks involved in growing your business, and discuss how many hours you need to devote to your business each week.

2. *Outline the benefits.* Explain how your business helps your family as a whole and how it can offer individual benefits. Ask them to visualize these benefits through "dream boards." Family dreams could include a vacation, a new car, or a new home. Include individual dream boards, too. Skates, clothes, and bikes are great motivators!

3. *Enlist their help.* Let your family know that you need each of them, and that their contributions and support are critical to the success of your business, and, by extension, of your family.

4. *Assign tasks.* List business and household tasks, and assign them according to age and ability. Tasks may include:

   – Creating and distributing fliers and promotional material

   – Helping at trade shows

   – Stuffing and stamping envelopes

   – Labeling and sorting

   – Computer work, such as recordkeeping and inventory

   – Household chores, such as laundry, cleaning, cooking, and shopping

5. *Provide a script.* Write out a 30-second response that your children can memorize and use when answering the phone or when questioned about mom's new business. The kids will feel more comfortable having something in writing and will leave a positive impression with family and friends.

6. *Stick to it!* A plan is just words on a page unless you implement it. At your next meeting, ask for feedback and adjust your plan accordingly. Then follow it!

After the first time or two, you'll get a sense of how often your family meetings should take place. For some women, once a month is sufficient; for others, a weekly meeting helps everyone stay on track. The important thing is to make these gatherings a priority and to schedule them regularly.

Finally, remember that the tone of your meeting doesn't have to replicate that of a corporate boardroom. Keep the gatherings light and fun, so that family members look forward to the time spent together. Plan to have pizza delivered on family meeting night, or call a Saturday morning meeting where everyone climbs into your bed in his or her pajamas. Combining business and fun makes everyone feel closer and strengthens the bond between your family and your business.

Setting Your Agenda Today and Tomorrow

1. Schedule your first meeting.

2. Start a running list of family- and business-related issues that need to be addressed in your meetings. Perhaps the laundry is piling up, or maybe you have a mailing going out in a week's time. Prior to each family gathering, you can use this list to jot down an agenda and your goals for the meeting. ∎

∎ Get Creative with Child Care

By Kristie Tamsevicius
Empowering women to achieve breakthrough success

BALANCING YOUR ACT

As a direct-selling mom, you juggle the roles of head chef, chauffer, nursemaid, wife, and more. ***Being there for your kids may be the very reason you have a home-based business, yet this myriad of roles makes carving time out for your business challenging at best.*** By developing a wide variety of cost-effective childcare options, you can achieve a balance between spending time with your children and building your business.

There are times when working at home while watching the kids goes without a hitch. They're playing a game in the other room, doing their homework at the kitchen table, or gabbing with their friends while you're making your calls, filing your paperwork, and crossing items off of your To Do list with efficiency. There are other times, though, when parenting and working requires a superhuman ability to focus. Once, as I was doing a phone interview with the local media, the *Pokémon* theme was blaring on the TV, a toy was singing, "If you're happy and you know it, clap your hands," and my son came over saying, "Mommy, Mommy, Mommmmmeee . . ." The reporter was amazed that I could concentrate on writing an article for my newsletter with such distractions. The key is honing the ability to let go of the distracting voices while still listening for cues that your children really need help.

BRINGING IN THE RELIEF PITCHER

No matter how well you multitask, there are occasions when you need undisturbed time to devote to your business. Here are some ideas for getting the relief you need:

- **Hire a sitter to come to your home.** In the summertime, you can find local high school and college kids who will keep the children entertained for a few hours rather inexpensively. Otherwise, you can ask friends, neighbors, and customers to recommend sitters who are willing to do day care in your home.

- **Swap babysitting and working time with another mom.** If you have a friend who also has her own home-based business, you can trade work and sitting times. For example, if you work in the morning, she can watch your kids. In the afternoon, she can work while you take over the childcare duties.

- **Set up a childcare co-op.** Arrange with two other moms in your neighborhood or on your team to take all three kids for one afternoon. By taking turns watching the brood, the kids will form lasting friendships while each mom gets two afternoons per week to work on her business kid-free!

- **Work swing shifts with your husband.** You can watch the kids while your husband works, and then he can take over while you work the next shift. The disadvantage to this approach is that you don't get a lot of quality time to spend with your husband.

- **Work around the kids' schedules.** You can get chunks of work done while the kids are in school, or while they're sleeping in the early morning or at night. If you have a baby or toddler, you can work while they are taking naps.

- **Ask your family for help.** Going to grandma's house can be an adventure. If you have extended family, they may be willing to watch the kids while you work.

- **Enroll your kids in a class.** Most local parks and recreation districts offer dozens of inexpensive classes for children of all ages. Go through the course catalog together with your children, and have them pick out the classes that most interest them.

- **Park your kids at the pool.** Invest in a summer pass for your local public pool and take advantage of the recreational swim hours. As long as your kids can swim, most public pools allow school-age children to swim without a parent being present. You can get two to three hours a day of uninterrupted work while your kids are splashing in the sun.

- **Sign your kids up for day camp.** Many parks and recreation districts offer inexpensive day camps. When they're not in school, consider signing your kids up for day camp one or two days each week. They'll have fun and you'll have peace of mind.

Assessing Your Options

1. Realistically assess how well you're juggling your many roles, and whether some form of childcare would help you achieve your personal and professional goals.

2. Determine how many hours each week you'd like help with the kids, and choose one or more strategies from the previous list.

3. Do the research or make the calls to get the help you need. ■

■ Be a Hero in Your Wife's Business

By Mark Semple

A hero helping husbands of direct-selling women

GIVEN IN MARRIAGE

Are you the husband of a direct-selling woman? She may want or need your support to grow her business, and you may want to do whatever you can to support her, but you may not know how. *By gaining knowledge about her business and adopting strategies that support her efforts, you can help her become successful and enrich your marriage in the process.*

THE ART OF SUPPORT

Let's be realistic: Your wife *can* achieve success flying solo. If that's the way she chooses to pursue her business, it's okay. As husbands, we must respect the fact that it is *her* business, and that she has the right to run it any way she desires.

However, your wife can be substantially more successful if she draws on your talents and encouragement. My wife knows she can count on me anytime for anything she needs.

The opportunities for providing support are endless. The key is to let your wife know you are available to help. Note that this may cut into a ball game or a fishing trip, but it will be worth it in the long run. Trust me on this one.

Give Her Your Time

The single most important element in providing support is to help your wife have the time she needs to run her business. Obviously, there is only so much time in a day, and she must juggle her family, personal, and business needs. The more you can do to help make time available to her, the more she can contribute to the family. Ask her how much time she needs to devote to her business each week, then think of the ways in which you can help her to carve out those hours. These might include:

- Taking on more of the routine chores and household upkeep

- Improving your skills in planning meals, buying groceries, and cooking

- Relieving her of mundane activities, like counting inventory or running to the post office

- Taking the kids out for a movie or to the park

Learn about Her Business

Help her with bookkeeping, read the company materials, share in her training, and accompany her to seminars. If you understand her business, you are in a position to contribute ideas that really count. You could even assist her with hosting events. If she is unable to attend a show for some reason, you could step up to the plate and do it for her. This is a "Major Support Moment."

Use Your Talents

Chances are, some of your skills complement those of your wife. As an IT professional, I support my wife by taking care of anything technology-related. As your wife shares ideas about how she'd like to grow her business, you can offer suggestions and participate in putting her plan into action. Remember that you have a perspective that she does not. Using your male intuition (yes, ladies, it does exist), you can suggest marketing strategies or ways to streamline her inventory control, or help her create a workspace that allows her to thrive.

Be an Active Participant

Volunteer to assist with any of your wife's events. These could include seminars, shows, festivals, and training meetings. She will appreciate your willingness to be involved in her business, and you will have the opportunity to spend more time with your wife.

Motivate Her When She's Down

Like most pursuits in life, her business will have peaks and valleys. By staying positive and providing her with reminders of her successes and goals, you will play a crucial role in her business.

Your First Steps as a Champion

1. Sit down with your wife and ask her how much time she needs to devote to her business each week. Ask her what level of involvement she would like from you. Tell her that she can count on your support.

2. Make a list of the ways in which you can help your wife, whether it's taking the kids to baseball practice, attending a seminar with her, or painting her office the shade of blue she's always liked. Present her with the list and let her choose what she'd like you to do.

3. Have fun! Yes, it's a business, though not business as we know it. Your wife's driving force is passion; she loves what she sells and does. Participate and contribute, and always have fun in the process. ■

■ Share Life Lessons with Your Children

By Michelle Knapp
Daughter of a direct-selling mom

MY HEAD START IN LIFE

When it seems your business is encroaching on your family life, you might wonder whether your direct-selling career is as good for your children as you hoped it would be. *You can replace any guilt with a sense of pride in knowing that your children will grow up understanding the value in working hard for something they want,* how it feels to lead others and make a difference in other people's lives, and that they can realize their dreams.

I'll admit there were moments when I thought my mom's company was the bane of my existence, but as an adult I recognize the tremendous blessings associated with having a mom who owned her own home-based business. In retrospect, the lessons I learned from my mom's involvement in direct selling vested me with experience that other college graduates attain only after years in the workforce.

From the time I was 10 or 12, I helped my mom with presentations in our home. The products my mother marketed were so integral to our lifestyle that it was easy for my brother and me to add our ideas and even to give parts of presentations. She would, for example, ask me to share a positive experience I had with one of the products that she marketed. As I grew older, I learned how to present entire sections of her meetings. My mom never pushed me, but she would involve me to the extent that I was comfortable. She always made her business "the family business."

After we graduated from high school, my brother and I became involved in the business ourselves and began traveling with our mom to Europe. By this time, we felt completely confident doing training meetings on our own. In retrospect, I am amazed that I possessed the confidence to professionally interact with complete strangers from around the world who were often two or three times my age.

My mother also instilled in us the confidence to pursue our own dreams. She taught us that our accomplishments were limitless, and because her vision was not restricted by a certain salary, neither was ours. This could have been dangerous, except that we learned that our happiness and financial prosperity are directly related to how many people we help and serve. If we ever wanted

> **O**ur life revolved around lifting others up, not getting ahead of them.

something we couldn't afford, my mom would say, "Well, I guess we'll just have to reach out to more people and make more of a difference, so that we can get that!" Through our home-based business, I understood that advancement was predicated upon helping others succeed. Our life revolved around lifting others up, not getting ahead of them. Through her example of leadership, my mother taught me to always generously serve others. This approach made her business thrive, and permanently affected my outlook on life and my attitude toward work.

My mother was successful in involving us in her business because she didn't compartmentalize her personal life and her professional life. As she interacted with parents at Little League games and school activities, they often became interested in her line of work. Because the business was such an integral part of our lives, it was completely natural for her to share the opportunity with other families. In fact, one of her most successful distributors is a woman she met over 18 years ago, because of a friendship between my brother and her daughters.

I must mention that Sunday was the one day of the week devoted entirely, without exception, to the family. It was important for us to know that, although the business permeated many areas of our family life, our family was ultimately the more important of the two.

Making It Work—and Fun—for Kids

1. Sit down with your family and set business goals that reward the entire family, such as going on a special vacation.

2. Turn your next humdrum business chore into a fun activity by having your children invite friends over to help with a mailing, and ordering pizza or watching a movie.

3. Encourage each family member to make a "dream poster." Have them incorporate pictures from magazines that represent what matters most to them, and let them know that their dreams are as important as yours. As you support your children in reaching their dreams and goals, your children will be more likely to support and encourage you in your business. ▪

■ Attend Life University

By Paola Horvath
A daughter transformed by the power of books

MY POSTGRADUATE SURPRISE

After I graduated from college, I was a little worried about adult life—school was all I'd known for the previous 17 years. A couple of months after I graduated, I moved to Seattle and began looking for a job. The hunt got long and I got scared. This is when my direct-selling parents approached me with their idea for "postgraduate work."

One night as dinner nourished our brains, my parents began to lay their thoughts on the table. I did not say a word, not wanting to accept just *any* idea that my parents had to offer me. The last thing I wanted to hear was how to plan my future and what kind of job I should get. But, my expectations were wrong. Their idea was *good!*

They described *Life University*, which they had designed as a game to give me a greater love for learning and personal growth; a chance to learn how to design my life to be exactly as I want it to be; and an opportunity to discover some of the things schools don't teach, like how to find my purpose, the truth about money, and insights to achievement and success.

The rules of the game were this: They would give me a list of books, tapes, and seminars on all sorts of "real life" topics. Next to each resource they'd indicated the dollar value they were prepared to pay me in exchange for reading the book, listening to the tape, or attending the seminar. After finishing a resource, I would have to answer these four questions for them in writing:

1. What did you find most interesting about the subject matter?

2. What do you question about the subject matter?

3. How does this information apply to your own life?

4. What will you do, if anything, with this new knowledge?

They also asked me to record my thoughts and ideas in a written journal "for my eyes only." One more thing: They said I could use the money *only* to invest in some form of portfolio that I would then learn to select, manage, and grow.

I saw immediately that Life University would give me the opportunity to learn everything that my parents learned later on in life. With each lesson, I would be paid a certain amount that could be invested into my future. And, I was free to back out whenever I wanted. I realized that if I attended Life University, there was nothing to lose!

I started reading books, listening to tapes, and watching videos. I kept a journal and after each Life University experience, I wrote a summary of my thoughts. During the process, it dawned on me—I am really lucky! Not many parents do this for their children. In fact, whenever I told friends about it, they said they thought it was so cool and they wished they had something like it.

> **I** *am really lucky! Not many parents do this for their children. In fact, whenever I told friends about it, they said they thought it was so cool and they wished they had something like it.*

Through Life University, I gained more than I had imagined possible. I learned about the purpose of life, finding a purposeful career, becoming prosperous and successful, financial investments, communication skills, spirituality, and many other topics. I implemented my new skills effortlessly, and developed a new desire to succeed. I found a job in a salon that many would consider brainless, but I made it purposeful by raising environmental awareness—discovering earth-friendly chemical alternatives and recycling. Later I was offered more and more purposeful jobs with worthy salaries in my field of study. Even more important, I am excited about my career!

So, how did my parents succeed in this maneuver? They stayed out of the way. They did not put any pressure on me. They seemed pleased and satisfied with whatever growth I enjoyed. They simply let me experience Life University.

What kept me going? I realized that my parents were not gaining anything from this. It was purely for me and I could take it or leave it. As I read each book, I reminded myself that the words I was reading were not coming out of my parents' mouths—that the information was coming from an outside source. By maintaining an open mind, I stayed on track and took advantage of the opportunity. Now I know how to make any job purposeful. Now I experience my life more completely, grateful, because like Life University, its potential is so much greater than I could ever imagine.

Starting Your Own University

1. Make a list of your favorite self-improvement resources and assign a value to each one, making sure that the total of potential payments is an amount you are able and committed to award your young adult to invest, in case he or she maximizes the opportunity.

2. Present your young adult with an invitation letter to attend Life University, and, if he or she decides to participate, sign an agreement that you will both abide by the rules of the game. For a sample invitation letter and agreement, see http://www.morebuilditbig.com/gifts.asp. Enjoy watching your child learn and grow in a whole new way! ∎

■ Create a Super Space for Your Business

By Kristie Tamsevicius
Empowering women to achieve extraordinary results in their business

FROM GODDESS TO EXECUTIVE

One of the great privileges of the direct-selling profession is being able to work from home. But the freedom of your career comes with challenges. The sink is full of dishes, your son left his crayons on your desk, and the laundry is piled up in the corner. A well-designed home office helps you transition from the role of domestic goddess to high-powered direct selling executive. Just like Clark Kent changes in the phone booth to become Superman, *as you enter your office space, you turn into queen of your direct-selling empire*. Instantly, your mind shifts from the list of household chores to strategies for earning the big bonus next month and winning that Hawaiian vacation.

DESIGNING WITH IMAGINATION

Here's how to plan the perfect workspace—one that keeps you organized, inspires you, and boosts your productivity.

Plan a Space That Meets Your Needs

- **Space.** Imagine your dream space. Where is it? What items does it contain? Do you need to be where you can keep an eye on the kids? Do you need a meeting space? Will you have customers or other consultants stopping by?

- **Location.** Choose a space in your home that best supports your needs. Whether it's a spare bedroom, a corner of the living room, a large closet, an attic, or a converted garage, find a room that has enough space for the equipment and furniture you need.

- **Storage.** While not every direct seller keeps inventory on hand, those who do need a space to store product. Make sure that the space you choose has ample room for shelving and storage. Make a list of the items you handle on a daily basis. Do you need a bookshelf or wall holders for catalogs and brochures? With the proper storage to keep your office tidy, you'll have a more organized workspace.

- **Furniture.** Next, outfit your workspace with a desk, bookcase, and filing cabinets. Whether you choose a simple desk, an office armoire, or a complete L-shaped unit, make sure you'll have the desktop space you need to keep key items at your fingertips. Splurge a little and get yourself a comfortable and ergonomic chair. It's a back-saving, worthwhile investment.

- **Equipment.** Plan spots for your computer, phone, and fax. Buying an all-in-one printer/scanner/fax machine is a smart choice that saves you desktop space and money.

Put It Together in a Way That Makes Sense

- **Organization.** Place key equipment to complement your workflow. Create centers for the tasks you frequently perform. Put all of your hostess gifts, order forms, and catalogs in one area. Other areas may include a shipping center, a faxing center, and a printing center. Boxes and bins are great for keeping smaller office supplies organized.

- **Ergonomics.** Place your keyboard, lighting, and monitor at proper heights. By being good to your body, you can function at peak performance and prevent injury from incorrect positioning.

Create an Inspiring Atmosphere You Love

- **Personal.** Now's the chance to create the office of your dreams. Make your office a space that truly inspires you. Choose a paint color that brings you joy. Pamper yourself with treasured photos, candles, and artwork. Add a dash of color with a potted plant or vase with flowers on your desk. Finally, include inspirational quotes, a dream map, and visual reminders of your goals—powerful tools to keep you motivated and on the track to success.

- **Clean and tidy.** There's nothing better than starting the day with a clean desk. Get in the routine of either cleaning your desk at the end of the day or doing a five-minute tidy first thing in the morning.

- **Well lit.** Don't skimp on overhead and task lighting. In addition to creating ambiance in the room, proper lighting keeps you from straining your eyes.

Starting Your Dream Office Today!

Get a jumpstart on your home office by taking the following actions in the next 48 hours:

1. Walk around your home and visualize your office. What space feels good and inspiring to you? Choose the perfect space and clear it out.

2. Flip through catalogs and magazines. Clip pictures of furniture, décor, and items you'd like to include in your dream office. By clarifying the details of your perfect workspace, you'll more easily spot those items as you come across them.

3. Look for smart buys. Scan the newspapers, store fliers, and online office store coupons for sales and special offers. ■

■ Lead with Your Feminine Strengths

By Dr. Denis Waitley
Enlightened instructor in feminine leadership

HONORING YOUR NATURAL TALENTS

Women often lack the confidence in their ability to lead others to success, and see their lack of experience or training as a detriment to their future success. ***When you tap into your inborn traits and honor your natural talents, you realize that leadership is yours for the taking.*** You can then approach your business with new confidence and the motivation to attain a leadership position within your company.

CLIMBING THE LADDER

Here are some of the reasons why women possess qualities that make them natural-born leaders.

Women Take Action

- **Women are starting companies at twice the rate of men.** The number of female-owned businesses in North America alone has grown to nearly 10 million. Women-owned companies employ one out of every four workers and generate more than $2.5 *trillion* in annual revenues.

- **Women take education more seriously.** In North America, about 90 percent of women complete high school, compared with 86 percent of men; 30 percent get college degrees versus 26 percent of men.

- **Women are breadwinners.** Women are the main income producers in one out of four two-income households in North America.

- **Women look at the big picture.** Women, more often then men, make the final decision on which home to buy. They consider functionality, practicality, location, convenience, services, and safety. Men consider the design, general appearance, location, and costs.

Women Are Flexible

- **Women encourage experimentation and tolerate mistakes.** In today's best-managed companies, employees are urged to "color outside the lines" and to speak up and make suggestions. Women are less opinionated and more flexible in considering alternative approaches.

- **Women can adapt more readily to change.** Because women have been more responsible for attending to the emotional needs of others, which are very fluid, they learn to read between the lines and come up with creative solutions for accommodating people.

- **Women try to resolve conflict more peacefully.** We live in a borderless world where different cultures collide via instant communications, so the ability to gain consensus among differing interests is paramount to our survival.

Women Value Quality of Life

- **Women are waiting much longer to get married.** Marriage is no longer a woman's sole indicator of success. Education, service, career development, and self-actualization also are important considerations.

- **Women are more conscious of their health, not just their looks.** The nutrition and fitness industries are driven primarily by women. Although women have longer life expectancies than do men, women also want quality of life for themselves and their families.

■ **Women are more intuitive.** While men tend to look at the bottom line numbers, women look at the whole person. In an "infomercial world" loaded with get-rich-quick schemes and fads, it is important to go to the "gut" or intuition when assessing a business or personal relationship. Women seem to be able to spot a phony better than most men.

Women Are Team Players

■ **Women readily delegate authority.** In simpler times, the egotistical boss could survive. Now leaders must empower others. Women don't need to take the credit for success and are comfortable sharing both the responsibility and the spotlight.

■ **Women have better networking skills.** Today, success is based more on relationship power than position power. Being a team player and team leader are more important to success than being a charismatic superstar.

■ **Women understand how important personal contact is in networking.** No e-mail, voice mail, or gift will ever replace the value of taking time to be there in person for someone you care about.

■ **Women have better listening skills.** Through centuries of playing a supporting role, women have fine-tuned the ability to listen for the core passion or need of the other person by asking questions and empathizing, rather than presenting.

Women Are Already Leaders

■ **Women are better at recognizing and reinforcing positive behavior.** Because women have the major role in early child development, they understand that good behavior needs constant reinforcing, and that bad behavior is changed more readily with the carrot than with the stick.

■ **Women can and will be elected to lead their countries.** A University of Chicago survey reports that nine out of ten voters would vote for a qualified woman to lead the United States.

Golda Meier, Margaret Thatcher, Indira Ghandi, Sandra Day O'Connor, Condoleeza Rice, and many other prominent women have paved the way for future female leaders.

Looking in the Mirror

1. Make a list of the natural leadership traits you see in yourself.

2. Write down how each trait benefits your business.

3. Honor and celebrate your innate leadership abilities and consciously use them to your best advantage. ■

Enlightened Leadership

8

*A*fter receiving many accolades from readers about the leadership perspective offered in *Build It Big*, we decided to fully embrace what we have fondly come to refer to as "Enlightened Leadership" by dedicating an entire chapter to this very topic.

As we come to know those who are truly successful in this business, we learn that they share a certain style of leadership: one that is grounded in integrity, wrapped in a spirit of service, and tied up with a genuine love for those they lead. Enlightened leadership not only impacts individual teams, but also passes through the generations of organizations, enriching their culture and leaving legacies of excellence that others will follow.

We purposely chose leaders of different molds to contribute to this chapter. Their teams range in size from a few hundred to tens of thousands. Their styles of communication vary from high tech to high touch—and everything in between. Yet their common spirit enables them to lead others toward their dreams and inspires loyalty among their team members.

Drink in the words of wisdom on the following pages, and soak up the commitment of these leaders to stay the course, regardless of the obstacles that emerge. Revel in the knowledge that you have the opportunity to influence others in a deep and lasting way. As you put these visionaries' words into action, become the enlightened leader you are meant to be—one that you would follow toward your own dreams.

■ Attract Excellence with Principled Leadership

By Laura Kaufman
Leading with integrity and heart

STARTING AT THE TOP

Leadership begins at the top and spreads throughout the entire organization. Unfortunately, poor leadership duplicates and spreads just as easily as good leadership. Therefore, you must deliberately *create your team's culture based on principles of excellence that resonate with the people you want to attract.* When you practice excellence in the principles of trust, respect, service, integrity, and authenticity, and instill them throughout your organization, you create an environment where your team members can become the best they can be.

FIVE GUIDING LIGHTS

The Principle of Trust

Trust must be the cornerstone of your team. You must have faith in your team members, believe in them, look for the best in them, and keep their confidence. You communicate your understanding that people learn best by doing, even when they sometimes make mistakes, by giving your team as much autonomy as possible. When you delegate responsibility to a team member, by asking her to do training at a meeting, for example, you exhibit confidence in her abilities and encourage her to lead. Ultimately, trust leads to a culture of self-sufficiency, self-confidence, and the desire of your team members to step outside of their comfort zones and fully realize their potential.

The Principle of Respect

Respect for those within your team means honoring who they are as women, being willing to consider and value the ideas and skills they bring to your team, and guiding them without interfering in their process. In adhering to the principle of respect, you take on the role of coach, knowing that each member of your team is inherently competent and that her unique qualities add to the success of the team. When you communicate to your team member that she is valuable, you help her to see herself as valuable. This builds her self-esteem and encourages her to become a confident leader.

The Principle of Service

Service to others represents a commitment to assist those on your team in developing their talents, and to always put their best interests first. It doesn't mean that you are a doormat, nor does it mean expending effort on women who are not willing to learn. It does mean, however, that when a situation requires you to make a choice between what is best for you and what is best for the team, you opt for the team. When you consistently choose to do what is best for them, your team members feel your commitment to service, and adopt it as their own guiding principle. They go the extra mile in service to their customers, thus ensuring the success of the team.

The Principle of Integrity

Integrity means always doing what is right, no matter how difficult that may be. It is being who you say you are and doing what you say you will. As a leader, know that someone on your team is always observing you, and that she is forming her opinions of the business based on your actions. When you consistently operate from integrity, your team will produce to their full potential. When challenges surface, your team will not go astray if they know—beyond a shadow of doubt—that they can always count on you to do the right thing.

The Principle of Authenticity

Authenticity means being open and honest, even about your own human frailties. You rely on your strengths and seek growth and assistance in areas where you are weak. When you come from a place of authenticity, you can openly say "I don't know" or "I made a mistake." Your team member then understands that we are all in the process of learning, and that she can be who she is and still make it to the top.

Pinpointing Your Strengths

In the next 48 hours, review each of the five areas of principled leadership. Here's how:

1. Draw a circle, divide it into five parts, and label each area with one principle.

2. In each area, draw one dot. Place the dot close to the rim if you are strong in that principle, in the middle if you have some skills in that area, and close to the center if you need significant improvement.

3. Connect the dots. Is the result round?

4. For the three dots closest to the center, identify an action you can take to strengthen that principle. Although you will probably have to go outside your comfort zone, remember that stretching helps you grow! ■

■ Discover Your True Agenda

By Laura Berman Fortgang
Keeping the focus on what's important

WHOSE AGENDA MATTERS MOST?

Everyone who has succeeded at direct selling knows she could not have done it alone. Yet, getting great results from others can be frustrating and difficult at times. Pushing your agenda and motivating others to reach a goal can feel fruitless if your only motivation is to succeed. That may sound strange because of course you want to succeed. But you might want to put your agenda aside momentarily to make motivating others easier. If you *shift your agenda to what your team members need* instead of just what you need (results), you will get better, easier outcomes all around.

SHIFTING FROM YOUR AGENDA TO HERS

Coaching another means having her best interest at heart; otherwise, it's not coaching. With only your interests at stake, it is better named persuasion, teaching, or sometimes even seduction.

Think of every person you work with and ask yourself, "What is my agenda for her?" If all your answers have to do with how she can perform better and deliver better sales numbers, stop yourself and shift your focus. Now ask: "What does Mary (or any team member) need from me?" The answer may have nothing to do with the mission at hand. Maybe she needs some resources to help her troubled teen, or perhaps she needs a call to show her you care about her outside of the business, or it could be she needs the name of her local Toastmasters group to have a place to improve her presentation style. The more you can help her get what she needs, the easier it will be for her to achieve what you need her to.

It may cross your mind that spending time doing these kinds of things will distract you from the bottom line or turn you into a caretaker. That may sound logical, but not if you put it into a different context. When you have the new agenda of caring about what is in it for each team member, you can quickly see who is really prepared to contribute to the team and how. You will know more about people immediately and will save yourself time barking up the wrong tree if ultimately someone cannot deliver. Also, you'll build the loyalty of each member and help her find the time and presence of mind to perform better for you and for herself. It will never be a waste or a distraction from the bottom line to meet the true needs of your team instead of just your own.

Coaching others effectively means having an agenda that everyone succeeds, but the trick is letting them succeed their way without pressure or being made to feel dumb or wrong. That takes a lot of finesse as a coach and especially as someone who has a lot at stake in the game. In putting the other person first, you will be tested and tried. Your fighting spirit and desire to win may want to take over at the slightest urging, but if you can fight that response, and choose to truly be there for *their* success, you will have more to celebrate. You'll also have the satisfaction of knowing you took the high road and didn't use people for your gain at the expense of their happiness and peace of mind. That's not to say you'd do that knowingly, but it can happen unwittingly just by being someone who thinks big and wants the best.

Most important is remembering that by investing a small amount of time helping someone motivate herself, you can save months of trying to do the motivating for her. Coach and inspire *for her* and not you and you will have a loyal, winning team.

Your New Agenda for Easier Results

In the next 48 hours:

- Write down the name of every member of your team.

- Next to each name, write your agenda for that member. Then write down what you think *her* agenda is.

■ Brainstorm and write down ways you can help her reach *her* agenda.

■ Add these activities to your calendar and To Do list, and as they come up, do them.

As time goes on, you'll watch the return on your investment grow! ■

■ Travel the Ethical Road to Leadership

By Gary Ryan Blair
The Goals Guy

TRACTION ON A SLIPPERY SLOPE

Character is the backbone of effective leadership. Of course, other leadership virtues are important, but without good character a leader's long-term impact is negative and marginalized. If, for example, you are promoted to a new level in your company, but you achieve the promotion by purchasing more personal inventory and enrolling people under fictitious names to meet the qualifications, can you really be considered a success? Even if you unintentionally cede the moral high ground, can your achievements be respected if the means make you want to blush in embarrassment? *When you find yourself on an ethical slippery slope, you must acknowledge the problem, establish the mindset to fix it, and then make amends to those you've harmed.* Ultimately, your integrity, honor, and reputation both precede you and linger after you move on. When you lead by example and demonstrate solid ethical behavior, you are not only benefiting your team and your company, but you are also making a difference for the entire direct-selling profession.

When it comes to ethics and values, the ultimate litmus test is *behavior.* Your behavior is a physical manifestation of your values, and reveals your moral strengths and weaknesses. In a word, behavior never lies. Doing the right thing, for the right reasons, is the way to live a successful life and run a successful business. But behaving in harmony with your beliefs, values, and good intentions is one of the biggest challenges you face. It's a lot easier to fight for principles than to live up to them.

CLIMBING BACK UP

The direct-selling profession presents numerous opportunities to wander off the path of ethical behavior. What would you do, for example, if you knew that your prospect had a relative in the business? What if, while working a trade show booth, you had the opportunity to follow up with someone who had been working with someone else in the booth? To remain in integrity, always ask a new prospect if she is working with another representative from your company. After all, how would you feel if someone recruited your customer?

If you've ever found yourself at an ethical crossroads and have chosen a path that isn't in alignment with your values and core beliefs, it is crucial that you get back on track. You can reverse the tide and restore your ability to live an ethical, values-based life by subscribing to the following principles.

Awareness. You must remain aware that this problem exists. You must be conscious of the consequences of moral decay. You must also faithfully monitor your own behavior and take inventory of any compromises you have made regarding your own character.

Shared concern. When you share the concern for our industry, for future generations, and for one another, you discover and develop within yourself a sustained and unshakable resolve to effect meaningful change in your own standards and behavior, as well as those of your team and society at large.

Put belief into practice. As Socrates suggests, "All human virtues increase and strengthen themselves by the practice and experience of them." You must act in accordance with your highest values, and experience the benefits of practicing what you believe. If you've done something you regret, you must admit it to those involved, whether it's your customer, team member, upline, or someone else in your company. Together, you can find a solution that works for everyone.

Then pick yourself up, reconnect with your values, and recommit yourself to living in alignment with your principles. For true success, you must focus your mental, emotional, and spiritual energies on pursuing the highest goal: that which is right and good.

Walking the Path

1. Ask yourself this question: Am I following my company's policies and procedures when speaking with prospects and working with my team? If so, in what ways?

2. If you've slipped into situational ethics and committed a moral misdemeanor, outline your strategy for righting the wrong. Consult with your upline, address the problem, apologize for your behavior, and give those affected your genuine pledge that it won't happen again.

3. Make a list of all the ways that your team can participate in assisting the profession as a whole to be viewed with ethically high standards, and present it at your next team training. ■

■ Honor Their Dream

By Dr. Shirley B. Carmack
Sharing a lifetime of experience to uplift and inspire

ACCEPTING THAT LESS MAY BE MORE

As you review your team's performance, you might feel frustrated that you don't have enough stars. Shouldn't more of your team members want to build organizations of their own? The truth is, women have a variety of reasons and motivations for joining a direct-selling company. Yet, many leaders either don't understand the range of motivations their team members possess or, if they do, they fail to respect and honor those differences. *By recognizing the motivational patterns of direct sellers and making the most of each one, you can honor and celebrate each of your team members while maintaining realistic expectations that bring you peace of mind.* As a result, your team members feel valued, reap the rewards they desire from their businesses, and are more likely to stay with the team for the long term.

PERCEIVING AND PRIZING THE PATTERNS

The motivations of direct sellers fall into five basic categories:

1. **The Wholesale User.** This woman wants to use the products or services at a discount, rather than to generate income. Engage her with a special incentive to earn free or discounted products. You may, for example, tell her that she will receive a certain dollar value in free products by referring a new team member.

2. **The Socially Oriented.** This woman gets involved because she likes being around people. She enjoys the fellowship and camaraderie, but seldom does much business. Engage her by asking her to play the role of greeter or ambassador at a team function, or to arrange an annual potluck dinner for the team.

3. **The Short-Termer.** This woman wants to earn a specific amount of money to attain a specific goal, such as buying holiday gifts or financing a vacation. When her goal has been reached, she disappears. She may show up again to earn some more money, and then disappear again when she reaches that goal. Engage her by encouraging her to always have a short-term goal she is excited about.

4. **The Consistent Part-Time Earner.** This woman builds a solid part-time business that continues to grow modestly. She's happy earning a consistent $500 to $2,000 per month to add to her family's income. Engage her with recognition of her consistent achievements and by asking her to share her experience with others in the group.

5. **The Career Builder.** This is a serious-minded businesswoman who does what it takes to be a top money earner. Because her goal is to develop a full-time career, she is persistent enough to overcome disappointments. Engage her with personal mentoring that helps her develop the skills she will need to lead a growing organization.

Honor and Cherish Today

1. Within 48 hours after you enroll your next team member, conduct an interview to determine her motivation for joining your business.

2. Devise a strategy for mentoring that fits with her motivational pattern.

3. Honor her motivation and commitment, and let her know that she's a valuable member of your team. ∎

∎ Launch Every Success with a Quick Start System

By Michele McDonough
Training others to grow teams

STREAMLINING THE TRAINING PROCESS

While it's your responsibility to provide the support, training, and encouragement that each new team member needs to get off to a great start, you might become confused and overwhelmed when many new distributors start at different skill levels and at conflicting times. ***Putting a Quick Start system in place automatically gives new team members the tools, techniques, and business plan to move forward.***

The system will save you time, eliminate confusion on the part of the distributor, and provide a template that your team members can use for their recruits.

The key to creating your Quick Start program is writing scripts and materials that you can use with each new distributor. Developing checklists and handouts to give to your new recruits emphasizes your professionalism. To be able to duplicate your success with every recruit, you must memorize or document the scripts or agendas you use in phone calls and teleconferences. Make it easy for emerging leaders on your team to use your Quick Start system by developing materials that "train the trainers." The more turnkey you make the process, the easier it is to duplicate the success.

The faster your team members get trained and start selling, recruiting, and doing their own training, the faster your business can grow. Solid training leads to confidence. Confidence leads to activity. Activity leads to revenue. Revenue leads to cash in everyone's pockets! This, in turn, leads to even more confidence, activity, and recruits.

YOUR QUICK START CHECKLIST

- **New Distributor Orientation.** Through a phone call or in person, find out your new team member's "Why" for starting her business. Ask about her short-term and long-term goals. Depending on the number of new distributors in your organization each month, you can do this one-on-one or in small groups via conference calls.

- **Plan of Action.** Help her lay the foundation for her plan of action by helping her identify the amount of sales, the number of new recruits, and the total team volume she needs to meet her goals. She can then fill in the action steps she needs to take to fulfill those specific objectives.

- **Successful Start Handout.** Compile a list of steps your new team member can take in her first 24 hours, 7 days, and 30 days of being in business. This will keep her focused, give her a sense of accomplishment and ensure she gets off to a great start. Make sure the list includes specific actions, such as reviewing company audio-video material, using company products regularly, and reviewing the contents of her business kit.

- **New Distributor Training.** Either in person or via teleconference, conduct training for your new distributor on the basics of launching her new business. Most companies provide an outline for new distributor training, so look to your company for guidance. If that resource isn't available, you can find a sample distributor-training outline on http://www.morebuilditbig.com/gifts.asp. Training should cover topics such as getting her first appointment, creating her 30-second commercial, key product education, possible scripting, and the why and how of early sponsoring.

- **New Distributor E-Support.** Create a series of e-mails to send to new team members every Monday. Incorporate brief tips and suggestions for starting their business and include an element of inspiration.

- **Scheduled Success Calls.** Schedule a time for your new team member to call you once a week for her first four weeks in business. Refer to the coaching chapter in this book for guidance on how to conduct effective and efficient coaching calls with your team.

- **Meet and Greet.** Make your new distributor feel a part of her new direct-selling family by ensuring that she attends an upcoming live event where she will meet top leaders and other new distributors. Welcome her on a team conference call or in a printed or electronic newsletter. Above all, let your new distributor know that you see the greatness in her and that she is now a part of a caring community that wants to see her succeed.

Building Your Quick Start Today and Tomorrow

1. Review your current training program against the checklist.

2. If your current program isn't complete, fill in the gaps.

3. Is your system duplicable? Could one of your team members easily use it with her own team members? If not, work on polishing your scripts, handouts, and checklists. ∎

∎ See the Wholeness behind the Hurt

By Shirley Casavant
Discovering the greatness in others

FROM HARMED TO HOPEFUL

As a direct-selling leader, no doubt you are pleased when someone joins your team to improve a life she already loves. But what about the woman whose hopes and dreams have been doused by a lost job, a broken marriage, or the grind of the day-to-day? Many leaders would advise you to say, "Next," and focus your energy on someone who has more capital. *When someone comes to me wanting the big picture of personal and financial growth that I have painted for her, I prefer to say, "Nurture," and help her to be her best.*

Look past a recruit's current circumstances to see the person she truly is, and look for and help her see her strengths. A change in your attitude means you can recognize the potential for both her greatness and the greater potential for change. After all, who is the more grateful for success, someone who has failed little or someone who has failed a lot? Embrace the prospect with challenges and you take part in changing a life forever. Not only will you see her do greater things in her business, you will see her become a more positive influence on the world around her.

∎ **Bring out her story.** Sit with each woman in a private place and just let her tell you about herself. By bringing out the hurts and highs of the past, you can know her strengths and address her weaknesses. Then you can tie it all together, explain why she is where she is at the moment, and then bring her along one step at a time.

- **Address her strengths.** Let her know what she has and show how her strengths can fit in with her business. You can suggest the steps that are necessary to start on the road to personal and financial success, explain all the ways it can be done, and talk to her about how she can do it.

- **Kindle her dreams.** As you build up her attributes while being honest with her about her capabilities, she starts to open up more. Eventually, she begins to dream again, and smiles happen. Then she can build a "game plan," establish her "quest," build her belief in herself, and overcome her hurt with solutions.

- **Make each step attainable.** As each step is met, her self-esteem builds. With the first income from her business, she can take baby steps in creating solutions to her life's challenges. Ultimately, she wants to know she has what it takes to go forward. You are the key to that discovery.

Watching Her Bloom

1. Think of two people on your team whose abilities you may have questioned because of the challenges they face in their lives, and rethink your assumptions.

2. Outline a plan to give them the encouragement and support they need to achieve greatness in their lives.

3. Implement that plan with a willing heart. ■

■ Soar with a Sense of Belonging

By Dr. Shirley B. Carmack

Sharing a lifetime of experience to uplift and inspire

RETENTION WITH HEART

Does it seem your team is plagued by a revolving door? Today, more women are starting direct-selling businesses than at any other time in history. Yet thousands soon give up—and you've likely seen some of them among your recruits.

As I built a network of more than 10,000 distributors in the past 20-plus years, I learned why some stay and some go. ***When your organization has heart, your recruits find the heart to stick with it.*** You nurture your own success as well as theirs when you extend a welcoming hand, offer a comforting hug, and provide an encouraging word in the moment it matters most.

When a prospect meets your team for the first time, you want her to have a wonderful experience of *family*—of being welcomed and embraced by people who care. You want her to develop a sense of belonging that can help her through the challenges ahead.

Where do you learn how to create this sense of community? I often tell the leaders in my organization to *look up* for inspiration! Then I share this deceptively simple story from Dr. Robert McNeish that so beautifully illustrates how leaders can create supportive unity in their teams.

LESSONS FROM THE GEESE

Fact: As each goose flaps its wings, it creates uplift for the birds that follow. By flying in a "V" formation, the whole flock adds 71 percent greater flying range than if each bird flew alone.

Lesson: People who share a common direction and sense of community can get where they are going more quickly and easily because they are traveling on the thrust of one another.

Fact: When the lead goose tires, it rotates back into formation and another goose flies to the point position.

Lesson: It pays to take turns doing the hard tasks and sharing leadership. As with geese, people are interdependent on each other's skills, capabilities, and unique arrangements of gifts, talents, or resources.

Fact: The geese flying in formation honk to encourage those up front to keep up their speed.

Lesson: We need to make sure our honking is encouraging. In groups where there is encouragement, the production is much greater. The power of encouragement (to stand by one's heart or core values and encourage the heart and core of others) is the quality of honking we seek.

Fact: When a goose gets sick, wounded, or shot down, two geese drop out of formation and follow it to help and protect it. They stay with it until it dies or is able to fly again. Then they launch out with another formation or catch up with the flock.

Lesson: If we have as much sense as geese, we will stand by each other in difficult times as well as when we are strong.

Fact: When a goose falls out of formation, it suddenly feels the drag and resistance of flying alone. It quickly moves back into formation to take advantage of the lifting power of the bird immediately in front of it.

Lesson: If we have as much sense as a goose, we stay in formation with those headed where we want to go. We are willing to accept their help and give our help to others.

Flying High with Team Values Today

When you're looking for specifics on how to instill the values of the geese into your team, review the following articles:

1. To build a formation that creates lift for all: "Create Culture to Connect and Motivate Your Team," by Donna Johnson

2. To get someone back in formation: "Reveal Her Re-engaged Vision," by Rysia Crockett

3. To rotate leadership: "Excite Your Team with Interactive Meetings," by Courtney Wright

4. To honk encouragement: All the articles in the coaching chapter

5. To demonstrate loyalty to all team members: "Honor Their Dream," by Dr. Shirley B. Carmack ■

■ Bolster Your Confidence in Conference Calls

By Scott W. Orlinski
Providing services that connect people worldwide

A NEW TOOL FOR TEAM BUILDING

Although you've heard about the effectiveness of conference calling, you might be reluctant to start using the technology. ***Learn how to run conference calls so you can get past your techno-jitters and start using calls to build your team.*** You'll gain a new respect and confidence in yourself for conquering your fears, and a new ability to develop your team and its culture—perhaps even to global proportions.

THE ABCS OF CONFERENCE CALLING

Strategy. Your conference-calling strategy is an action plan that delivers necessary communication to your team in an organized, scheduled fashion. A powerful conference call strategy you can implement might look something like this:

- *Weekly team call.* Include sales data, recognition, and a short training topic by a guest speaker; lasts a maximum of 30 minutes.

- *Weekly recruiting call.* Designed for team members with guests interested in your opportunity; lasts a maximum of 45 minutes.

- *Weekly leadership call.* For top leaders only, this 20-minute call is a great way to get input on organization.

- *Monthly training call.* To help educate team members, this 60-minute call conveys more information and drills down into details.

The right service. Once you have developed your strategy, the next step is to find the right conference call service provider. A deciding factor in selecting a service is whether or not their customer support enables you to talk to a "real" person if you run into a challenge. Service providers' features vary; be sure to evaluate these:

- Flat-rate versus toll-free

- Reservations versus reservationless

- Presentation mode that mutes listeners

- Live call count

- Recording option

- Security features

- Ability to have many participants

- Optional replay line

For additional guidelines on selecting the right conference call service to meet your needs, please visit http://www.morebuilditbig.com/gifts.asp.

Overcoming the techno-jitters. For anyone, the first few conference calls are a bit intimidating. These tips on how to optimize your call's success will help both moderators and team members.

- Have the moderator dial in five minutes early to greet callers, or have background music playing until the moderator arrives. This assures your callers that they are on the right call and prevents them from hanging up.

- Don't use speakerphones, as they pick up background noise and sometimes cause "clipping." If a speakerphone is a necessity, find one that is "full digital duplex," and allows all parties to speak at the same time. To eliminate background noise, use the speakerphone's mute option when no one on your end is speaking into it.

- Don't use cellular or portable phones, as they may cause static or break-ups and result in low-quality recordings. If the moderator is using a cellular phone and is disconnected, all conferees may be disconnected from the line.

- If you are using three-way to connect people on the conference bridge, make sure you call the conference bridge last in your sequence.

- Turn off call waiting to avoid interruptions or beeps.

- Avoid placing your phone on hold, as the background music will play to everyone on the conference call.

- State your name every time you speak, as other participants may not recognize your voice.

- At the start of your call, announce the key command for participants to mute their individual lines.

- Prior to the call, provide guest speakers with any speaking etiquette or conference call rules.

- If a technical issue develops, remain calm and make light of the situation. Know how to reach customer support to resolve the problem.

- Give the moderator personal identification number (PIN) only to your speakers, and change it every few months for security.

Call times. Most company calls are at 9:00 PM and 10:00 PM EST, Sunday through Thursday. For greater attendance, schedule your calls for 7:00 PM EST on a weekday or during a weekend afternoon.

Launching Your Conference Calls Today

Building a community through conference calling will give you a powerfully educated, top performing team that other leaders will envy. In the next 48 hours, put the following steps into action:

1. Develop a conference calling strategy and a call agenda.

2. Select a service provider that meets your needs. For information, search "technology" on the DSWA Web site vendor page.

3. Send your team a conference call schedule and start building your first event! ■

■ Nurture Growth with a Team Library

By Pamela J. Heller

Supporting transformational change in others

THE POWER OF SELF-IMPROVEMENT

Sometimes, the best way to ramp up your business growth is to accelerate your personal growth by using self-improvement books and tapes. Because my continual focus on personal growth heightens my knowledge and motivation, utilizing resource materials has had a sustained impact on my success and my outlook on life.

Often, the distributors who most need to undertake self-development either aren't aware of the resources, don't have the money to purchase the available materials, or don't value themselves enough to invest in the books and CDs. When a direct seller doesn't have access to self-improvement materials or hesitates to use them, she falls behind those who incorporate them into their business strategy.

When you create a lending library for those you lead, you can demonstrate and share the value of self-improvement materials. This promotes a flourishing team culture that views personal growth as a stepping-stone to financial success. Ultimately, you help your team more quickly realize their dreams and reach their goals, which in turn does the same for you.

BIBLIOTHERAPY FOR TEAM MEMBERS

The idea of operating your own lending library may sound overwhelming, but you can begin your library today—with a single book—and grow your collection one book, tape, and CD at a time. Then, when a team member comes to you with a challenge she is experiencing, coach her as you normally would, then end the training by recommending a tape set or book that she can use for further education. If the title is in your library, offer to lend it to her.

To start and maintain your lending library:

1. Keep a master list of all the books, audiotapes, and videos in your collection.

2. Place a library card pocket in the back of each book and on each tape set. (Pockets are available at http://www.winnerinyou.com. Click Products, then Sales Aids, then Lending Library Card Kit.)

3. Establish clear guidelines for checking out material. Require, for example, a completed card for each item; a maximum borrowing period of two weeks; that the borrower maintain the condition of the item; and that only one item be borrowed at a time.

4. Keep the cards of checked-out items in a file box so you know exactly who has each item.

5. Purchase a rolling cart or suitcase to take your most popular selections on the road.

6. Consider mailing items to long-distance team members who are actively building their business. Ship using media mail rates to cut down on expenses.

7. Review the cards from checked-out items every two weeks, and e-mail or call those who have overdue materials.

If you're wondering, "Does everyone return the material?" the answer is, "Very few." This is okay, though—maintaining the library is part of the cost of doing business. If your book or tape set has helped more than one person, then the work has been done. When an item disappears, be sure to replace it, especially if it was one of the more popular resources in your library.

Preparing Your Library

1. Locate all your personal growth books, audiotapes, videos, and CDs for inventory.

2. Using a spreadsheet or paper and pen, list all of your material by title and author.

3. Order library card pockets to help you track the items. ∎

∎ Excite Your Team with Interactive Meetings

By Courtney Wright
Taking trainings to the next level

MORE THAN INFORMATION DISPENSERS

Team meetings are a wonderful way to recognize the efforts of team members, celebrate successes, foster relationships, and provide training. Team members come to get new ideas to incorporate into their businesses and their lives as well as to share ideas of their own. A challenge arises when you have so much information to share that you start to seem like a talking head rather than a leader. *Your meetings can take on new life when you make them more interactive, putting the focus on* **their learning** *rather than* **your teaching.** The direct benefit to you is that your team will leave your meetings with internalized learning and inspiration to act.

CUTTING OFF THE TALKING HEAD

Education is the core of the meeting so it's important to choose topics that address the needs of your organization and individual team members. Active learning is retained learning. Listed below are tried-and-true exercises that involve your team members and make your meetings more exciting:

- *Discussion groups.* Everyone loves to share their ideas but it can sometimes be nerve-wracking to do so in front of a large group. Small discussion groups ensure that each person's voice is heard in a safe environment. Divide team members into smaller groups, have them select a team reporter, and work on a specific topic. After a period of time, reporters share their group's findings with the rest of the meeting attendees. One topic for example is to discuss ways to increase sales at shows.

- *Demonstrations.* Let someone else be a star! Have team members showcase what they do best. Spotlight their expertise to benefit your entire organization. Choose a team member to present her sales demonstration to the group. Let team members take turns explaining the benefits or special features of highlighted products. Ask a strong recruiter to demonstrate how to close a deal. Giving a demonstration cements her skills while enhancing team learning and providing exceptional recognition.

- *Role-playing.* Provide opportunities for everybody to literally "get into the act." Use role-playing to simulate a real-life situation. Mistakes can be made in a safe environment and positive feedback can be given for improvement. A few team members can perform a role-play, or the entire group can be divided into pairs to play roles. Offer a script to follow or a situation to act out. Ask meeting attendees to perform a mock sponsoring interview, follow a hostess coaching script, or practice making reorder calls. It's a proven fact that we learn best by doing, and this type of exercise is a great way to hone team members' skills.

- *Brainstorming.* Most challenges are not solved by the first thought that comes along. Getting the best solution requires considering many possible solutions. In brainstorming, the group is given a challenge or issue and comes up with any ideas related to the topic—no matter how wild a suggestion may sound. All ideas are recorded, and evaluated only after the brainstorming is complete. Give your team a specific challenge and let them come up with a list of solutions. One challenge could be: "You haven't held any shows yet this month but there is still one week left. What can you do to book and hold four shows in that week?"

- *Quizzes and lists.* Use questioning techniques in the form of oral or written quizzes to test your team members' knowledge or to examine a new product or company policy. *Make sure that you do this in a fun and informal manner and that nobody feels like they are in school taking a test.* For example, you could have them list the top ten features of a new product. You could also examine their understanding of the hostess incentive program by asking true and false questions.

Your goal for each meeting should be for your team members to leave feeling inspired, motivated, and more knowledgeable than when they arrived. With a little advance planning you can make sure that your meetings are interactive events that inform and excite your team members and motivate them to take action.

Adding Interaction in the Next 48 Hours

1. Select a training topic for your next team meeting.

2. Choose and plan two interactive exercises to make learning fun and exciting.

   In the weeks following the meeting, seek feedback from team members and discover if they are putting what they've learned into practice. ■

■ Fill Your Pipeline with Value-Driven Events

By Ruth Van Buren
Traveling the world with a message of financial freedom

GIVING AWAY VALUE TO COLLECT GOLD

When you begin your direct-selling business, it's easy to think of people to call about your new product and opportunity. But after you've contacted everyone on your initial list, you have a new challenge: "How do I find new prospects?"

Over the years I've found my best business builder is to **get people to an event where they learn and take away value.** These events expand my network into the community, enhance my reputation and credibility, and ultimately create more leads. Customers and prospects are a natural result of value-driven events.

The key to success is to start by offering *value-driven* events, which first and foremost offer valuable education to the participants. Pinpoint a niche market for your product, then identify a topic that interests its members. For example, you could offer:

- A "Health Issues" workshop that includes a discussion of supplements

- A "how to" class for a craft or hobby, featuring your special supplies

- A makeover event where guests are transformed with your products

- A child-rearing class for parents featuring educational toys as the focal point

- A stress-reduction retreat presenting topics of breathing and meditation, as well as stress-reducing products

Make sure that you and perhaps a few associates can address the topic in a half-day workshop.

After you've hosted enough value-driven events, you'll have enough customers with interest in your business that you can host a *recruitment-driven* event, such as a seminar "For Women Only" that shows them the many benefits of having a business in their own home.

GROWING WITH VALUE-DRIVEN EVENTS

It's easiest to start with something simple that you can handle yourself.

- Look for an opportunity in your community to do a seminar. Investigate church groups, clubs, school groups, women's groups, and so on.

- Find a location that is convenient and centrally located to your target market.

- Create a flier and invite local people in the community to attend. Get information about your event into any newsletters, Web sites, or regular e-mails published by your host group.

- Make the seminars fun, interesting, and even exciting by having your associates present different segments of the seminar.

To reach even more deeply into your community, you can create an event featuring a local expert or present to a local business. As your network grows, you'll have the opportunity to create more sophisticated events. You can approach people who are successful in a profession related to your market about becoming a distributor in your business and cross-marketing your products in their existing events. If they are not doing events, create events together to serve their clientele.

Today's Action for Your Next Event

1. If you are just starting out, think of a valuable topic you'd enjoy presenting to your target market. Identify three community groups who would be interested and contact them.

2. If you have a team, ask the members what kind of event they'd enjoy creating to educate and attract prospects.

3. If you have a large organization or are well connected in your community, look and see who is a center of influence. Speak with them about cross-marketing your product in their events and seminars. ■

■ Support and Expand Your Long-Distance Team

By Krystal Kitchens Grant
Reaching across the miles to educate and uplift

TAPPING INTO THE POWER OF THE INTERNET

Many direct-sales companies are now embracing the global economy created by the Internet, and are encouraging their representatives to recruit nationally or even internationally. This freedom opens many exciting opportunities for finding new recruits, but leaves prospects hesitant to commit without a nearby support system and leaves sponsors with the challenge of supporting long-distance team members. ***By learning about and taking advantage of Internet technology and online services, you can overcome the difficulties posed by geographic distances.*** In addition, by demonstrating to prospective local recruits that you offer a complete support system to long-distance members, you may find more of them ready to join your team.

ACQUIRING THE TOOLS OF THE TRADE

- E-mail is the most efficient communication tool available, as it provides cost-free, nearly instant delivery of information, documents, and photographs. Most Internet service providers offer free accounts, as does Yahoo! (http://www.yahoo.com) and other free online services.

- Instant Messaging (IM) programs offer your team members a way to contact you for quick answers whenever you're online. It's also a great method for brainstorming, and by informally chatting with team members, you develop a more personal rapport than through e-mail. America Online (http://www.aim.com) offers free IM, as do other online services.

- Newsletters are a great way to communicate with your team by summarizing updates and information and providing recognitions on a weekly or monthly basis. Newsletters can be hosted on a Web site or distributed to team members via private e-mail. Constant Contact (http://www.constantcontact.com) offers a great tool to create professional-looking newsletters—even if you don't have Web design skills.

- Consider creating an online group to provide your team members with a sense of community. Yahoo! (http://groups.yahoo.com) offers free groups that are perfect for supporting your team. Groups consist of e-mail lists, where each person's e-mail is sent to all members on the list, so group discussions can be held via e-mail. Each group has a pseudo-Web site, where photos, databases, polls, files, links, a calendar, message archives, and more can be stored and accessed only by group members.

■ Team members can attend live "training chats" from the comfort of home—no need to hire a sitter or drive long distances. In a chat room, attendees can converse in "real time," asking questions, getting answers, and brainstorming. For those unable to attend, training chat transcripts can be saved and uploaded, e-mailed, or archived, so that all team members can receive the training benefits. Chatzy.com (http://www.chatzy.com) offers free chat rooms for small groups, and upgrades are available for a reasonable fee.

Keep in mind that, while it's possible to provide quality support via the Internet, nothing takes the place of voice-to-voice and face-to-face interaction. It's important to continue holding regularly scheduled coaching calls with each team member. As a long-distance team leader, you should plan to attend your company's national convention, and should strongly encourage your team members to attend as well. Use the opportunity to personally connect with each member and to hold meetings that sustain your long-distance team.

Ready, Set, Surf!

Today and tomorrow complete as many of these tasks as you can, then add the rest to your calendar:

1. Create a separate e-mail address that you only distribute to team members. Create a subfolder in your e-mail program to store all of your team-related e-mail so that you can find messages quickly. Commit to responding to your team's e-mail as soon as you log on each day.

2. Create a free Yahoo! group for your team to call home. Upload every helpful file, article, or document you have into the shared files section. Add useful links to the links section. Personalize group settings for your team. Then send an

invitation to join the group to every person in your
organization.

3. Decide upon a newsletter format and a date to publish or
   send the newsletter each month, then schedule time to
   gather information to include in your first issue.

4. Pull out your calendar and schedule an online training for
   your team. Plan for a general question and answer session,
   and to gather requests for specific training topics.

5. Sign up for a free Instant Messaging service. Choose a screen
   name and install the software on your desktop. Share your
   screen name with your team members, and invite them to
   contact you when they see you online. Make a commitment to
   sign on to this program whenever you are on the Internet. ▪

▪ Create Culture to Connect and Motivate Your Team

By Donna Johnson

Creating a sense of family where everyone is welcome

SHEPHERDING THE FLOCK

In the beginning, every new recruit feels lost and alone on the
front line and unconnected to your company. ***By creating a culture
for your organization that's appropriate for its level, you can let your
new team member know that she might be in business for herself, but
that she is not in business by herself.*** She feels connected more quickly,
and is inspired and motivated to advance through the levels as your
organization grows. Plus, watching the bonding, cooperation, integrity, and teaming within your organization is a wonderfully satisfying
reward.

You don't need to wait until you're in a top position to start creating an organizational culture. Always build a bridge to your upline, sideline, team, and company. For instance, when you start sponsoring, you can say:

> Mary, not only are you a part of (*your company name*), but you are a part of my team, and I'm so excited that as a district manager, I'm building toward a VP position. You're also a part of the Great Harvest Region, and the Spirit Wings Nation. You are in business for yourself, but not by yourself. Our job is to help you reach your goals!
>
> I've created a list for you that includes our team's calls, events, incentives, and contact information. Let's three-way to our upline. I've told them about you, and they are anxious to meet you!

Imagine how connected your recruit would feel if your welcome included this script!

CREATING TRADITIONS

Regardless of your leadership level, you can contribute your own traditions to your organizational culture that are appropriate to the size of your team and to your income.

Entry-Level Leader

- Provide each new team member with a checklist that outlines steps she can take in the first two weeks to get her on the road to success.

- Create a name for your team, and then use your team name in all your communication to team members.

- Create other cultural elements for your team: pick a team color; choose a team motto; think of a unique name for each meeting you hold on a regular basis; or come up with a team mascot.

- Host a popcorn and movie night for your team, and show your company's training video.

- Every Monday morning, hold a "meet and greet" over coffee for your team and their prospects.

- Coordinate a monthly no-host dinner at a local restaurant for your team members and their spouses.

- Be an encourager, and send out a weekly e-mail or named news-letter touting team members' successes and including words of inspiration and advice.

Experienced Leader

- Incorporate your team name into items such as magnets, Post-its, and other inexpensive motivational giveaways for your team members.

- Select a monthly theme, such as "service" or "integrity"; then at month's end, get the team together so each member can share how she incorporated the theme into her life and business.

- Hold a monthly session with leaders to give them a preview of new materials, company announcements, and exciting news from your upline.

- Organize a monthly outing for leaders and their families, such as a picnic at the park, a trip to the zoo, or a swim party.

Regional Leader

- Create a Web site that includes your region's name, mission, and logo; depending on your Internet Service Providor, you may be able to offer members team e-mail accounts, with ad-dresses using *TeamMember@RegionName.com*.

- Send a letter to every new recruit, welcoming her to your team.

- Create long-distance connections with a *Leader's Master Mind Call*—a regularly scheduled teleconference where your leaders can brainstorm ways to motivate their team members, address a common challenge, and keep themselves and their teams moving forward.

- Have each leader hold a fundraising event with her team to raise money for a worthy cause.

National Leader

- Host an annual weekend recognition retreat for team members who have achieved specific goals.

- Host a multiday annual event for team members and their families to experience training and fellowship.

Culture Club

In the next 48 hours:

1. Develop a list of elements that you can use to create an organization culture appropriate to your leadership level.

2. Create a time line for implementing your organizational culture.

3. Research resources that you'll need in order to create giveaways, recognitions, and so on. ■

9

Success Strategies

*T*he success you achieve in life and in business is in direct proportion to the pace at which you are learning and growing!

The contributors to this chapter embody the principle that personal and professional growth leads to excellence and achievement. Although they are not immune to life's pitfalls and the weaknesses of human nature, each leader navigates the waters of life with assuredness and confidence. They have developed the mindsets, habits, and strategies that manifest as success in their lives and their businesses.

Like the final chapter of the same name in *Build It Big*, these insights are the icing on the cake. Appreciate and implement the specific advice each leader shares, but go further and benefit from their commitment to personal growth and the positive results it brings. They serve as a shining example of the best in our profession—leaders who are consistently open to learning, who see potential teachers in everyone they meet, and who suffuse their businesses with a sense of purpose and joy.

As you allow the presented wisdom to seep in, renew your commitment to self-development, learning, and personal growth. As you continue on your journey, you are sure to achieve your dreams.

■ Connect One-to-Many with a Newsletter

By Sharon Davidson-Unkefer
Million-dollar earner who is leading the way

BUILD YOUR "KNOW, LIKE, TRUST" FACTOR

Frequent and heartfelt communication is one of the keys to being an effective and inspiring leader. But as your team spreads throughout the country and maybe even the world, you can no longer communicate one-on-one as frequently as you'd like. *To prevent communication breakdown, produce a regular newsletter for your team that helps them grow from knowing you, to liking you, to trusting you, and to feeling a part of your family.* In the traditional sales world, they call this the "know, like, and trust" factor. You'll have better communication, strong connections, and a sense of family that inspires your team members to stay the course and grow their businesses.

THE ART OF THE NEWSLETTER

Whether you lead a team of 12 or 12,000, a monthly newsletter is a simple and effective means for you to communicate one-to-many with your organization. It offers an opportunity to share your heart, celebrate your team members' successes, and educate and inspire others to the top. You don't have to have any special talents or be an exceptional writer (you can get help with that) to produce a newsletter. What you do need is a desire to make a difference and a willingness to learn a few techniques.

An effective newsletter incorporates some or all of the following components:

1. *A personal message from you.* Make your message heartfelt and genuine to set the tone of family and celebration.

2. *An inspiring theme and quote.* Share something that is timely that has helped you continue toward your vision.

3. *An inspirational message around your central theme.* This is the message they will carry with them for weeks, so be sure to make it count!

4. *Edification of the profession, your company, and the corporate team.* Never miss an opportunity to instill pride in your distributors, pride in the profession, pride in your company, and pride in your products.

5. *Product testimonials that educate and inspire.* These are particularly important for new distributors, who may not have collected their own success stories to share as they sell and sponsor.

6. *Distributor recognition.* Put the spotlight on your team, crosslink, or anyone who is accomplishing great things. Look for ways to celebrate team triumphs, such as reaching a quarterly volume goal or achieving 100 percent attendance at a company-sponsored event. When possible, recognize in story form so others can take the story and use it.

7. *Calendar of events.* Promote upcoming local, regional, and national events, complete with dates, places, contact names, and phone numbers. Include your travel itinerary as well, so distributors can meet you when you are visiting a nearby city.

If you are sending your newsletter via e-mail, recipients might forward it to friends and prospects anywhere in the world! Make sure their first impression of you, your team, and your company is a positive one by following these simple tips:

■ **Keep it short and sweet.** People will lose interest if your newsletter is too long. The optimal length is one to four typewritten pages.

■ **Save time, paper, and hassles with an electronic newsletter.** With technology, you can connect with your entire organization with the click of your mouse. Learn the basics of e-mail etiquette, such as remembering to BCC (blind copy) all of the recipients and avoiding the use of ALL CAPS (which signifies shouting).

■ **Keep it professional.** In addition to making sure your content is 100 percent accurate, have a proofreader check your writing. Select a layout that is easy to read, with good size margins and adequate white space. Finally, separate sections with colorful headings and include quality images when appropriate.

Do your best to guide and inspire your readers—make your newsletters positive, thought provoking, and informative. When you openly share your successful business-building strategies, you foster a positive environment for your team and benefit your company, your profession, and perhaps the spirit of community in ways you might never know.

Commit to Connect

1. Decide that you are going to create a regular communication tool for your team.

2. Begin a hanging file folder or create a Word document where, throughout the month as you think of it, you place ideas for content. When it comes time to compile your newsletter, you will already have a head start.

3. Take the leap. Your first few newsletters will be simple, but heartfelt. As you grow as a leader, your newsletter will get easier and better. For now, just enjoy the opportunity to connect! ■

■ Automate Your Success with Heartfelt Handouts

By Susan Raab
Champion of the Cause for Clear

CLONING YOURSELF ON PAPER

How many times have you given someone a handout only to have her ask you the very same questions the handout was supposed to answer? She didn't read it, did she?

You create a handout hoping it will spread the news without your being there. You sit at your computer with the information about your event, your training, or your business opportunity. With so many options—fonts, sizes, and clip art—how do you know which to choose? When people barrage you with questions the handout was supposed to answer, you might wonder if you made the right choices, or why you bothered with the handout at all.

People *do* read, but they're jaded by today's information glut. ***Make your handouts resonate with your readers' values and you'll capture their attention.*** They'll be intrigued and engaged, more likely to retain what they've read and take action on it. Plus, you'll improve your reputation for professionalism to boot. Here's how to create your vision for a handout that touches your reader's heart as surely as if you were holding her hand.

VALUES THAT FUEL VISION

Answer these questions to determine *what value* your content offers your reader. You might come up with responses like the sample answers below when you're creating a handout for someone who's interested in your business opportunity.

1. What does your content do for your reader *immediately*? Try to answer in eight words or less. *"Makes it easy to decide to join my team."*

2. What about this information turns your reader on and makes a connection with her? *"That she can achieve her dream in a step-by-step, manageable way with my support for her learning and growth."*

3. How can you measure the value the content offers your reader? *"It gets her off to a quick, smooth start."*

Answer these questions to discover how best to *communicate* that value.

4. What's most likely to limit your reader's attention while she's reading? *"Family commitments, her concerns about her commitments and her time."*

5. What are your reader's heartfelt goals for the outcome of reading the content? *"To be taken seriously and to look smart and capable. To reinforce her decision to join even after she's 'cooled off.'"*

With these answers as a guideline, you can make better choices about what to put in the handout.

- Identify *who* you are talking to, so she will feel smart about not wasting her time. *"Thank you for your interest in joining my company."*

- Share your intent with the reader. *"This information makes it easy to decide to join us."*

- Help her reach her *goal* of deciding to join by showing her that it is a smart business decision. No frills—just realistic, objective nuts and bolts.

- Make it *easy to read* in a busy environment by using bullet points and headings instead of paragraphs.

- Build her *confidence* by reminding her of the unique support you offer her, as well as your company's support.

- Make it *heartfelt* by sharing your values—your dream for everyone on your team.

- Keep her motivated by reminding her of the benefits of joining. *"See how having your own business is the smart choice?"*

- Get her off to *a good start* by giving step-by-step instructions for what to do next.

With this kind of plan, you'll find a handout comes together more quickly, and you'll distribute it with more confidence, knowing it reflects your values as well as your reader's.

Today's Actions for Heartfelt Handouts

While many handouts are one-time promotions, others become part of your repeatable success system. When you take the time to think through and polish these handouts, you'll benefit for years: first, when you give it to your own prospects, and later, when your team members use it to build their own organizations.

1. Review the publications you distribute to more than five people. Look at your e-mail newsletters as well as posters, recruiting and sales handouts, and training materials.

2. Pick the three that are most important to building your repeatable success system.

3. For the most important publication, ask yourself the five *what* and *how* questions. Identify ways to improve the publication before you send it out again.

4. Schedule time to make those improvements, as well as to review and improve the other two publications. ■

■ Discover DISC for New Communication Power

By Dr. Robert A. Rohm
Personality Plus Creator

VISIT HER PERSONALITY PLACE

Just as it's easier to talk to your friend face-to-face than from across a gymnasium, it's easier to get your message across to her when you communicate in her personality style. For you to use her communication style, you must first understand yours, be able to recognize hers, and understand that you can communicate in her style without losing your own.

Most people have predictable patterns of behavior and specific personality types. There are four basic personality types, also known as temperaments. *Understanding your friend's personality type allows you to communicate in her style.*

The overriding benefit to communicating with your friend in her style is that she will understand your message more readily. Understanding your message means that she can align with you more quickly and easily, as long as she agrees with your point of view or desires.

DIVE INTO D-I-S-C

The four personality types are like four quarters of a pie. Before looking at each of the four quarters, let's look at the pie in two halves: **outgoing** and **reserved.** Think of it this way: Some people are more outgoing, while others are more reserved.

There is another way to divide the pie. It can be divided into *task-oriented* and *people-oriented.* Some people are more task-oriented, and some are more relationship-oriented.

Outgoing people are more active and optimistic. Reserved types are more passive and careful. One type is not better than the other. Both types of behavior are needed, and both are important. Outgoing types

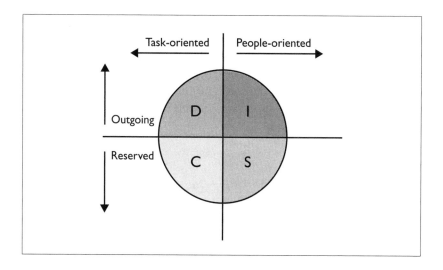

need to learn how to be more steady and cautious. Reserved types need to learn how to be more dominant and inspiring.

Task-oriented types need to learn to relate better to others and become more interactive and sharing. People-oriented individuals need to learn to be more focused on doing tasks or things. They need to be more directing and correcting.

Now, we can look at the pie divided into four quarters. We can visualize the four parts: *D, I, S,* and *C.* Those people who are predominately outgoing and task-oriented we say are "*D*" types. Those who are predominately outgoing and people-oriented are "*I*" types. Those who are predominately reserved and people-oriented are "*S*" types. Those who are predominately reserved and task-oriented are "*C*" types.

- The "*D*" type can be described with words such as dominant, direct, demanding, decisive, determined, and doer.

- The "*I*" type can be described with words like inspiring, influencing, inducing, interactive, impressive, and interested in people.

- The "*S*" type can be described as supportive, steady, stable, sweet, sensitive, and status quo.

- The "*C*" type can be described with words like cautious, calculating, competent, consistent, contemplative, and careful.

By now, you have probably thought, "I feel like I have some of all these traits. I have some D–I–S–C in me." Exactly! You are a unique blend of these four traits. Each of us is "wired" differently. Some traits are more dominant in us than others. Research shows that in about 80 percent of the general population, people have at least two areas that tend to dominate their personality style, while the other two areas are less dominant.

Note that no one is purely a "*D*" or an "*I*" or an "*S*" or a "*C*." Everyone is a unique blend of these four types. If someone says that she is an "*I* / *D*" personality blend, that means that she is highest in the traits of the "*I*" (inspiring type), and that she is next highest in the traits of the "*D*" (dominant type). This, of course, is true of the other traits, as well.

Put the Pieces Together

In the next 48 hours, be aware of personality styles:

1. Spend some time to really understand the DISC system—the dominant characteristics of each personality style.

2. Notice the behavior of those around you during the next two days, and try to identify dominant and subdominant behaviors.

3. Select two family members and two team members and identify the dominant or secondary style they exhibit. ■

■ Master the Obi-Wan Approach

By Mark Victor Hansen
The Ambassador of Possibilities

ACTING "AS IF" UNTIL YOUR GOALS ARE ACCOMPLISHED

Just because you set a goal does not mean you are going to achieve it. Why? Because successful individuals—winners—do things that separate them from simple goal setters: They believe, feel, speak and act "as if" what they want is already happening.

I call this acting "as if" style the "Obi-Wan Approach." You remember Obi-Wan Kenobi. He's the top-notch Jedi from the *Star Wars* movies, one of Luke Skywalker's teachers—a master of acting "as if." He displays this mastery brilliantly in one scene from the original *Star Wars*. Obi-Wan and Luke, who are smuggling secret plans hidden in one of their robots, are challenged by a storm trooper (one of the bad-guy police) when they approach a town. With complete confidence, Obi-Wan tells him, "These are not the droids you're looking for." The storm trooper repeats, "These are not the droids we're looking for," and lets them enter the spaceport. Other *Star Wars* characters call this a "Jedi Mind Trick." But it's really not a trick—it's the convincing of one's *own* mind to bring about a certain result. Obi-Wan was not *hoping* the storm trooper wouldn't recognize the droids; he was *convinced* he would not. He shows how complete control of one's thinking can manifest itself into physical form.

PUT ON YOUR JEDI ROBE

When it comes right down to it, the power to begin and the power to win come from within. ***You must think, speak, and act as if your goals have already been accomplished.*** When you master these disciplines, you'll have laser-beam focus and impenetrable faith that everything you want is already yours.

Think "As If!" To put your mind to work, you must ask your higher power to give you your heart's desire. But ask only once. Asking for the same thing over and over shows a lack of faith. All that should follow your request is vigilant belief that you are—not *will be* but *are!*—receiving what you asked for. Believe and be thankful that it is coming to pass. Remember: Your prayer has already been answered—your thinking makes it so.

Speak "As If!" Words have power. You are merely announcing your future experience in advance. If this didn't work, companies wouldn't spend billions of dollars a year on marketing and press releases, and politicians wouldn't have speechwriters. Everything we say has a mental and a physical impact on the world around us. So speak with conviction and enthusiasm. Create self-fulfilling prophecies every time you open your mouth!

Act "As If!" In the second *Star Wars* movie, when Jedi Master Yoda confronts Luke about his inability to complete a task, Luke tells him he is "trying." Yoda replies: "Do! Or do not. There is no try." Trying is another word for "maybe" or "hoping." Yoda knew the bottom line: You either accomplish something or you don't. You either believe you will succeed or you don't. There is no in between. Maybe you're saying, "But what if I want to close my first sale? I've never done it before, so I can't succeed immediately. Does that mean I'm a failure?" *Absolutely not!* If you ask for the order and get a No, you have still succeeded. In the beginning, chances are that you'll be a lousy closer, but you *are* closing. You're not *trying* to close. The more closing you do, the better you'll get.

USE THE FORCE, YOUNG JEDI!

Thinking, speaking, and acting "as if" your goals are already accomplished are the factors that span the divide between success and failure. First, you must truly believe in your heart that you not only deserve everything you want, but that it is already yours. If people don't believe in you and tell you No a million times, and *you* still believe that you can accomplish your goals, those naysayers don't have a chance in the world of stopping your dreams.

You must speak *only* of success and prosperity. Negative words attract negativity from mental, verbal, and physical realms. You must demonstrate that you believe by behaving "as if" your wishes have become a reality. By combining all of the elements of the "Obi-Wan Approach" you show that you have faith in God, faith in yourself, and faith that you will see all of your dreams come true.

■ Spell Your Image P-r-o-f-e-s-s-i-o-n-a-l

By Marion Gellatly, AICI, CIM
Director of the DSWA Image Center

LOST OPPORTUNITIES

If you've ever donned a set of sweats to run to the store, apologized to a client or team member about the messiness of your workspace, or rummaged through your purse to locate a business card, you're probably missing out on business opportunities. An important component of success in today's direct-selling industry is conveying your professionalism via your image. *Projecting a professional image requires that you are ready to conduct business—anywhere, any time—with the right attitude, behavior, communication, and appearance.* Developing your image is a key marketing strategy that produces immediate results.

RECOGNIZING AND REALIZING PROFESSIONALISM

Visualize the "professional" you aspire to be. Identify someone in your company who you admire. She probably has qualities, traits, and a uniqueness that convey her professionalism and success. Observe how she behaves, how she conducts business, how she communicates, and how she treats others. In all likelihood, what sets her apart is:

- Her "can do" attitude

- Her clear communication

- Her impeccable wardrobe and grooming

- Her courtesy and integrity

Developing Attitude

In face-to-face situations, your attitude precedes you. A "can do" attitude will have a positive impact on your interactions with others and will lead you to believe in yourself and your abilities.

- Smile, extend your hand, make eye contact, and speak in a friendly tone.

- Adopt useful attitudes, such as warmth, enthusiasm, confidence, resourcefulness, and helpfulness.

- Avoid negative attitudes and behaviors, such as complaining, hostility, rudeness, superiority to people in lesser positions, anger, and pessimism.

Communicating Clearly

Because one of the most important communication tools for a direct seller is the telephone, your answering technique conveys an image of both you and your company. View every call you make and receive as an opportunity to build good public relations.

- Invest in a dedicated phone line for your business or use separate voice mailboxes to differentiate family calls from business calls.

- Answer your business phone with your full name and a voice that "smiles."

- Only answer your phone when you have time to talk; otherwise, let the call go to voice mail.

- Don't chew gum, eat, or drink while on the phone.

- Keep your business cards in a case and carry them with you at all times.

Polishing Your Visual Image

Like it or not, people are often judged by their appearance. A book *is* judged by its cover, a home *is* judged by its curb appeal, and you *are* judged by your dress and grooming.

- Emphasize quality over quantity in your clothing purchases.

- Base your business wardrobe on classic pieces of clothing.

- Flatter your body type.

- Maintain your shoes and keep them scuff-free.

- Keep your nails reasonably short and well manicured.

- Keep your hair clean and your hairstyle updated.

- Wear little or no fragrance.

Practicing Courtesy and Integrity

How you behave, how you treat others, and how you conduct your business reflects on your professionalism and on the professionalism of the direct-selling industry.

- If you commit to deliver your product by a certain date, make sure it happens. If there's an unavoidable delay, let your customer know about it as soon as you know.

- A token of appreciation sets you apart as a professional, so send notes of thanks to your customers.

- Organize your workspace before a meeting or a customer visit to send a positive message that you are in control of your business.

- Turn your cell phone off if you're in a meeting or in a public area where it will disturb others.

- Learn how to make proper introductions and use that skill regularly.

- When being introduced or introducing yourself, stand up and initiate a handshake with your thumb up and out.

- Attach your nametag on your right shoulder when networking or in a meeting.

Finally, remember that a professional image is not something that's acquired or worn like an article of clothing. Developing it is a process that evolves over time.

Your Image Review for Today

1. Think of someone from your upline who can be a role model of professionalism and pinpoint the qualities that set her apart.

2. Honestly assess your attitude, communication, appearance, manners, and integrity.

3. Choose one item to work on from each evaluation area. ■

■ Plug Your Energy Drains

By Jennie England, PCC, CPCC
Co-creator of the DSWA's Principle-Centered Coaching program

RECAPTURING THE FREEDOM OF ACCOMPLISHMENT

Are you feeling a drain of energy from those unfinished tasks? How about the thank-you note to the hostess of your last party or the follow-up phone call to your potential new recruit? What about the piles of paper that have accumulated in your office and stare at you each day? Or the ten e-mails in your "To Be Answered" file that you separated out so you wouldn't lose track of them and intended to answer them when you had more time? The truth is, our hectic lives are filled with too many obligations, stresses, and pieces of unfinished business. We feel constantly behind, frustrated, overwhelmed, and disempowered. *You can recapture the energy you spend keeping track of the things you "should" do by taking care of the tasks or eliminating them altogether.* In doing so, you'll feel a sense of pride, peace, and well-being—and, of course, energy!

We pay a heavy price for procrastination—the price of drained energy! We put tasks on the back burner and try to forget them. But do we? Most often, they lurk in the back of our minds, robbing us of our sense of peace, accomplishment, and especially our energy to do the things we love.

DISCARDING THAT DEPLETION

The ironic thing about tasks that drain your energy is that, when you actually write that thank-you note, you find it takes a maximum of ten minutes. And you wonder why you wasted so much valuable time and energy avoiding it.

The key to plugging your energy drain is changing your perception. When facing piles of paper, don't think of the piles. Instead, think of spending 15 minutes to make a dent in one of the piles. It's amazing how much difference 15 minutes a day for a week can make. Because getting started is the hardest part, 15 minutes sounds manageable and can motivate you into action. Anytime a task looks too big, just take a bite of it and often it turns into a meal. Voilà—the pile is gone!

If the e-mails are filed out of sight, but not out of mind, answer two a day to unload your self-imposed burden. Then, schedule a daily time to handle the e-mail that needs more than a two- to five-minute response. Schedule a time in your daybook when things are as quiet as they get and make those phone calls that you're prone to put off. You can also set a time limit for each call and stick to it. Soon, you will be caught up. Give yourself a well-earned reward!

To help you with your motivation, remember that there is a certain positive energy that surrounds a task when it first needs our attention. For instance, when a gift is first received, your grateful energy is strong and can support you in responding with a quick thank-you note. This energy is then expressed in the note you write, which makes it more alive and personal. If you don't respond in the moment, the empowering energy evaporates as time goes by, the task becomes more of a burden, and then finally a drain on your energy.

Clearing Your Drains Today and Tomorrow

If you've got some undone tasks that you know have become drains on your energy, try the following steps to catch up:

1. List all the energy drains you have in your life. You may want to put them into categories, such as business, personal, family, and home. Prioritize the categories and the energy drains within each category. Estimate the amount of time it will take to complete each energy drain. Allow a little more time than you first estimate to ensure your success in eliminating it.

2. Determine the amount of time you can spend on clearing your energy drains each week, then calendar a time or times for clearing the drains.

3. Enjoy the relief and sense of accomplishment that you feel by creating the means to clear your energy drains. For fun, make a list of some of the things you might want to do with your newfound energy! Perhaps you'd like to take some inspiring walks in nature, do some motivational reading, or spend more time with your family. ■

■ Honor Your Cause, Courage, and Commitment

By Lora Enabnit
Courageously caring and sharing

CHUGGING TO SUCCESS

Like the "Little Engine That Could," you've been working your business and climbing up the mountain day after day, week after week, month after month. You've had your share of successes, yet one day you find that you can't move another step forward. Your energy to keep going up the mountain falters, fear blocks you, or your attention wavers. ***By developing and strengthening three critical characteristics—cause, courage, and commitment—your personal growth and the success of your business will become consistent and natural.*** When that happens, you're better equipped to continue chugging along, letting nothing get in the way of making your vision a reality.

A Cause Based in Passion

What does a lack of passion look like in your business? You succumb to distractions and your work becomes less of a priority. Your business may seem tedious and boring. Passion provides the fuel to keep going because its fulfillment gives ever-fresh satisfaction to your soul. Passion is crucial to your long-term success, because to keep going, you sometimes need motivation from a deep source.

Courage with a Purpose

What does a lack of purpose look like in your business? You let your fear prevent you from sponsoring your first person, offering the business opportunity to a relative for whom it would be a perfect fit, or speaking in public. Purpose helps you take action in spite of your fears. It governs your priorities, and when you focus and learn about your top priorities, you gain courage to take risks. The willingness to take risks is critical to fulfill your commitments to your cause.

Commitment with Clarity

What does a lack of commitment look like in your business? You leave work undone, you don't follow up with your customers or follow through with your upline, and you miss opportunities for advancement and success. Commitment expresses our passion and purpose in the world because it requires *action*. Action arising out of commitment is what it takes to make your dreams for prosperity come true.

Climbing the Mountain

1. **Cause:** Write down three of the passions that drive your desire to be successful. This will be your cause.

2. **Courage:** Write down three of the fears that prevent you from taking action. Write down strategies to overcome those fears. Implement those courageous strategies and fulfill your cause.

3. **Commitment:** Write down three ways in which you fulfill your commitments to your business. Write down three ways in which you do not. Congratulate yourself on those you fulfill and commit to changing those you do not. This is your path to prosperity. ■

■ You Are the Message

By Beth Jacobs
Leading with calm, collected confidence

CALMING THE STORM

As you juggle many roles and fill the needs of everyone from your family members to your team members, it can feel as though the winds of chaos are swirling around you. Just when you feel you can't handle one more challenge, another is laid at your feet. How do you respond? Do you take a deep breath and calmly address the problem? Or, do you feed the storm by tensing your body, rushing into a meeting, and venting your frustrations to a team member? If you succumb to the chaos and express overwhelm to your team member, do you notice how uncomfortable she becomes? When you appear rushed and overwhelmed, you undermine your team's confidence in you and convey the message that leadership brings chaos into one's life. *In contrast, when you maintain a sense of calm confidence, no matter what the challenge, you earn the confidence of your team.* In the process, you free others to do their best, unfettered by upset and uncertainty. You also inspire others to follow in your footsteps and aspire to leadership.

REVEALING YOUR FOUNDATION

I've learned that the easier I make leadership look, the more my team members want to follow in my footsteps. The truth is, I don't always feel centered and at peace, but I do my best to project an image of calm, collected confidence. You can do the same.

Feeling Confident

Inward poise is one of the secrets of personal magnetism. Developing a calm center is largely a matter of focusing your concentration on your long-term goals and vision, and having the faith and confidence that you will achieve them. When you can keep an unwavering eye on the big picture, the challenges you meet along the way remain in perspective. You can then employ patience and flexibility to create an environment where solutions can emerge.

Show your flexibility by adapting quickly to unexpected circumstances while maintaining your self-control and composure. Show your patience by bearing trials calmly and without complaint; manifesting forbearance under provocation or strain; and remaining steadfast despite opposition, difficulty, or adversity. In the positive environment your flexibility and patience create, you only need to tell your team to overcome the adversity—they will surprise you with the ingenuity of their solutions!

Looking Confident

The image you project is both a matter of how you feel and how you look. When you feel good—both outside and inside—you feel prepared for the selling process and feel happy to be a part of the direct-selling profession. Start your day off right by dressing professionally the first thing in the morning. This way, if an unexpected customer calls and needs to stop by, you are calm and prepared. You have eliminated the stress of frantic showering and changing at the last minute.

Throughout the day, be sure that your body language communicates enthusiasm and conviction. When you stand tall, make eye contact, and speak with a smile, your inner glow and confidence shine.

Sounding Confident

The manner in which you speak is as personal as your fingerprint. Your mastery can be communicated in the calm tone of your voice when you're facing a challenge, in the warm tone you use when you're welcoming your customers and team members, and in the enthusiastic tone you use when you're talking about your products.

You also express confidence when you listen more than you speak, when your choice of language befits your position, and when your integrity shines through in your truthful words. Most of all, your calmness creates an impression when your customers and team members never hear you utter a negative word about another person, never hear you disparage a situation, and never hear you express doubt or pessimism about the future.

Remember that, when you have the attitude that roadblocks are to be expected and overcoming them offers opportunities to grow, you can face them gracefully.

Instant Messenger

Today and tomorrow:

1. Assess how others perceive you—especially by your team and your prospects. If you aren't sure, or need validation, call a close colleague and ask her for an honest appraisal of how you present yourself.

2. On a piece of paper, describe the image you want to project to others, both in terms of your appearance and your speech. Be as specific as you can.

3. Make a list of any current behaviors and speech patterns that hinder your ideal image, and list positive behaviors and speech patterns you can use instead. Then, start practicing!

■ Success Leaves Clues

By Jack Canfield
Success strategist extraordinaire

WHO'S ALREADY DONE WHAT YOU WANT TO DO?

One of the great things about living in today's world of abundance and opportunity is that almost everything you want to do has already been done by someone else. It doesn't matter whether it's losing weight, running a marathon, starting a business, becoming financially independent, triumphing over breast cancer, or hosting the perfect dinner party—someone has already done it and left clues in the form of books, manuals, audio and video programs, university classes, online courses, seminars, and workshops.

If you want to retire a millionaire, for instance, there are hundreds of books ranging from *The Automatic Millionaire* to *The One Minute Millionaire*, and workshops ranging from Harv Eker's "Millionaire Mindset" to Marshall Thurber and D.C. Cordova's "Money and You." There are resources on how to make millions in real estate, investing in stocks, starting your own business, becoming a super salesperson, and even marketing on the Internet.

If you want to have a better relationship with your spouse, you can read John Gray's *Men Are from Mars and Women Are from Venus*; attend a couples' workshop; or take Gay and Kathlyn Hendrick's online course, "The Conscious Relationship."

For virtually everything you want to do there are books and courses on how to do it. Better yet, just a phone call away are people who've already successfully done what you want to do and who are available as teachers, facilitators, mentors, advisors, coaches, and consultants.

When you take advantage of this information, you'll discover that life is simply a connect-the-dots game, and all the dots have already been identified and organized by somebody else. All you have to do is follow the blueprint, use the system, or work the program that they provide.

WHY PEOPLE DON'T SEEK OUT CLUES

When I was preparing to go on a morning news show in Dallas, I asked the station's makeup artist what her long-term goals were. She said she'd always thought about opening her own beauty salon, so I asked her what she was doing to make that happen.

"Nothing," she said, "because I don't know how to go about it."

I suggested she offer to take a salon owner to lunch and ask how she had opened her own salon.

"You can do that?" the makeup artist exclaimed.

You most certainly can. In fact, you have most probably thought about approaching an expert for advice but rejected the idea with thoughts such as, Why would someone take the time to tell me what they did? Why would they teach me and then create their own competition? Banish those thoughts. You will find that most people love to talk about how they built their business or accomplished their goal.

But unfortunately, like the makeup artist in Dallas, most of us don't take advantage of all the resources available to us. There are several reasons why we don't.

- ■ It never occurs to us. We don't see others using these resources, so we don't do it either. Our parents didn't do it. Our friends aren't doing it. Nobody where we work is doing it:

- ■ It's inconvenient. We'd have to go to the bookstore, library, or local college. We'd have to drive across town to a meeting. We'd have to take time away from television, family, or friends.

- ■ Asking others for advice or information puts us up against our fear of rejection. We are afraid to take the risk.

- ■ Connecting the dots in a new way would mean change, and change—even when it is in our best interest—is uncomfortable. Who wants to be uncomfortable?

- ■ Connecting the dots means hard work, and frankly, most people don't want to work that hard.

Seeking Out Clues Today and Tomorrow

1. Seek out a teacher, coach, or mentor; a manual, book, or audio program; or an Internet resource to help you achieve one of your major goals.

2. Seek out somebody who has already done what you want to do, and ask the person if you can interview him or her for a half hour on how you should best proceed.

3. Ask someone if you can shadow her for a day and watch her work. Or offer to be a volunteer, assistant, or intern for someone you think you can learn from. ■

Used with permission. © 2005 Jack Canfield.

■ Learn to Let Go and Grow

By Pam Shaw
Teaching teamwork and teambuilding

EXPANDING YOUR COMFORT ZONE—ONE STEP AT A TIME

To advance your direct-selling career, you must spend your time on the tasks that provide the highest payoff. Unless you delegate the duties that don't require your personal attention, you'll be too overwhelmed to focus on growing your business. Yet, even knowing that delegation is a smart business move, you may resist it because you don't want to surrender control. ***To move away from this Catch-22, approach delegation with simple steps that will engage the support of an entire team and allow you to remain in—and then expand—your comfort zone.*** When you do, you'll have time to concentrate on the tasks that contribute most to your business, and have more time to spend with family and friends.

DELEGATING WITH APLOMB

- ■ **Delegate gradually.** Start by hiring an assistant a few hours a week to perform small tasks, and gradually expand her duties. Each new task should have enough complexity to challenge her while not overwhelming her.

- ■ **Let go of your need to control.** As you gain trust and confidence in your assistant, you'll feel more comfortable releasing control and working on the aspects of your business that only you can do.

- **Maintain some privacy.** Hire an assistant who can work both in your home office and at her home. You need space and privacy to grow your business.

- **Be prepared.** Keep a delegation list and a delegation file. The list has two columns; one itemizes duties she has mastered and is responsible for, while the other annotates tasks for which she needs training. The delegation file acts as her "In box," where you place the papers and notes she needs to handle.

- **Be flexible in the process, but committed to the outcome.** Recognize the validity of individual work styles. Supervise your assistant, but don't smother her. If she's getting the job done, give her independence in her approach.

- **Get out of Dodge!** You have your assistant, so go out and build your business. It's possible that a single extra appointment each week will pay for a week's worth of help.

Choosing What to Delegate

In choosing what to delegate, first make a list of everything you do in all facets of your life. Your list might include:

- **Home and Family:** Carpooling, housecleaning, cooking, gardening, and paying the bills

- **Office:** Technology (equipment and Web site maintenance); correspondence (e-mail, snail mail, and welcome letters); paperwork (copying forms and filing); supplies (stocking prizes and business supplies); inventory maintenance (re-ordering, labeling, and organizing); and schedule (arranging and confirming appointments)

Then ask . . .

- What am I doing that I don't enjoy? *Hiring someone to clean my home was the smartest thing I've done.*

- Which are the high payoff tasks that I want to keep? *I stay in projects that bring the most money for my time.*

- Which tasks take me toward my goal? *I spend as much time as possible in the leadership role of sponsoring, training, and coaching.*

- Which tasks take me away from my goal? *I avoid anything administrative.*

- For which tasks does someone else on my support team have more experience? *My husband is a whiz at all things technical, so he handles that.*

- What am I not willing to let go of? *I pick up my son from school because it is a time when he opens up and shares about his day.*

Once you've enumerated tasks that you are willing to delegate, decide who you would like to have on your support team. Don't be afraid to engage multiple people. Teens in the neighborhood can watch your kids, college students can help you with administrative tasks. Your husband may want to help with the finances, and so on. The tasks that are left become the basis for your assistant's job description.

Taking the Plunge

1. Make a list of everything that you do, then go through the list of questions and analyze the tasks that can be delegated.

2. Identify who you want on your support team, either by name or by skill set.

3. Now, make the calls! If you've identified needs for several different kinds of helpers, focus on starting with just one until she is up to speed, then adding the next. ∎

■ Quiet the Doubter Within

By Marcia Wieder
America's Dream Coach®

MOVING TOWARD OUR DREAMS

The business of direct selling requires that we face challenges that are outside our comfort zones. When we do, it awakens our Doubter within, which causes us to retreat and not reach for our dreams. The primary way we sabotage our dreams is by saying things like, "But, what if?" and imagining the worst. We say, But, what if I . . .

- fail?

- succeed?

- say or do the wrong thing?

- don't know the answer?

- get clients or team members?

- don't get enough clients?

- can't quite cut it?

- don't make enough money?

By learning some simple ways to quiet our inner Doubter so that it does not control or disempower us, we will keep moving toward our dreams.

NAMING AND CONFRONTING OUR FEARS

Commit to Your Dream

If you feel afraid or indecisive, this simple exercise can help you stabilize. Draw a line across the center of a paper. On the top, write your dream in as much detail as possible. On the bottom, write out your reality about this dream, including your fears, doubts, and "But, what ifs?" Then, ask yourself this essential question: Are you more committed to your dream or to your fear?

Two things will cause you to be more committed to your fear: not having a clearly defined dream, and projecting your worst fears onto your dream. When fear is placed in its proper place, as part of reality, it simply becomes something to manage, so it is easier to be more committed to your vision.

Interview Your Doubter

At different intervals along your path, you'll often run into the voice of your Doubter. Left unattended, this voice can be disruptive. But, by interviewing the Doubter with the following questions, we can capture the insights and wisdom it has to offer.

"The way I sabotage (*your name*)'s dream is _____."
Example: "The way I sabotage Susan's dream is by having her doubt herself and quit."

"When I am running (*your name*)'s life, I _____."
Example: "When I am running Susan's life, I keep her too busy to focus on what's important."

"What I need from (*your name*) is _____."
Example: "What I need from Susan is for her to have faith, to get help, to breathe."

List Your Doubter's Obstacles

Your Doubter can provide a list of real or imagined obstacles based on its fears and concerns. Imagined obstacles are limiting beliefs, while real obstacles require a plan. Wherever there's a real obstacle, design a strategy to manage it. Make a list of your obstacles and identify which ones are limiting beliefs and which ones require strategies. For example, an obstacles list for your dream to grow your business might include:

- I don't know how. (belief and strategy)

- I'm afraid I will fail. (belief)

- I don't have the money. (strategy)

- I'm too tired. (belief and strategy)

Replace Limiting Beliefs with Empowering Beliefs

Beliefs are never neutral. They either move you forward or hold you back. The way to move from limiting beliefs that hold you back to empowering beliefs that move you forward is through choosing to believe in yourself and your dreams. Make this choice and practice internal dialogue that overrides your Doubter until this new outlook becomes part of your identity.

Design Strategies to Manage Real Obstacles

For most of us, obstacles involve something we dislike, are not good at, or that we have no idea how to tackle. When that task is essential to the success of your venture, it could be your demise. The strategy for handling real obstacles is to decide if it is something you're going to tackle yourself. If so, decide how you're going to learn a new skill. If not, find someone who can do it with you and seek out a mentor. Or hire someone or barter with someone to do it for you. Then, get back into action in the areas where you excel.

Four Steps to Freedom

1. Interview your Doubter, and then list the internal beliefs and external obstacles that prevent you from achieving your dream.

2. For each belief, write down a positive counterargument; for each obstacle, write down a strategy.

3. Choose one belief and one strategy to implement in the coming week.

4. Demonstrate that you are more committed to your dream than your doubt by *taking action.* ■

■ Stock Up Your Personal Pantry

By Wally Amos
Helping people feel good about themselves

THE FIXINGS FOR GOOD FORTUNE

All good cooks will tell you the key to their success is the quality of their ingredients. With the finest herbs, spices, seasonings and condiments at their fingertips, they can turn the simplest of foods into a gourmet meal. So it is with the quality of our lives. *It is the day-to-day ingredients of decisions made, actions taken, and people we spend time with that we use to create a fulfilling, successful, "gourmet" life.*

TASTY, TRIED, AND TRUE

Challenges over the years have taught me, one by one, the essential ingredients I've needed to bring into my kitchen to stock what I call my "Personal Pantry." Let's consider these indispensables as our spices for life.

Basics. These ingredients are key in just about any recipe you undertake, like salt. Even when they're not specifically mentioned in the recipes, you can bet a good cook will be sure to include them in varying proportions, as needed:

■ Honesty

■ Integrity

- Positive loving attitude

- Faith

- Fun

- Responsibility

- Commitment

- Reality

- Imagination

- Energy

- Serendipity (common name: Luck)

- Intuition

- Humility

- Giving (your unconditional sharing of self)

Survival spices. As their name implies, these spices are the ones that will see you through just about any kind of challenge:

- Unconditional love

- Spirituality

- Self-respect

- Trust

- Determination

- Clarity

- Balance

- Courage

- Self-awareness

- Confidence

- Tenacity (common name: Stick-to-it-iveness)

- Indefatigability

- Resourcefulness

- Perspective

- Good judgment

- Practicality

- Relationships

Entrepreneurial extracts. These are what you should keep in stock to concoct successful business enterprises:

- Superlative mentors

- Teamwork

- Individuality

- Enthusiasm

- Vitality

- Personality

- Decisiveness

- Leadership

- Passion

- Vision

- Originality

- Forthrightness

- Ability to focus on answers and solutions

- Networking skills

- Willingness to work hard (common name: Elbow grease)

- Productivity

- Competence

- Problem-solving skills

- Attention to detail

- Self-sufficiency

- Thrift

Relationship rules. These are the ingredients that keep friends and loved ones around your table:

- Generosity

- Ability to receive

- Respect

- Tolerance

- Friendship

- Spontaneity

- Playfulness

- Appreciation

- Thoughtfulness

- Gentleness

- Amiability

- Fair-mindedness

- Credibility

- Forbearance

- Empathy

- Loyalty

- Sensitivity

- Active listening

Cook's Note

It may seem that some of the ingredients in my Personal Pantry are contradictory, but you know, when you get ready to create a dish, you rarely, if ever, use everything at your disposal! It all depends on what you want to cook. Meat dishes call for herbs and spices that are totally inappropriate for cakes and cookies. On the other hand, I don't think many recipes can do without a pinch of salt.

In life, as in the kitchen, balance and adjustment are everything and almost everyone I know tweaks even their tried-and-true recipes, adjusting them a smidge every time they prepare them. Circumstance always dictates what you choose to use, but the point is to make sure you have what you need in stock!

The Golden Rule of Recipes

Here is the bottom line for any recipe: Specific combinations of ingredients *A, B, C,* and so on are going to result in Product *X*. If you, the cook, are not satisfied with Product *X*, it is up to you to alter the combination and proportions of the ingredients that you selected. If your final product pleases you, then you'd better pay attention to what you used to create it.

Now, because what I am talking about are Recipes for Life, how can we apply this Golden Rule to who we are and what we do? It's simple! If all events of your life—your ingredients—have combined to produce the person you are today, and if you are happy with those results, then it stands to reason that you've got a successful recipe going: *A, B,* and *C* produced an *X* you like. This approach can make us all much more accepting of what happens in our lives. Even when some stuff doesn't feel too good at the time it goes into the mix, it can still ultimately be part of something very tasty. In many cases, what tastes bitter by itself adds depth and richness to a dish.

By the same token, if you're disappointed in Product *X*, then you'd better rethink the ABC's of your ingredients. It's always a question of balancing the recipe 'til you get what you want. Just remember: You're the cook!

Stocking Up the Next 48 hours

1. Take inventory of your Personal Pantry.

2. Pick three ingredients you would like to have in greater supply.

3. Add to your confidence in your supply of those three things by acting like you have plenty! ■

■ Get in the Game of Life

By Les Brown
The master motivator

FAIL YOUR WAY TO SUCCESS

You probably entered this profession with great intentions and a healthy dose of commitment. But many people are simply unable to handle the fear, the challenges, and the obstacles that inevitably come their way. *Stay in the game by establishing a personal growth regimen, detoxifying your life, and taking risks.* You'll wind up among the very few to stay in the game long enough to score.

Today, nearly 50 million people worldwide have taken a leap toward living their dreams by starting their own businesses with one of the many fine network marketing or party plan companies. Imagine—50 million people who have put their heart on the line so they can have a shot at making their dreams come true! From New York to Nairobi, the entrepreneurial spirit burns bright in people just like you. What we know about these brave souls is that some will become rich beyond their wildest dreams, others will achieve a lifestyle that brings joy to those they love, and still others will reap the rewards that can't be measured by their bank account.

> **I**t's the fear of the unknown, the fear of looking foolish that keeps the majority sitting on the sidelines, wanting desperately to play the game, yet unwilling to risk defeat.

You may be asking, What determines my destiny in direct selling? What will put me in the ranks of the ones who make it big instead of the legions of the ones who just make it? What talents do they posses that set them apart from the rest? One characteristic stands out above all others: They are willing to fail their way to success.

An Equal Playing Field for All

Your direct-selling business is your chance to become the person that you've only dreamed of being, but that you know is inside of you. Your business gives you a shot at earning an income that isn't determined by your education, that isn't based on your connections, but that's a result of your willingness to put on your game face and run ahead of the pack. This profession is an equal playing field where you get to be the star yet still have the support of a team. Your coach cheers you on, your plan fuels your passion, and your product gets you off the couch and out building your business!

So if we're all on an equal playing field, with others to cheer us on and a company that provides us with the right equipment, why doesn't everyone succeed? In my view, it's fear of failure. Not everyone is willing to endure the heartache and struggles that come up when we strive for something greater than we have ever achieved before. It's the fear of the unknown, the fear of looking foolish that keeps the majority sitting on the sidelines, wanting desperately to play the game, yet unwilling to risk defeat.

Staying in the Game

If you have a dream, a vision for something greater than yourself, make a promise to yourself to stay in the game. Pick yourself up every time you get knocked down. That is what separates the ones who build it big from the ones who do not.

Develop a daily self-development regimen. You are in the business of personal growth—first, the growth of yourself and then the growth of those on your team.

> **W***hat's your dream? What deep desire keeps you up at night? What vision gets your heart pumping?*

- Read 10 to 15 pages of something that fills your brain with positive, affirming, and thought-provoking ideas you can apply to your own life.

- Listen to 30 minutes of an audio message that helps you develop the personal and life skills to prepare you for the opportunities that are just around the corner.

- Brainstorm at least 30 minutes a day on creative ways to get closer to your goal. If possible, get outside, listen to music, and be around nature to open up your mind to new possibilities.

- Write down goals that are way outside your comfort zone and review them every morning and night. Choose goals that make your heart pump and your hands sweat! That's how you'll know you have stumbled upon a vision that will drive you through even the toughest times.

I remember the day I decided that I would someday buy a home for my mother, Miss Mamie Brown. My heart ached with desire. I wanted it so badly—I can remember being willing to do anything to achieve my goal.

What's your dream? What deep desire keeps you up at night? What vision gets your heart pumping? Don't chase it away with excuses and doubt. Make it your reason for staying in the game!

> **T**he truth is, we look foolish if we get to the end of our lives not having gone for our goals.

Detoxify your life by assessing your relationships. Some relationships can literally make you sick. Their toxic energy clouds your vision of what you want for your life while their negativity infects you like a bad case of the flu.

Look around you and identify the people in your life as nurturing or toxic. Then, spend less time with the ones who bring you down and more time with the ones who make you feel good. It's that simple! If your net*work* determines your net *worth,* look around you to determine the direction you are headed. Be sure to align yourself with like-minded people who are making great things happen in their lives.

Be willing to take risks. Starting a direct-selling business is a risk. Make it okay to fail. Most people don't make the attempt because there are no guarantees. They don't even want to try because they don't want to look foolish. The truth is, we look foolish if we get to the end of our lives not having gone for our goals.

Life is like a roll of toilet paper—the closer you get to the end, the faster it runs out! I love this saying because it reminds us that life is not a dress rehearsal! We have only one life to live and we must make every day count. Making things happen in your life requires faith, or an unshakeable ability to believe, regardless of your circumstances.

Get going! So many people make a career of "getting ready" to start. They have one more product to learn about, one more fact to memorize, yet they never get around to talking to others. Don't justify staying out of the game.

Give it your honest effort and you will eventually get better. Get yourself in the game. Develop yourself, detoxify your life, and take risks. When you're in the game, you never fail—you only fail forward.

■ Additional Resources

ABOUT THE DSWA

The Direct Selling Women's Alliance is a community of individuals who are engaged in the pursuit of their dreams through one of the fine network marketing or party-plan income opportunities available today. Our membership is comprised of women (and men) representing independent direct sellers from around the world and more than 275 direct-selling companies.

Jane Deuber,
Nicki Keohohou,
and Grace Lee

The mission of the DSWA is to make an authentic difference in your direct-selling career and your life! We are teachers, cheerleaders, friends, coaches, confidants, and mentors who offer industry-specific education by the top leaders, speakers, trainers, and experts the profession has to offer. We respect your choice to grow your direct-selling business and will work to provide you with all that you need to become the person you are meant to be.

DSWA MEMBERSHIP BENEFITS

As a member of the DSWA, you enjoy extensive benefits, both online and in your local area. Every day you'll have access to the private areas of our 400-page-and-growing Web site, as well as bi-weekly teleclasses on topics uniquely related to your business, an extensive Learning Library of articles and tips, and a support network that understands and respects your passion for your business.

You can also become active in your local DSWA Chapter or Success Circle. These monthly meetings provide a safe and welcoming place for direct sellers who choose to learn, grow, and support one another. You'll receive industry-specific training in a setting where members are bound by a common goal of success and a love for direct selling. Discover the excitement of meeting women in your community who respect your career choice and want to support you and your direct-selling business! With new chapters and Success Circles starting each month, there may be one near you. If none are established in your area, consider becoming a founder and making a difference in your community.

Learn how you can become a member of the DSWA for a minimal annual fee by visiting the DSWA Web site at http://www.dswa.org and the following pages:

■ Member Benefits: http://www.dswa.org/list_of_benefits.asp

■ Why Join the DSWA: http://www.dswa.org/member_area_tour.asp

■ Who Is the DSWA: http://www.dswa.org/who_we_are.asp

DSWA SUCCESS ENHANCING PRODUCTS

Discover these powerful Direct Selling Women's Success Enhancing Products!

■ *Build It Big–101 Insider Secrets from Top Direct Selling Experts,* Direct Selling Women's Alliance's premier issue of the Build It Big series of educational publications written for the direct-selling entrepreneur.

■ *The Build It Big Companion Workbook* takes you beyond reading and applying insights to explore fundamental concepts in depth. Through its exercises, you'll integrate vital beliefs into your mindset, bringing balance and new personal power to your life and business.

■ In *Managing Your Business Finances**, Vicky Collins, CPA, gives you a comprehensive, easy-to-understand approach to taking care of the "money side" of your business—once and for all!

■ In *Principle-Centered Coaching™**, Jennie England, PCC, CPCC, teaches a proven method of working with team members that supports them to move toward improved performance and more rewarding relationships.

■ In *Personal Power**, Marion Gellatly, AICI, CIM, guides you through the steps of designing a professional image that supports your success. From creating a fabulous business wardrobe to networking like a pro, this comprehensive program will accelerate your rise to the top!

■ The *Make It Happen Music CD*, is a collection of ten inspirational songs that will lift your spirit and ignite your passion for success! Every note is designed to help you maintain a mindset for success that will carry you toward your dreams.

* These CD sets come with a comprehensive e-workbook that serves as a guide for learning and implementing the ideas presented by the DSWA's team of experts.

To learn more about these and other exciting DSWA products, visit the DSWA store at http://www.dswa.org/dswa_store.asp.

■ Distributors/Leaders

Jackie Baugrud

Director, The Angel Company

The Angel Company's Top Seller for the past three years, Jackie was awarded their first two incentive trips and Demonstrator of the Year in 2004. She feels blessed to help other women realize and achieve their dreams.

Sandra Bergstrom

Group Director, Home Interiors

One of Home Interiors' Top 10 Directors in the Nation in 2004, Sandra has been recognized at seminars as having the #1 Best Contemporary Design, and has trained hundreds of consultants to achieve success.

Barb and Clem Birch

Gold Executives, Watkins

During their 11 years together at Watkins, Barb and Clem have built the Birch Team throughout the United States and Canada. They know firsthand how engaging each other in business has transformed their relationship and made their life together magical.

Robin Blanc-Mascari

Diamond Executive, Oasis LifeSciences

With 25 years background as trainer, speaker, and coach in the corporate world, Robin brings enlightened leadership to her initiatives to develop leaders, welcome female associates, and support those with special challenges in the Oasis LifeSciences community.

Gloria Brice

Executive Representative, Country Bunny Bath and Body

Through her direct-selling career, Gloria has grown into a more focused, organized person; strengthened her family; and found joy in the opportunity to be a blessing to and make a difference in the lives of others.

Sue Burdick

National Marketing Director, NSA

With an infectious desire to succeed and a heartfelt delight in helping others find their true potential, Sue was awarded the prestigious Founder's Award by NSA President Jay Martin for achieving over two million air miles in support of NSA distributors worldwide.

Tami Carbone

Executive, Sensaria Natural Bodycare

With a passion for meeting her customers' needs and a love of sharing her business, Tami received Sensaria's first and only Platinum Award for sales, leadership, and recruiting, as well as #1 in promoting supervisors and two incentive trips.

Dr. Shirley B. Carmack

Founder, GNLD Wellness Center

Expressing her lifelong desire to help others, Shirley has pursued a career in Anesthesia, studied psychology, and been active in direct selling for more than 25 years. Her special calling is to help people rise above the limitation of race, gender, and economics.

Shirley Casavant

Founding Member, International Galleries Inc.

A strong leader, mentor, and pioneer in the networking marketing industry, Shirley has 35 years' experience in direct selling. IGI has honored her with many leadership-level awards, but her favorite is the Mentoring Award, because she believes building self-esteem in others is building their dreams.

Rysia Crockett
Executive Director, Warm Spirit

Called to create optimal health, personal development, financial liberation, and life freedom, Rysia complements her direct-selling career by owning and leading The Finished Product, a company that offers training, recruiting, and operations management support.

Sharon Davidson-Unkefer
500K Premier Select, XanGo, LLC

In partnership with her husband, Sharon occupies her company's top position and earned the top check with group volume of $11 million in August, 2005. She is adding 13,000 to 15,000 new distributors per month and growing, thanks to strong recruiting, events, communications, and hands-on help for her team.

Pat Dempsey
Senior Executive Director, AtHome America

In her 14 years with AtHome America, Pat has personally sold over $500,000 in Homewares, recruited over 250 HomeStyle Specialists, earned the incentive trip each year, and received numerous National Awards—this year second place Executive Team Sales for the second year in a row and third place for Recruiting.

Gayle Driscoll
Regional Marketing Director, Oxyfresh Worldwide

Having built a standout business through hard work, entrepreneurial savvy, and constant team-building efforts, Gayle and her husband recently received the Oxyfresh $10,000 Super Star award for their strong commitment to the field and their team.

Cori Dyer
Presidential Advisory Board, Synergy Worldwide

Within four months of starting her direct-selling business, Cori was earning five figures a month in residual earnings. She created a simple system for recruiting and training over the Internet, and within three years expanded into seven countries around the world.

Lora Enabnit

31 Star Double Platinum Presidential, Mannatech

Expressing their passion for helping others reach their optimal health and financial goals, Lora and her husband have consistently been one of the top four income earners at Mannatech—earning over seven figures annually—and received its most prestigious honor: the Top Business award.

Joyce Feraco

Independent Demonstrator, Stampin' Up!

Joyce balances her life as military wife and mother of six with her thriving business. Her personal career sales exceed $700,000. Her personal sales and recruiting reached Top Ten for eight and five years respectively. She was her company's first Demonstrator of the Year, and counts her three years on its Advisory Board her biggest honor.

Barbara Fishpaw

Diamond Infinity Designer, Home and Garden Party

With her "secret weapon"—her husband John—Barbara is grateful for being crowned King and Queen of Sponsoring their first year, sharing incentive trips with their sons, and seeing members of their team recognized as tops in sales and sponsoring. In 2005, they've attracted over 8,000 new recruits and team sales of over $100 million.

Krystal Kitchens Grant

Gold Director, Top Line Creations

"The luckiest woman alive"—in love with her family, her hobby, and her career—Krystal has earned her company's BMW incentive, spoken and trained at five conventions, and in her first 18 months with TLC, built a team of more than 1,700.

Chris Harney
National Sales Director, Longaberger Company

Believing "direct selling is a way to have it all!" Chris has reached her company's highest sales field position and built a team as large as 1,500. With decades of coaching experience, NLP and HNLP Master Practitioner and other credentials, she shares her wisdom as a motivational speaker and seminar leader.

Pam Heller
Senior Executive Unit Leader, Avon Products, Inc.

Most rewarded by empowering her team members' success, Pam has surpassed her dreams by building a multi-million dollar company from home with a team of over 1,000. With determination, she grew her business each time she moved to support her husband's career, and now is the only top-level achiever in her state.

Kathleen McGraw Heyn, JD
National Vice President and Independent Consultant, Arbonne International

Having exchanged an 18-year partnership in a prestigious law firm for a home-based business, Kathleen no longer trades time for money. She quickly replaced her income, delights in her unlimited residuals, enjoys teaching and training others, and is honored by her company's Vice President Leadership, Area of Consistence Excellence, President's Circle, and other awards.

Jeanette Holtman
Senior Director, Creative Memories

Leading her team by modeling top-level sales and sponsoring, Jeanette has received numerous awards, including the National Spirit of Success Award, and believes that in direct selling, if you work hard, you *will* be rewarded.

Paola Horvath

Independent business owner

The stepdaughter of DSWA Cofounder Jane Deuber, Paola grew up in the world of direct selling and has always longed to learn, grow, and help others. Today Paola and her husband are proud new parents and independent business owners, thrilled and blessed by their association with a respected and rapidly growing company.

Beth Jacobs

National Senior Executive Director

Beth is an experienced direct seller, recruiter, trainer, and coach. In 16 years with her company, Beth has built a $9,000,000 business; developed a top-selling, top-recruiting team; earns trips and awards every year; and is among the Top 20 individuals in her company for first line cluster sales as well as overall cluster sales.

Donna Johnson

Executive National Vice President, Arbonne International

Fulfilled by helping other people become successful, Donna joined Arbonne early in its development, became its first National Vice President, and now leads a team that includes nine first-generation VPs.

Laura Kaufman

Team Elite, Photomax–a division of NuSkin Enterprises

Once trapped in the American Dream of owning an art gallery, Laura has discovered in direct selling the freedom of creating a multiple six-figure income for her family, the satisfaction of assisting many of her team members to do the same, and the pleasure of sharing the journey to achievement with others.

Christy King

Independent Diamond Infinity Designer, Home & Garden Party

With three small children and a husband doing shift work, Christy needs the flexibility of her own home business and delights in helping others find similar success. She is among her company's top 75 leaders, a member of the Million Dollar Court, and twice a member of the Queen's Court for sponsoring.

Leigh Kirk
Senior Regional Vice President, PartyLite

Dedicated to helping others reach their income and professional goals, Leigh has been PartyLite's top income earner for over ten years and was the first to earn over $1 million in one year. Today she sets a good example for her team by maintaining a strong personal business.

Debb Klingel
National Sales Manager, Weekenders USA

Still thrilled by her 14-year adventure in direct selling, Debb has realized her passion through helping other women take control of their lives and become more than they ever dreamed possible—making their unit #1 in the nation twice!

Michelle Knapp
Group Director and Kandesn Instructor, Sunrider International

Entering the network marketing industry at age 18, Michelle has had considerable experience training and teaching worldwide, with distributors in Great Britain, the Netherlands, Belgium, Ireland, Austria, Spain, Switzerland, and Finland.

Kim Leopardo
Senior Team Mentor, Tastefully Simple

Growing her business along with her family, Kim has received her company's highest honor, the Gung Ho Spirit Award. As a top recruiter and charter member of the Gold Leaf Executive Club, Kim frequently speaks at national and regional conferences.

Gayle McDonald
Executive Director, The Body Shop At Home

A master of team development for The Body Shop, Gayle has been the #1 leader in organizational sales and the #1 in organizational recruiting for three years, as well as leading her distributors to the #1 Team in Sales Growth every year.

Suzanne McGee
Executive Director, Cookie Lee Jewelry

Suzanne became an Executive Director in 11 months, setting a company record, and was recognized for sponsoring 100 consultants in just over 2 years. Now a national trainer for Cookie Lee, Suzanne often travels throughout the United States helping others build their businesses.

Jacqueline McGrath
Executive Sales Director, Epicure Selections

The recipient of Epicure's prestigious Caring and Sharing Award, Jacqueline thanks her amazing team—the largest organization of Epicure consultants—which has earned the title of Top Sales and Top Sponsoring for three consecutive years.

Mary Nelson
Ambassador, Free Life International

While a top earner in real estate, Mary saw that she could double her income only by doubling her hours, so she became a student of leveraged income. Now a multimillion-dollar earner, business trainer, and national speaker, Mary has spent the past decade teaching others how to create leveraged residual income.

Karen Olson
Senior Executive Director, Signature HomeStyles®

Joining the company as a single woman with a high school education and achieving success at every stage of her 21-year career, Karen leads an organization of over 500 representatives and 19 leaders with sales of over $2 million. In 2004 she received the Million-Dollar Earner award.

Debbie Rotkvich

Executive Field Vice President, lia sophia Fashion Jewelry

During her 14 years with *lia sophia*, Debbie has followed the leaders who walked the walk and drawn over 2,000 people to her team, which this year sold just under $20 million.

Carmen Saucedo

Executive District Director, Jafra Cosmetics International

A leader who develops leaders, Carmen has mentored thousands of Hispanic women to create businesses that enhance lifestyles for generations to come. Carmen's District spans the country with over 500 managers, 40 district directors, and 30,000 consultants of all ethnicities, backgrounds, and life experiences.

Katherine Sigrist

Senior Leader, Homemade Gourmet

Joining Homemade Gourmet in 1999, Katherine became a Founding Director in August, 2001. A Founding Member of the Consistency Club, she has been #1 in Top 10 Unit Sales every year since. Last year, she was also #4 in Top 5 Team sales and entered the $1,500,000 Volume Breakers Club.

Dianne Thompson

Senior National Executive Director, BeautiControl

In less than a decade, Dianne reached the $1,000,000 earnings goal and went on to become BeautiControl's first Senior National Executive Director. A #1 performer in every category, she has attracted over 15,000 members to her team, and supports every level from consultant-in-training up to Senior National Executive Director.

Ruth Van Buren

Executive Director and National Kandesn Advisor, Sunrider International

In 23 years with Sunrider, Ruth has built large organizations in over 15 North American and European countries. She has also trained in many Asian countries, served 14 years on Sunrider's Executive Advisory Board, and has produced business tools including "Creating Your Dreams."

Leslie Vitzthum

5-Star Manager, Body Wise International

A top-level performer, respected leader, and trainer, Leslie regularly presents seminars on business development, achievement, and leadership. Body Wise has honored her with the Golden Microphone Award for excellence in public speaking, and the inaugural Body Wise Factor award for outstanding leadership.

Joy von Skepsgardh

Platinum Ambassador, Amazon Herb Shop

When Joy was inspired to start her direct-selling business, she set a company record by becoming a Platinum Ambassador in 13 months. She leads over 2,000 distributors and celebrates a sales volume of over $1,000,000 annually, and received the Amazon Herb Company Leadership Award in 2002 and 2004.

Sandi Walper

Executive Diamond Distributor, Immunotec Research

Immunotec's first distributor, first million-dollar earner, and first Executive Diamond distributor, Sandi finds fulfillment in her freedom to choose her work style, the opportunity to help those who are ill, and the wonderful friendships she's developed among the 25,000 on her team.

Ann White

National Vice President, Warm Spirit

Living proof that success follows passion and purpose, Ann was the top earner nation-wide and became National Vice President in 2003. That year her team, the sensational Spirit of Success, ended with over $3,000,000 in sales, over 3,400 members, and more Managers, Executives, Directors, and National Vice Presidents than any other unit.

Dennis and Ruth Williams
Royal Ambassadors, Nikken, Inc.

Dennis and Ruth are most proud of making a positive difference in the lives of thousands of people, including helping 35 of their friends (so far) become members of Nikken's Millionaire's Club; becoming Royal Ambassadors and receiving a special reward of $1 million; and serving on the Nikken Executive Sales Board.

Jodi Wilson Siegel
Two Star Director, Southern Living at Home

As a single mother of three boys, Jodi enjoys the freedom, flexibility, and income of her direct-selling career. Finding joy in watching women blossom and expand their strengths, Jodi has developed a team of over 700 consultants from Alaska to Florida, and earned every incentive trip.

Courtney Wright
Executive Director, Homemade Gourmet

During her six years with Homemade Gourmet, Courtney has developed five breakaway directors and a unit of over 1,000 team members. Number two in team sales, Courtney has won several incentive trips and the Silver Spoon Award. She enjoys developing leaders, working with her team, and bringing families back to the dinner table.

■ Speakers, Trainers, and Experts

Wally Amos

Founder of Famous Amos Cookies

The father of the gourmet chocolate chip cookie industry, Wally shares the principles of entrepreneurial success and generously uses his fame to support educational causes. His honors and awards include the President's Award for Entrepreneurial Excellence, the Horatio Alger Award, and the Outstanding Business Leader Award. To contact Wally, call 858-292-9106, write to Marcia@bluefeathermanagement.com, or visit http://www.wallyamos.com.

Carly Anderson

Master Certified Coach to Leaders and Emerging Leaders

Carly Anderson is a masterful leadership coach and expert on virtual learning. Her e-book *How to Lead Effective and Engaging Tele-Seminars* teaches leaders how to be inspiring and create interest and accountability in their teleconference team calls.

To contact Carly, call 949-716-9265, write to carly@carlyanderson.com, or visit http://www.carlyanderson.com.

David Bach

Chairman and Founder of FinishRich Inc.

David is a best-selling author, speaker, and creator of the FinishRich® seminar series, which highlights his quick and easy-to-follow financial strategies. David carries the unique distinction of having four books in the Finish Rich Series appear simultaneously on the *Wall Street Journal, BusinessWeek,* and *USA Today* best-seller lists. To contact David, visit http://www.finishrich.com.

Gary Ryan Blair

Founder of The GoalsGuy

A visionary and gifted conceptual thinker, Gary is highly regarded as a speaker, consultant, strategic planner, and a coach to leading companies across the globe. More than 80,000 organizations and 4 million employees use the GoalsGuy handbooks, training programs, and coaching services. To contact Gary, call 877-462-5748, write to gary@goalsguy.com, or visit http://www.goalsguy.com.

Les Brown

An authority on maximizing human potential, Les teaches and inspires millions of people through empowerment speeches, motivational materials, and personal development programs. Les received the National Speakers Association's highest honor: The Council of Peers Award of Excellence (CPAE), and was selected one of the World's Top Five Speakers by Toastmasters International. To contact Les, call 800-733-4226, write to speak@lesbrown.com, or visit http://www.lesbrown.com.

Jenny Bywater

Founder of The Booster

In 1981, Jenny founded The Booster to offer the little things that make a big difference in your results. She has developed more than 4,000 products, delivered the fun in numerous motivational speeches, and helped over 400,000 direct sellers build their businesses. To contact Jenny, call 800-553-6692, write to jennybb@thebooster.com, or visit http://www.thebooster.com.

Jack Canfield

Cocreator of Chicken Soup for the Soul

Jack has been a leading authority in the area of self-esteem and personal development for the past 30 years. He leads three organizations—The Foundation for Self-Esteem, Self-Esteem Seminars, and Souperspeakers.com—to bring self-esteem resources and training to people in any walk of life. To contact Jack, write to info4jack@jackcanfield.com or visit http://www.jackcanfield.com.

Michael S. Clouse

An internationally recognized direct-selling expert, Michael is an experienced personal success coach and a dynamic educational speaker. In addition to over 50 published articles on network marketing, Michael is the author of *The Fifth Principle, Recipe for Success,* and *Learning the Business One Story at a Time.* To contact Michael, call 888-639-3722, write to msc@nexera.com, or visit http://www.nexera.com/msc.

Vicky Collins, CPA

DSWA Prosperity Panel Member

Author of *The Direct Selling Women's Guide to Managing Your Business* and a respected trainer, Vicky helps direct-selling professionals throughout the United States take control of their financial destiny, legally reduce the taxes they pay, and save thousands of dollars with integrity. To contact Vicky, call 214-824-6890, write to vicky@vickycollins.com, or visit http://www.vickycollins.com.

Joseph H. Craft, CPA

Senior Partner, Craft, Lee & Sievertson CPAs, PLLC

As one of the nation's leading home-based business specialists, Joe serves clients in all 50 states. He has also written tax cutting books and frequently speaks at national and regional conferences that focus on home business issues. To contact Joseph, call 270-443-1450 or write to joe@clscpa.net.

Jane Deuber, MBA

President and Cofounder of the DSWA

Jane's experience as a distributor, company founder, and industry consultant gives her an in-depth understanding of all facets of direct selling. As an author and trainer, Jane empowers direct-selling leaders through the DSWA's Principle-Centered Success Program, which integrates professional coaching skills into the foundation on which successful organizations are built. To contact Jane, call 888-417-0743, write to jane@mydswa.org, or visit http://www.dswa.org.

Belinda Ellsworth
Founder of Step Into Success

Through her results-oriented programs for conventions, workshops, and leadership conferences, Belinda has motivated and empowered thousands of consultants, managers, and executives worldwide. The Success Express, her online resource training center, offers the latest in education, motivation, inspiration, and personal coaching in one easy-to-use place. To contact Belinda, call 734-878-1075, write to belinda@stepintosuccess.com, or visit http://www.thesuccessexpress.com.

Jennie England, PCC, CPCC
Professional Coach, Cocreator, and Author of the DSWA's Principle-Centered Coaching CD and E-book

Jennie has a passion for bringing the DSWA's Principle-Centered Coaching skills to direct sellers via telecourses, training seminars, and coaching for individuals and groups. The founder of Wisdom in Action, Jennie has 25 years' experience working with individuals, businesses, and organizations in the areas of communication, leadership, and teamwork. To contact Jennie, call 831-624-2525, write to Jennie@wisdominaction.net, or visit http://www.jennie@wisdominaction.net.

Doug Firebaugh
Chairman and CEO of PassionFire International

Doug has been in direct selling for more than 19 years. He loves this industry because it is the bastion of free enterprise: the greatest way to embrace financial, time, and personal freedom. To contact Doug, call 972-998-3473, write to dfirebaugh@yahoo.com, or visit http:// www.passionfire.com.

John Milton Fogg
Founder of GreatestNetworker.comUnity

John's book, *The Greatest Networker in the World,* is the best-selling book on direct selling, with over 1 million sold around the world. In addition, John has written or edited more than 25 books and tapes that together have sold over 3 million copies. To contact John, write to jmf@greatestnetworker.com or visit http://www.greatestnetworker.com.

Laura Berman Fortgang, MCC

Recognized internationally as a pioneer in the personal coaching field, Laura is the best-selling author of *Take Yourself to the Top, Living Your Best Life*, and *Now What?* Her work has been featured on *Oprah, Today,* and in print media around the world. To contact Laura, visit http://www.laurabermanfortgang.com.

Bruce Gardner

Freedom Accounting and Tax Service

A home-based business specialist, Bruce helps clients keep more of what they make. To contact Bruce, call 270-443-1450, write to bruce@craftandcompany.net, or visit http://www.craftandcompany.net.

Marion Gellatly, AICI, CIM

President of Powerful Presence

Marion loves to help people achieve Personal Power, sense *wow!* in their appearance, and feel confident in their business communication and etiquette. She presently serves as president of Association of Image Consultants International, the premier global image organization with members in over 30 countries. To contact Marion, call 831-625-2000, write to mlgellatly@powerful-presence.com, or visit http://www.powerful-presence.com.

Kosta Gharagozloo

CEO, Team In Motion

Kosta operates the extremely successful Team In Motion, with over 90,000 Lexxus distributors in over 40 countries—all from the comfort of his home in Canada. Thanks to his direct-selling career, he became Lexxus International's youngest millionaire at age 31. To contact Kosta, visit http://www.teaminmotion.com.

Mark Victor Hansen

Cocreator of Chicken Soup for the Soul

For more than 25 years, Mark has helped people and organizations reshape their vision of what's possible. With Chicken Soup partner Jack Canfield, Mark created what *Time* magazine calls "the publishing phenomenon of the decade." With partner Robert Allen, Mark's current best-seller is *Cracking the Millionaire Code*. To contact Mark, write to service@markvictorhansen.com or visit http://www.markvictorhansen.com.

Rhonda K. Johnson

Managing Partner, Accountable Solutions

A respected speaker, trainer, tax professional, and networking diva who has been active in the direct-selling industry for more than 20 years, Rhonda has helped hundreds of direct sellers maximize legitimate tax write-offs and succeed by keeping more of what they make. To contact Rhonda, call 866-282-3127, write to rhonda-johnson@socal.rr.com, or visit http://www.accountablesolutions.biz.

Beth Jones-Schall

Founder and President, Spirit of Success, Inc.

Beth started as a sales consultant and grew to the positions of director of training and sales director, where she was responsible for leading more than 1,000 consultants. Now she is a powerful, proven speaker and trainer who equips others for success. To contact Beth, call 813-654-1540, write to beth@spiritofsuccess.com, or visit http://www.spiritofsuccess.com.

Nicki Keohohou

CEO and Cofounder of the DSWA

Active in the direct-selling profession for more than 30 years, Nicki has personally worked with thousands of direct sellers from around the world and is on a mission to empower more people to achieve their dreams through a career in direct selling. To contact

Nicki, call 888-417-0743, write to nicki@mydswa.org, or visit http://www.dswa.org.

Grace Keohohou Lee

Vice President and Cofounder of the DSWA

Having grown up among direct sellers and eventually becoming one, Grace appreciates the dedication it takes to achieve success. She wants more women to be able to leave the "job" that keeps them away from their family and home. To contact Grace, call 888-417-0743, write to grace@mydswa.org, or visit http://www.dswa.org.

Ronna Lichtenberg

Author of Pitch Like a Girl

A nationally recognized business author and lecturer, Ronna teaches women why it's sometimes hard to sell themselves and their ideas and what to do about it. As a consultant, Ronna helps companies fix troubled business and employee relationships, and create new ones that are valuable to all concerned. To contact Ronna, call 646-336-7566, write to ronnal@askronna.com, or visit http://www.askronna.com.

Michele McDonough

Industry Consultant and Trainer

A respected business consultant, coach, and trainer with over 18 years in direct selling, Michele understands each company's need to serve its distributors. In the numerous sales, promotion, and training programs she's developed, Michele helps distributors harness the power of geometric growth within their organizations. To contact Michele, call 949-466-2707 or write to mmcdon4946@aol.com.

Ilene Meckley

Called the "Queen of Training in Home-Based Businesses," Ilene has conducted over 1,000 training seminars and presented keynote speeches at regional and national conventions throughout the United States and Canada. She is making home-based business the profession of choice. To contact Ilene, call 800-383-2039, write to il-ene@ilenemeckley.com, or visit http://www.ilenemeckley.com.

Denise Michaels
Founder of Marketing for Her

For over two decades, Denise has been a successful marketer, speaker, trainer, and coach, sharing her keen observation of the Mars/Venus marketing differences between the sexes. Her latest book is the myth-shattering *Testosterone-Free Marketing: The Yin and Yang of Marketing for Women.* To contact Denise, visit http://www.marketingforher.com.

Peter Mingils
President and CEO, PM Marketing/Networkleads

As a successful direct selling executive, Peter recognized the potential of lead generation to build businesses. Now his company is a top provider of the leads, systems, and training necessary to build a home-based business. Peter is active in the industry as a vendor, distributor, trainer, and consultant. To contact Peter, call 888-491-1093, write to peter@networkleads.com, or visit http://www.networkleads.com.

Scott Orlinski
President, Smart Office Solutions

Scott is a highly respected and accomplished leader, businessman, and educator. From the executive offices of Smart Office Solutions to the online classroom at Strayer University, he educates and moti-vates with extraordinary knowledge and power. To contact Scott, call 800-891-8601 x108, write to scott@smartofficesolutions.com, or visit http://smartofficesolutions.com.

Karen Phelps
Founder, Phelps Positive Performance Inc.

An author, trainer, and international speaker, Karen brings 22 years' experience in direct selling to her students. While pursuing her career goals, she managed to be there for her family's important life events. She believes you can too, and get what you want! To contact Karen, call 248-673-3465, write to Karen@karenphelps.com, or visit http://www.karenphelps.com.

Paula Pritchard

Paula is known worldwide as one of the top network marketers and trainers—a person of utmost integrity in a very competitive industry. She has proven her business-building methods work, leading the expansion of four companies into Europe. Her book *Owning Yourself* details her methods. To contact Paula, write to paula@mlm-madesimple.com or visit http://www.mlmmadesimple.com.

Susan Raab

President and Founder of Content Wheel

With a passion to speed ideas that help people improve their lives, Susan is the award-winning creative force behind hundreds of nonfiction titles. As an executive, founder, and designer, she's brought the Power of Clear to corporations like Sony, Microsoft, and McGraw-Hill, as well as entrepreneurs, authors, and self-publishers. To contact Susan, call 831-626-0406, write to susan@contentwheel.com, or visit http://www.contentwheel.com.

Caterina Rando, MA

As a master certified coach and author of the national best-selling book *Learn to Power Think*, Caterina passionately helps women succeed in direct selling. She is also a dynamic keynote speaker and the entrepreneurship expert for Staples.com. To contact Caterina, call 415-668-4535, write to cpr@caterinar.com, or visit http://www.caterinar.com.

Kathy Robbins

Kathy has reached the top position with five network marketing companies and helped in the expansion of four of those companies to Europe. She is known as one of the best trainers and consultants in the industry. To contact Kathy, write to kathy@mlmmadesimple.com or visit http:// www.mlmmadesimple.com.

Dr. Robert A. Rohm

President, Personality Insights, Inc.

Robert helps his clients create better teams and build better relationships. For example, in 1996 the Arizona Diamondbacks hired Robert to help draft potential players by personality style. In 2001, the Diamondbacks won the World Series—faster than any other team in baseball history! To contact Robert, call 770-509-7113, write to robert.rohm@personalityinsights.com, or visit http://www.personalityinsights.com.

Dr. Maryann Rosenthal

Clinical Psychologist and Author

Maryann is a trusted authority on instilling self-discipline and self-leadership skills in adults, adolescents, and young children. She co-authored *The Seeds of Greatness System* with Dr. Denis Waitley, and in her clinical practice, provides the tools clients need to make confident decisions for high performance achievement. To contact Maryann, visit http://www.theseedsofgreatness.com.

Deborah Rosado Shaw

Founder of Umbrellas Plus, LLC and Dream BIG! Enterprises

Raised in the nation's poorest congressional district, Deborah's strategies for success formed a bridge from tough inner-city beginnings to award-winning entrepreneur and advisor to Fortune 500 CEOs. A powerful voice in the market, she has presented keynotes and seminars on issues of personal empowerment, diversity, business strategy, sales, and entrepreneurship. To contact Deborah, visit http://www.edreambig.com.

Kristie Tamsevicius

Speaker, author, and consultant, Kristie is an entrepreneurial expert who has helped thousands of people start and succeed in their online businesses. She is the founder of Webmomz.com, president of Branding on the Net, and author of three books including her newest, *I Love My Life: A Mom's Guide to Working from Home*. To contact Kristie, call 847-244-8450, write to kristie@kristiet.com, or visit http://www.kristiet.com.

Dr. Denis Waitley

One of America's most respected authors, keynote speakers, and productivity consultants, Denis is the author of 14 books and 10 best-selling audiotape programs. With his partner Dr. Maryann Rosenthal, Denis has developed a new value-based program, *The Seeds of Greatness System*, which has been called "the instruction manual that should have been delivered with each child." To contact Denis, visit http://www.theseedsofgreatness.com.

Marcia Wieder

America's Dream Coach

Marcia is a top-rated author and presenter on visionary thinking, goal achievement, and team building to companies such as Avon, The Pampered Chef, and Creative Memories, and reaches tens of thousands more through appearances on shows like *Oprah* and *Today*. To contact Marcia, call 415-435-5564, write to marcia@dreamcoach.com, or visit http://www.dreamcoach.com.

Lisa M. Wilber

Owner, The Winner in You

Avon's number three money earner in the United States, Lisa has a team of more than 2,000 representatives who sold over $10 million in 2004. Lisa is an accomplished speaker and reaches thousands more through the media. To contact Lisa, call 800-258-1815, write to lwilber@aol.com, or visit http://www.winnerinyou.com.

Steve Wiltshire

Cofounder and CEO of Lifeline Coaching and Education, Inc.

Steven is a dynamic speaker, author, and acknowledged leader in coaching and training direct sellers. In his 20 years in the field, Steve held more than 5,000 shows, recruited 650 consultants, and developed numerous top leaders. To contact Steve, call 509-526-3837, write to support@lifelinecoaches.com, or visit http://www.lifelinecoaches.com.